Tora Holmberg
Annika Jonsson • Fredrik Palm
Editors

Death Matters

Cultural Sociology of Mortal Life

Editors
Tora Holmberg
Uppsala University
Uppsala, Sweden

Annika Jonsson
Karlstad University
Karlstad, Sweden

Fredrik Palm
Uppsala University
Uppsala, Sweden

ISBN 978-3-030-11484-8   ISBN 978-3-030-11485-5   (eBook)
https://doi.org/10.1007/978-3-030-11485-5

Library of Congress Control Number: 2019934107

Cover illustration: © Minfeng Wu / EyeEm / Getty Image Library
Cover design: Fatima Jamadar

This Palgrave Macmillan imprint is published by the registered company Springer Nature Switzerland AG.
The registered company address is: Gewerbestrasse 11, 6330 Cham, Switzerland

Preface

Every book has a story of its becoming: from idea to publication. So does ours. The anthology *Death Matters: Cultural Sociology of Mortal Life* came out of an established collaboration between scholars working in the field of cultural sociology. We had already been working together more or less closely affiliated with a particular academic setting, the research cluster Cultural Matters Group, physically located at the Department of Sociology, Uppsala University, Sweden. Taking this common affiliation as a point of departure was a given when wanting to explore death and mortality further. At first glance, our background in cultural sociology might indicate a homogenous theoretical perspective, methodological approach and/or empirical focus. But even though the geographical location of the research group and most of its members is located at a Swedish university, the chapters included thematically move beyond the national context. The chapters in this book study a range of cases, including memorialization of victims of death shootings in the US, responses to drone strikes in Iraq and self-help narratives in international scientific publications, as well as more local Swedish cases such as abandoned mining sites. The projects in this book still have one thing in common: the death/life complex. Death is present in all our scholarly work, albeit more or less directly. For some, it is at the core of inquiry, for example, when studying how objects left behind by beloved relatives become essential to memorialization processes, or how the mourning of deceased celebrities is being capitalized though digital labor. For these studies and others represented in this book, demise is the focus of research. For others, death appears from the "corner of the eye," through the encounter with dead places, the ever-present shadow of death in antibiotic resistance narratives, or the role of death in sexual behavior. We found coming from different angles within cultural sociology and from projects firmly situated in ongoing scholarly work to be a strength. Accordingly, we collaborated around the questions that are clarified in the introduction and developed throughout the book. We hope that, as much as we enjoyed working together with this project, you as a reader will enjoy the plurality of cases collected under the joint umbrella where cultural sociology meets death studies.

Uppsala, Sweden   Tora Holmberg
Karlstad, Sweden   Annika Jonsson
Uppsala, Sweden   Fredrik Palm
30 October 2018

Contents

Notes on Contributors

Philip K. Creswell is a PhD candidate in Sociology at Uppsala University. In his dissertation, he studies interpersonal networks, trust, and influence among political hackers and digital activists. He is interested in network theory, the study of social movements, and the role of informal activist networks in the organization and performance of digital activism.

Hedvig Ekerwald is Professor Emerita of Sociology at Uppsala University. Her research concerns youth in social movements, family life, mental health, and sexuality. She has a special interest in the feminist social scientist, peace researcher, and Nobel Prize winner Alva Myrdal (1902–86). Ekerwald is vice-president of the Research Committee on the History of Sociology of the International Sociological Association.

Henrik Fürst, PhD, is Senior Lecturer in Sociology at Uppsala University and has previously worked at the Swedish Defence University. In his co-authored contribution, he combines his knowledge of how actors assess people and things under uncertain circumstances and military sociology.

Hedvig Gröndal holds a PhD in Sociology. Her research interests lie at the crossroads of medical sociology and science and technology studies (STS).

Gröndal's PhD project concerned rational use of antibiotics, and she has published articles in, for example, *Sociology of Health and Illness* and *Science in Context*.

Tora Holmberg is Professor of Sociology at Uppsala University, Sweden. Holmberg's cultural sociology approach combines animal studies, STS, and urban theory, for example, in *Urban Animals: Crowding in ZooCities* (2017). She has co-edited several books, most recently *Animal Places: Lively Cartographies of Human-Animal Relations* (2018). She is the research leader of the Cultural Matters Group.

Karin Idevall Hagren, PhD in Scandinavian Languages, is a postdoctoral researcher at Uppsala University. Her research centers around language's function in reproducing meaning and social relationships. In particular, her research explores how discriminating and privileging discourses, including discourses of racism and nationalism, are reproduced through language.

Annika Jonsson is a Senior Lecturer at the Department of Social and Psychological Studies, Karlstad University. Her research concerns different aspects of how people continue to live with their deceased significant others. Her primary interest lies in how continuing bond practices are developed in relation to the cultural context.

Magdalena Kania-Lundholm, PhD, is a researcher at the Department of Sociology, Uppsala University. Her research focuses on the intersections between culture, power, and technology. In recent work, she explores the notions and meanings of technology non-use, media refusal, and voluntary online disconnection. Kania-Lundholm's work has been featured in journals such as *Sociology Compass*, *National Identities*, and *Media Culture & Society*.

María Langa, MSc., is a PhD student at the Department of Sociology of Uppsala University, Sweden. She is part of the *Seed Box*, a research group on Environmental Humanities at Linköping University. Langa received her degree at Universidad Nacional del Comahue (UNCo) in

Argentina. She is working on her dissertation project about the urban gardening scene in Sweden.

Nicklas Neuman, PhD, is a postdoctoral researcher at the Department of Food Studies, Nutrition and Dietetics, Uppsala University. His research interests cover a broad span of issues under the umbrella of "the sociology of food and eating." This includes food consumption and climate change, gendered divisions of domestic food work, and public health.

Tobias Olofsson is a PhD candidate at the Department of Sociology, Uppsala University. Olofsson's dissertation analyzes future-oriented evaluations in mineral exploration with a focus on uncertainty, temporality, commensuration, valuations, and risk reduction. Olofsson has been a visiting pre-doctoral fellow at Northwestern University, Evanston, IL, USA.

Fredrik Palm is Senior Lecturer in Sociology at the Department of Sociology, Uppsala University, Sweden. Palm's research is mainly oriented toward sexuality studies, including issues of the role of death in sexuality and sexual practices, combining psychoanalysis, discourse analysis, and feminist theory.

Ruth Penfold-Mounce is a Senior Lecturer at the University of York, UK. Her research focuses on crime, popular culture, and death. She leads the Death and Culture Network (DaCNet) and edits the *Emerald Series in Death and Culture*. Her publications include *Celebrity Culture and Crime* (2009) and *Death, The Dead and Popular Culture* (2018).

David Redmalm, holds a PhD in Sociology, and works as Senior Lecturer at Mälardalen University. Redmalm's main interest is animal sociology, and he has previously published articles on this topic in journals such as *The Sociological Review* and *Organization*.

List of Figures

List of Tables

1

Introduction: Why Death Matters

Tora Holmberg, Annika Jonsson, and Fredrik Palm

Introduction

On 6 February 2014, a giraffe named Marius hit the headlines all over the world. One-and-a-half-year-old Marius was living at the Copenhagen Zoo and was about to be euthanized due to overpopulation of giraffes and potential inbreeding. A few days later, the news declared that he was now dead and was about to be dissected and later fed to the lions, all in public view. Children were crying, and a general uproar followed. Chinese, Portuguese, and Canadian papers, among others, reported on the event. Displaying the killing of Marius—a personalized, healthy, young animal—created an almost global debate: When is the killing of

T. Holmberg (✉) • F. Palm
Department of Sociology, Uppsala University, Uppsala, Sweden
e-mail: tora.holmberg@soc.uu.se; fredrik.palm@soc.uu.se

A. Jonsson
Department of Social and Psychological Studies, Karlstad University,
Karlstad, Sweden
e-mail: annika.jonsson@kau.se

© The Author(s) 2019
T. Holmberg et al. (eds.), *Death Matters*,
https://doi.org/10.1007/978-3-030-11485-5_1

1

animals legitimate? Is the killing of one giraffe different from the billions of animals sacrificed in factory farming? But soon the debate shifted from concerns about the moment of the stunning, to involving the life of a zoo animal. What is a good life for encaged wild animals? Is it morally justified to keep them in captivity just for human pleasure? The mediated debate regarding the killing of a giraffe exemplifies a manifest cultural trait regarding how societies in general deal with death. As is often the case, death reminds us of, and points to, life itself.

While the vast majority of us will come to experience various kinds of losses during our lifetime, people encounter death indirectly all the time—through objects that once belonged to dead relatives, from media reports, and from art, literature, film, and other cultural sources. And so the contours of death regularly present themselves to us in our ongoing lives, when we walk through a dark alley, see a black plastic bag with unidentified contents by the roadside, or return home and find a family member sound asleep. Death intrudes on our everyday experiences and practices, and as philosophy has long reminded us, it is more than anything an inescapable feature of the human condition (Becker, 1973; Hegel, 1977; Heidegger, 2010). As the "only certainty in life," death serves as a reminder of the finiteness of human life (Van Brussel & Carpentier, 2014: 2). Rather than two separate moments or stages of existence, life and death are thus entangled in an interdependent process of becoming in which the term "living" would not mean much without its binary.

Sociology has long been aware of the fact that this interdependence profoundly informs nearly all social life (Berger & Luckmann, 1966; Bauman, 1992). Death is deeply embedded in the social fabric of what we experience, on an everyday basis, as "life." As Jean Baudrillard (1993) once showed, the ways in which society relates to and manages death are fundamental to how societies and the relationships between its social beings are structured. The story about Marius demonstrates how various textual and material sources of knowledge—the institution of the zoo, newspaper accounts, global media, and narratives on incest, vulnerability, and oppression of animals—give shape to such meaning-making processes. The historical, material, and cultural context is originally implicated in the ways in which death presents itself in any given society and in the individual experience of death and dying as it arises in the latter.

Norbert Elias pointed out that people's experience of death depends on culture: "It is variable and group-specific; no matter how natural and immutable it seems to the members of each particular society, it has been learned" (2001 [1985]: 4–5).

In accordance with this, the present volume takes a *cultural*-sociological perspective on death. We ask how our knowledge about death and dying emerges through concrete personal experience, but also how it draws on culturally shared narratives, social institutions, and material conditions. Death becomes real and life becomes mortal through the actions framed by economy, media, art, scientific knowledge, law, societal institutions, and so on. The book investigates the relationships between cultural repertoires and broader material conditions and events, be it in the form of ferocious attacks perpetrated by strangers, lethal outbreaks of mysterious infections, or the peaceful end of long lives. In this sense, it is the cultural production of death in discursive and material practice that lies at the forefront of the studies presented here. However, the volume also rests on the assumption that death is never simply reducible to some particular culturally determined meaning (Bauman, 1992). As we argue below, there is always something improper about it, something that escapes our grasp. The exit from life resists being singled out from life itself, appropriated, or contained. Rather, it is everywhere, not least in everyday life situations.

The title of this book is *Death Matters*. This probing concept has several connotations and functions for the volume as a whole. Foremost, it draws attention to the "more-than-cultural" processes of meaning-making and action. In this volume, death matter is the node where bodies, artifacts, identities, infrastructures, emotions, knowledge, capital, and places intersect. It refers to the stuff of mortal life. As a consequence and as stated above, death comes to matter everywhere. It matters to how we understand ourselves and organize our social lives. It matters to knowledge, experience, and practice in particular time-spaces. The meaning-making process may also travel temporally and spatially; for example, when the image of three-year-old Alan spread all over the world, creating mourning and collective action, or, when Marius' corpse within the Copenhagen zoo caused a moral conflict far beyond this confined place.

As will be further developed below, *death matters* as the manifestation that is constitutive of everyday life.

Following from this, the book has two broad objectives. *First*, it seeks to understand how death features and intrudes on contemporary culture by studying the role of death in current forms of everyday life. This implies that the objects of study are not necessarily clear-cut "death practices," that is, practices surrounding dying, burial, and memorialization. Instead, we argue that meanings that emerge in areas of social life quite distant from such practices can be just as important in our attempts to account for the more general role of death in a particular society.

Second, the anthology offers a cultural-sociological perspective, focusing particularly on how subjectivity and materiality in everyday life shape experiences or notions of death and dying. We thus provide a deeper understanding of how death comes to matter in contemporary society by targeting how it intersects with subjectivity and materiality. Marius, because he was turned into a subject, deserved to be mourned and remembered. As dead matter, he, because of this, presented a dilemma—which subjectivities warrant a ceremony of some kind and which can simply be used for food? In line with this, the chapters in this anthology analyze how specific processes produce certain versions of not only death and mortality but also of life itself. In this sense, we argue that it is essential to address how death, in specific spatial and temporal contexts, relates to and raises questions about agency, boundary work, and vulnerability.

In the following, we develop these arguments, situating the volume in classical as well as contemporary work in death studies and the cultural sociology of death. We then end the introduction by presenting the three parts of the book—*Places of absence-presence*, *Disease/bodies*, and *Persons and non-persons*—and the studies included in them.

Death Matters Everywhere, Every Day...

Communal constructions and functions of mortality are demonstrated by all of the historical, cultural, and material variations in how death comes to matter in society: from zombies to sea burials, crime noir to ghost exorcisms, hospices to black metal and Goth fashion (e.g. Foltyn,

2008; Penfold-Mounce, 2015). Yet, death is never restricted to matters directly associated with death. Hence, Thomas Laqueur has pointed out that death is omnipresent in human culture: "Like gravity or the air we breathe, it is always there, a part of being human that is so basic that it cannot be dissected out from the rest of life as we know it" (2015: XIV). In line with this idea, this volume argues that death ought to be considered as part of our ongoing everyday life, and not in terms of some deviation or exception to this life. Being mortal is a fundamental condition of human experience and filters through the lived experience of individuals as well as broader cultural everyday practices.

In this everyday experience, we argue that death often appears—as it tends to do most of the time for most of us who live in countries with low mortality rates—almost out of the corner of our eye. Death itches in our experience, "scratching at some inner door" (Yalom, 2008: 9), and it is often precisely by entering death from such an *indirect* angle that everyday meanings concerning life and death come to the surface. In line with this argument, everyday life constitutes the canvas for all of the death-related topics investigated in this anthology, be it a seemingly deserted old mine, newspaper articles about antibiotic-resistant bacteria, or online memorialization.

The omnipresence of death in everyday life should not, however, be understood only in terms of its various expressions as meaning, experience, practice, materiality, and so on. Another crucial quality of death is that it to some extent always escapes our attempts to create meaning and intelligibility. Death marks a point that society ultimately cannot control or contain and that despite endless efforts to exorcise it, either physically or symbolically, never goes away (Bauman, 1992; Becker, 1973; Higo, 2012). Despite, or perhaps because of, the overabundance of socially produced meanings of death, it remains something that is culturally uncontainable. In this sense, death appears to be essentially "queer." It lacks a proper place, or rather this place is precisely what our efforts to take control of life stumble over. Because death always already seems to resist the place that society gives it, it will also reappear in the wrong place. It is this logic of reappearance of what culture cannot contain that social thinkers have referred to as "the return of the repressed" (Žižek, 1999: 317, see, e.g. Baudrillard, 1993; Bauman, 1992; Freud, 1955). This presence is often subtle, bordering on absence.

From this perspective, the production of sociological knowledge on death is presented with an intricate dilemma: How can we expound our knowledge on death without appropriating it and making it a separate domain? Avoiding delimiting the domain to research on dying, mourning, and memorialization would then be a challenge for the field of death studies, which in recent decades has carved a space for itself through its interdisciplinary body of research. From the 1980s and onward, scholars of death studies have provided us with a plethora of intriguing studies on historical and contemporary social practices around death and dying. To name some of its most prominent concerns, the field of "thanatology" has explored phenomena such as epidemiology and demography related to death, grieving, and mourning, funeral practices and memorialization, end-of-life care and decision-making, as well as suicide (Fonseca & Testoni, 2011; Hakola et al., 2015; Hockey et al., 2010; Meagher & Balk, 2013; Stanton Chapple et al., 2017). These contributions have clearly paved the way for generating new knowledge on contemporary ways of constructing and managing death. And yet, one might wonder whether death studies does not tend to reduce the phenomenon of death to an object of those exceptional occurrences and domains of everyday reality that directly address death or its immediate consequences. If this were the case, it would risk losing sight of those instances in everyday reality in which death operates in a less straightforward manner, that is, in social spaces typically not associated with it. Still, it seems as if death studies, with a primary focus on evident "death topics," risk reducing death to an equally evident object of study. When death is addressed directly in obvious contexts, we might lose sight of those instances in everyday reality where death operates in a less straightforward manner, that is, in social spaces typically not associated with it. As Howarth (2007) argues, death in pre-modern societies primarily marked a transition from one state of being to another and thus did not constitute an absolute end. In contemporary Western societies, death is viewed both as a risk and as a certainty, and the obvious task at hand is therefore to increase longevity. When death is only equated with finitude, as is often the case, it demands our attention in special ways, and this might be one reason why death scholars tend to face death head-on instead of taking an interest in how death seeps into all sorts of social nooks and crannies.

The approach described above is unfortunate because it demands death's empirical visibility, or, rather, what we take to be its visibility. Restricting death to certain domains of society (central to thanatology and peripheral to most people's everyday experience) potentially results in the reification of its complexities, in particular failing to pay adequate attention to the crucial question of the interdependency of life and death. In contrast, this volume raises questions about the nature of death as a circumscribed object and about what practices a field like death studies could or even should study. If death cannot be contained, we ask how this should be taken into account by studies of death. In order to understand the place of death in contemporary society, should death studies not also include other forms of everyday life practices not explicitly dealing with mortality? In response to such challenges, the anthology *Death Matters: Cultural Sociology of Mortal Life* inscribes itself into the field of death studies, while at the same time challenging its core identity and its focus on an overly present object. Thus, on the one hand, our approach by necessity builds upon the shoulders of thanatology. For example, we too investigate mourning, memorialization, and post-mortality. On the other, the book also departs from the notion that common experiences in mundane life matter as much as the rare.

Cultural Sociology of Death and Dying

In order to realize the objective of studying death as it occurs in everyday social reality, this volume adopts a cultural-sociological framework. This said, cultural sociology admittedly comes in different varieties. The common thread is, of course, that it puts "culture" at the center of investigation, and rather than perceiving culture as predetermined by social structures, cultural sociology presupposes autonomy from other social spheres to certain extents. Rather than studying how power structures are sustained through the means of culture, cultural sociologists focus on how meaning-making and practice affect different areas of society (Larsen, 2013; Alexander, 2003). This means that cultural sociology starts from and analyzes cultural systems—that is, worldviews—and the ways in which people navigate in and through them (Durkheim, 1995 [1915]). In particular, it attends to how the interplay of cultural meanings, practices, and matters structure and challenge these cultural systems or worldviews, and this allows the cultural sociologist to explain how and why the worldviews are reactivated (Geertz, 1973; Lund & Trondman, 2013).

As our task is to explore death and its' role in society as the ultimate limit, we take the chance to use it as a case for developing an even sharper material-sensitive approach within cultural sociology. This means that when understanding and explaining, for instance, ongoing disputes over how to best handle antibiotic resistance, one might also consider the cultural lives of germs and how they interact with other actors at the clinic in a meaning-making process (Gröndal, 2018; Gröndal, Chap. 5, this volume). Another example is how representations of dead celebrities online are embedded in the fabric of digital affordances, capitalist frames, memorialization rituals, and users' habits and emotions (Kania-Lundholm, Chap. 9, this volume; Penfold-Mounce, 2018). These are then examples of "death matters," mattering processes and frames that propel death into the ongoing production of everyday life and experience.

As Thompson et al. (2016) note, sociology as a discipline has indeed been entwined with death since the very beginning. Already in 1907, Hertz made a significant contribution to the sociology of death by taking an interest in the dead body as a moral entity as well as in funerary rites around the world. He suggested that "when a man dies, society loses in him much more than a unit: it is stricken in the very principle of life, in the faith it has in itself" (Hertz, 1960 [1907]: 78), thus formulating an idea that has resonated in social sciences ever since—death is a threat to society. He also, much like Durkheim, pointed to the social nature of human responses to death and pursued a truly sociological understanding. In contemporary research there is likewise an extensive body of work on how, through social, collective processes, meaning is attributed to experiences and practices related to death and loss (see, e.g. Fulton, 1965; Glaser and Strauss, 1965; Kellehear, 2007; Klass et al., 1996; Niemeyer et al., 2014; Seale, 1998; Unruh, 1983; Walter, 1999, 2016). Nevertheless, as Kate Woodthorpe and Hannah Rumble (2016) point out, there is simultaneously a tendency within sociology as a whole to treat death as a very particular area of investigation. A proof of this is the lack of clear-cut sessions on death at sociological conferences. Sociology as a discipline thus seems to be ambivalent when it comes to death and death-related topics, which is interesting in itself.

A cultural-sociological perspective on death assumes that social phenomena always emerge as already historically, materially, and culturally produced. Cultural sociology systematically challenges reifying perspectives and suggests that death should be conceived of as a becoming. Such a position of course communicates with voices already present in death studies. For instance, Thompson et al. (2016) claim that sociology offers an invaluable perspective on dying, death, and bereavement because other disciplines, most notably psychology, fail to properly address the role of the social context. In this respect, they echo their sociological predecessors and the critique of psychology's reification of the individual. Likewise, working from solid sociological terrain, Tony Walter (2012) has studied modern societies' psychologizing of grief and medicalizing of dying and mourning. He shows how contemporary urban societies in fact manage death differently, in terms of significant structural factors as well as cultural features and institutions, and concludes that such psychologizing and medicalizing beliefs do not hold. He also points out that there is a certain tendency in death studies to reify the nation state—in many well-known texts a country's border is taken to coincide with specific practices and beliefs. On the other hand, there is also a tendency to use a broad brush and to assume that modernity similarly affects all countries that can be labeled as modern. All in all, Walter demonstrates the confusion that plagues death studies when it comes to knowledge claims, and thus he asks: What notions and death-related actions can be thought of as rooted in certain, specific contexts, and what findings can be generalized? Naturally, this is a problem sociologists face all the time, not only when studying death, dying, and mourning. By including numerous factors, such as migration, division of labor, information technology, collectivism, and religion/secularization, Walter asserts that we can analyze how death practices depend on social structures and cultural institutions that go far beyond the physical body or the individual mind (2012).

Yet psychology and medicine are not the only agents of reification. Of late, numerous theorists of culture have argued that notions such as meaning, constructions, and the social are as prone to reification as are notions of biology and mind (Alaimo & Hekman, 2008; Holmberg & Palm, 2008). In fact, the three themes that knit this volume together—namely everyday life, materiality, and subjectivity—are all linked to different versions of such a critique of reification. Our focus on everyday life is influenced by sociologist Henri Lefebvre and his notion that it is vital to approach the social fabric of society as an ongoing dialectic process. The "everyday" is precisely not an abstract or reified entity, but a time-space in becoming, and in order to grasp it he insists that we pay attention to how it emerges, for instance, through subjective lived experience. As a consequence, an exploration of death as part of this everyday would seem to require attending to people's experiences and everyday lives (1984).

In other words, this volume explores how issues of life and death are negotiated in practice through subjective meaning-making and material arrangements. In this sense, we treat subjectivity as a core dimension in the exploration of contemporary mortal life. As the case of Marius the giraffe demonstrates, the organization of life and death is closely tied to the ways in which subjectivity is understood. Does it involve a particular individual, a subject ascribed personhood, or a mass of unnamed zoo animals? Are the public represented as innocent children or as general consumers profiting from the bodies of captive wildlife? In this sense, subjectivity relates to both the construction of a subject and the nature of that subject—to the way in which subjectivity is attributed to or claimed by the dead, to how particular cultural practices negotiate the relationship between subjectivity and death, and to the materialization of death in subjective experience. As we shall see, a person may wield influence beyond the grave, but may also have been denied personhood while being alive.

The importance of recognizing subjective first-person experience has for a long time been an important way of challenging naturalized beliefs about social reality (Husserl, 1995; Oksala, 2016). Addressing subjective accounts of grief, one's own future death, or one's relation to dead kin in this sense affirms the lived experience of individuals and the role of such experience in the ongoing production of death in society, in contrast to, for instance, medical definitions of death. Importantly, it is only through this lived experience and other forms of sense-making that death develops into something more than a purely physical event. That is, it is only by way of some form of reflective or mirroring procedure that death is wrested from its natural in-itself and inscribed into social existence as something for-itself (Hegel, 1977). In the same manner, the phenomena of social death and loss of personhood attest to how biological and cultural life are not always synonymous. The concept of subjectivity, then, allows us to focus on intersubjective practices as spaces for the ongoing negotiation of human value. Thus, the focus on subjectivity and everyday life practice, among other things, lets us consider how humans and non-humans are being placed (and at times also place themselves) on a scale from valuable and fully individuated to worthless and unknowable.

However, we also claim that this focus on processes of meaning-making, everyday life practice, and subjectivity should not exclude giving attention to issues of materiality. On the contrary, the omnipresence of death serves as a constant reminder that materiality is always inherent in such processes. As scholars in science and technology studies claim, materiality is inseparable from cultural interpretations and agency, and to reduce it to inert matter would be just as reifying as excluding subjective experience from our understanding of society (e.g. Barad, 2007). Moreover, social relations take place somewhere, in physical places—such as the zoological garden—that shape and are shaped by subjective experiences. And this also holds for disembodied spaces such as those of social media, where dead bodies also materialize, and become normalized, through "morbid spaces" (Penfold-Mounce, 2015). Thus, experiences of the everyday cannot be singled out from material dimensions (Hockey et al., 2010). The notion that death matters in this volume implies that death is of vital importance for the meaning of life in general, but also that it *materializes* itself in our shared everyday life (Maddrell & Sidaway, 2010). As Hallam and Hockey have argued in *Death, Memory and Material Culture*:

[t]he multiple and ambiguous meanings that we find inscribed in space, place and objects, although diverse, all share a fundamental role in creating

and sustaining temporally located friendships between the living and the dead—and further situate the living in relation to their mortality. (Hallam & Hockey, 2001: 85)

Material dimensions of culture are intimately inherent and create conditions for both the reproduction and subversion of power relations, and this book highlights dimensions of subjectivity and materiality and their interdependence. In line with Donna Haraway, we claim that death and dying, like the body, must be conceived of as material-semiotic processes (1991).

To conclude, these critiques of reification are essential for our argument for a cultural-sociological understanding of death that emphasizes its ubiquitous and originally ambiguous nature in everyday life. In order to understand the importance of the cultural dimensions of death—as lived experience, practice, meaning-making, materiality, and so on—we aim to move beyond the boundaries of contemporary death studies. In this we ask if death studies as a research field does not risk getting caught up in a new version of reification insofar as it primarily attends to explicit death practices while in the process ignoring vital dimensions of the everywhereness and uncontainability that we take here as our point of departure.

Structure and Outline

The book is comprised of 13 chapters divided into an introduction, three subsections, and a concluding chapter. The chapters all relate and contribute to the "diagonal themes" of the materiality, subjectivity, and epistemology of the everyday, moving death from the margins of social life to the forefront of investigation.

The three chapters of Part I—*Places of absence-presence*—put the spotlight on *where* and *when* absence and presence are subjectively experienced and argue that spatial and temporal dimensions are crucial for understanding death in current forms of everyday life. It is a common saying that a deceased loved one leaves an empty space behind. Whether it is a neighborhood turned into a supposed "no-go zone," the home of a recently deceased person, an overgrown field, or a manor house kept alive by the last line of descendants, one senses a presence in that absence. Those who have gone leave traces, offering or imposing themselves on the present in the form of "ghostly matter" (Gordon, 2008) such as tales, memorialization rituals, and material evidence (McCormick, 2015). They remain as temporal-spatial phenomena through processes of memorialization, binding together here and there, now and then, linking the living to a lost past, but also to the unavoidable future of each living being. The once-alive—human or non-human—thus animates the present through an absence that reminds the living not only of a now absent past, but also of an absence yet to come. In this theme, such processes of memorialization are explored in terms of the ambiguous absences/presences they present.

The first chapter in Part I, Chap. 2, is written by Annika Jonsson, who investigates experiences of bereaved individuals in Sweden and the UK, particularly how the lost person is remembered and made present through material objects and places. In this sense, objects and places enable the grieving person to revive the bond or sense of affinity with the dead. Nonetheless, this benevolent role of materiality is always and already shadowed by loss and the more mysterious sense of being haunted.

This sense of haunting is also important in Chap. 3, featuring Tora Holmberg's study of manor and castle owners in contemporary Sweden. These custodians of the archaic legacies of what is referred to as the "mortmain" bear witness to a life heavily subordinated to fulfilling traditional conventions. Life on the manor is still pervaded by the rules and ideologies of ancestors, who—despite being long gone—exercise post-mortal agency through control over activities and property.

In the third and last chapter of this section, Chap. 4, we move from this burdened life of the manor, where the life of old still carries weight and imposes its way of life on the new, to the places the Swedish mining industry has left behind as traces of an earlier stage of modern capitalism. This is the object of Tobias Olofsson's chapter on the death of mining sites, which closes Part I of the book. Olofsson investigates how the political debate concerning dead and empty rural places feeds into carnal, ethnographical experiences of sites of old mines. The analysis demonstrates, however, that the place itself, through memories of industrial activities and budding vegetation, facilitates a critique of such discourses.

Part II dwells on a problem that follows from the material aspects of subjective experience that has been highlighted in detail above, namely that of the body. In order to be present and to encounter absences, one needs to be embodied. Bodies are both physical and social, and these dimensions are inseparably present in everyday mortal life. The material-semiotic body is often taken for granted and is not truly experienced until it is faced with a risk. Following this argument, the second part, and its four chapters, investigates what we term *Disease/Bodies*. Bodies marked by death and disease constitute a potential danger to society and its citizens, threatening the bodies of individual subjects as well as working as signifiers of moral, economic, and political systems. Therefore, it is not surprising that one of the major subjects of death studies concerns how death is related to issues of health and disease. Through, for example, healthism (Crawford, 2006; Rose, 1999) and medicalization (Conrad, 2007), the modern subject is thus warned that certain ways of eating or exercising will shorten or extend life while at the same time being bombarded by hedonistic injunctions to enjoy (Žižek, 1999) or to "live our lives to the fullest." This paradox puts the body at the center, as the marker of a "good life" as well as a "good death." The theme for Part II deals both with the medical discourse itself and with the social practices through which this discourse is filtered, primarily examining how death is embodied in contemporary practices related to questions of disease and bodily threats. In this sense, the presence of death is sometimes direct, and sometimes more indirect. And yet all of the chapters in the volume argue that death, in the studied contexts, becomes a profound concern, be it in terms of scientific knowledge, ethics, politics, or other forms of power.

In Chap. 5, Hedvig Gröndal studies how fear of disease and the threat against the human body materialize in discourses on antibiotic-resistant bacteria. In particular, her chapter analyzes narratives on antibiotics in the practices of Swedish medicine and animal farming. Although antibiotics were normalized early on through their use in animal husbandry, the Swedish case shows that, later on, this practice was heavily questioned in the medical context through the rise of antibiotic-resistant bacteria. In the latter discourse, antibiotic resistance has often been perceived as a global threat to humankind. Behind the mundane frugal use of antibiotics, then, lurks an appalling deadly threat to society as we know it.

Chapter 6, by Nicklas Neumann, focuses on stories about the embodied perception of a deadly disease: anorexia nervosa. The chapter re-analyzes quotes from published interview studies about recovery from the disease and demonstrates not only how the sufferers themselves relate, and have related, to their own deaths, but also how the disease is talked about as something with a life of its own, as something that has to disappear (die) in order for the person to stay alive. "Death," in this perspective, is both an existential dying and a physical demise, and the life of the disease emerges as the nodal point in the existential condition of the sufferer. The disease also, paradoxically, brings purpose to the life of the sufferer.

Fredrik Palm engages in Chap. 7 with a particular interpretation of the phenomenon of "bug-chasing," an extreme form of barebacking in which HIV-negative men engage in unprotected sex with HIV-positive men. It addresses the way in which bug-chasing has been described as a radical sexual, political, and even ethical movement, and it raises questions about the more exact role of death in the phenomenon. As in the previous chapter, something potentially deadly gives rise to a certain vitality, demonstrating the umbilical cord that connects death and life.

Finally, in Chap. 8, Hedvig Ekerwald examines attitudes toward the dead body in contemporary Sweden. The paradoxical blend of rational and irrational views among secular subjects is exposed through interviews with peers in relation to questions of cremation, autopsy, organ donation, and euthanasia. The novel approach of the chapter is that it seeks to analyze available and unavailable cultural repertoires concerning the dead body that are used by people when trying to grasp the abstract post-mortal becoming of their own body in the relationship between the decomposition of one's body and oneself as a person.

The last section—Part III—develops the human/non-human nexus and its importance for a cultural sociology of death. As stated above in this introduction, subjectivity is the name of the game for any exploration of mortal life. With the third theme's four chapters, subjectivity is further attached to the notion of personhood. What provides an actor the status of being acknowledged as a person and what disqualifies such claims? In short, the theme answers questions about the division and transgression between *Persons and Non-Persons*. Because the term "person" is central to the preceding chapters, it is in the third part more closely coupled with "non-person." The concept of "non-person" is used by Goffman (1961) in descriptions of people whose moral status is compromised such that they cease to be (experienced as) subjects. Today scholars refer to "social death" when analyzing this kind of existence (Card, 2013; Králová, 2015; Mulkay & Ernst, 1991; Patterson, 1982), a concept that takes us to the sociologically familiar domain inhabited by the classical figure of Antigone, or more modern equivalents such as the *Muselman* (Agamben, 1999). But the concept of non-persons can also situate us in the domain of that which never enjoyed personhood in the first place. In everyday life, this facet of non-personhood appears as that which does not belong to personhood—matter, nature, animal, artifact, and so on. Here the tension that permeates questions about personhood and subjectivity is explored in the context of suffering and death. The human and non-human beings focused on in this section all have one thing in common—their personhood is actively negotiated, advocated, or contested because they have died, are dying, or cannot die (in a biological sense). Throughout the chapters, it is also demonstrated how notions of meaningful and meaningless lives and deaths, and their subject positions are intertwined with artifacts, technologies, media, and matter.

In Chap. 9, Magdalena Kania-Lundholm investigates celebrity death and mourning as enacted in the context of social media. The question of personhood is actualized in a process in which the celebrity is turned into a valuable commodity, while on the plus side, perhaps enjoying social life after death. This chapter discusses how the often mutually exclusive logics of death and mourning are mixed together with the logics of commerce and profit through the process of *digital mourning labor*. This labor is immaterial but materializes in the form of profit generated by online networking sites and platforms. Consequently, value is not only extracted from users' digital mourning labor, but also from the symbolic meaning and value of celebrity death upon which global brands capitalize.

María Langa and Philip K. Creswell develop this theme of online memorialization in Chap. 10 in which they analyze how Black Lives Matter activists represent the victims of police killings in online media, which is a context where African Americans are criminalized both in life and after death. Here issues of personhood arise as different actors articulate their political claims in relation to the victims' stigmatized identities. Activists reconstruct the deceased's personhood by identifying them with a larger victimized collective and with the protestors themselves as potential victims of racialized police violence. In doing so, the dead not only become full persons again, but also postmortem actors. The dead join the fight against police killings of African Americans.

Other facets of subjectivity and personhood are brought to light in Chap. 11 by Henrik Fürst and Karin Idevall Hagren. They examine the framing of dead persons through an analysis of comments posted on YouTube in reaction to a video clip of a lethal drone strike in Iraq. Two cultural frames are identified—legitimate or illegitimate killing. With the legitimate frame, the drone strike is justified and those who are killed are blamed for their deaths. The other frame contests the killing as illegitimate, resulting in a view of the victims' "livability." The study shows the characteristics of war propaganda in a time pervaded by highly technologized warfare, by discourses of terrorism, and by new digital modes for communication.

Continuing the path of personalization and moving beyond the death of humans, in Chap. 12 David Redmalm investigates the discursive frameworks at play when conceptualizing the death of companion animals. In this context, pets enjoy a paradoxical status as an irreplaceable individual and as a consumable resource corresponding to a biopolitical rationale for breeding, buying, selling, and killing pets. This chapter suggests that pet keeping can be regarded as a demarcated zone where norms surrounding life and death can be played with, managed, and reproduced. The question at heart here is how much personhood a companion animal is permitted and how the boundary between human and animal is secured.

The purpose of any good conclusion is to emphasize the significant findings and value of the writing that has preceded it. In Chap. 13, Ruth Penfold-Mounce showcases the importance of the anthology by highlighting how it contributes to, and expands upon, the current parameters of death studies and cultural sociology. Departing from her own previous research on death in popular culture, she reiterates the value of this collected work on death from a variety of cultural-sociological perspectives. The reflective nature of the chapter aims to promote the idea that *Death Matters* are critical to a world in which death *does* matter.

The different chapters of the book can be read separately as case studies of the book's common theme. Or they can be enjoyed together as a coherent and progressive story of how death comes to matter in and through contemporary culture. We certainly acknowledge that this collection does not cover all aspects of cultural-sociological approaches to mortal life. However, it hopefully points to the potentials and constitutes a step forward in realizing such a research agenda.

References

Agamben, G. (1999) *The Man Without Content*, Stanford, CA: Stanford University Press.

Alaimo, S. and Hekman, S. (eds.) (2008) *Material Feminisms*, Bloomington and Indianapolis: Indiana University Press.

Alexander, J. (2003) *The Meanings of Social Life: A Cultural Sociology*, Oxford, New York: Oxford University Press.

Barad, K. (2007) *Meeting the Universe Halfway. Quantum Physics and the Entanglement of Matter and Meaning*, Durham, NC: Duke University Press.

Baudrillard, J. (1993) *Symbolic Exchange and Death*, London: Sage.

Becker, E. (1973) *The Denial of Death*, New York: Simon & Schuster.

Berger, L. and Luckmann, T. (1966) *The Social Construction of Reality. A Treatise in the Sociology of Knowledge*, New York: Penguin Books.

Bauman, Z. (1992) *Mortality, Immortality and Other Life Strategies*, Cambridge: Polity.

Card, C. (2013) 'Genocide and Social Death', *Hypatia*, 18(1), 63–79.

Conrad, P. (2007) *The Medicalization of Society On the Transformation of Human Conditions into Treatable Disorders*, Baltimore: The Johns Hopkins University Press.

Crawford, R. (2006) 'Health as a Meaningful Social Practice', *Health*, 10(4): 401–420.

Durkheim, É. (1995 [1915]) *The Elementary Forms of Religious Life*, New York: Free Press.

Elias, N. (2001 [1985]) *The Loneliness of the Dying*, New York, London: Continuum.

Foltyn, J. L. (2008) 'The Corpse in Contemporary Culture: Identifying, Transacting, and Recoding the Dead Body in the Twenty-First Century', *Mortality*, 13(2), 99–104.

Fonseca, L. M. and Testoni, I. (2011) 'The Emergence of Thanatology and Current Practice in Death Education', *OMEGA—Journal of Death and Dying*, 64(2): 157–169.

Freud, S. (1955) *Moses and Monotheism*, New York: Vintage Books.

Fulton, R. (ed.) (1965) *Death and Identity*, New York: Wiley and Sons.

Geertz, C. (1973) *The Interpretation of Cultures: Selected Essays*, New York: Basic Books.

Glaser, B. G. and Strauss, A. L. (1965) *Awareness of Dying*, London: Weidenfeld and Nicolson.

Goffman, E. (1961) *Asylums: Essays on the Social Situation of Mental Patients and Other Inmates*, New York: Doubleday.

Gordon, A. (2008) *Ghostly Matters: Haunting and the Sociological Imagination*, Minneapolis: University of Minnesota Press.

Gröndal, H. (2018) *Unpacking Rational Use of Antibiotics: Policy in Medical Practice and the Medical Debate*, (Doctoral dissertation) Uppsala: Acta Universitatis Upsaliensis.

Hakola, O., Heinämaa, S. and Philström, S. (eds.) (2015) *Death and Mortality: From Individual to Communal Perspectives*, Helsinki: Helsinki Collegium for Advanced Studies.

Hallam, E. and Hockey, J. (2001) *Death, Memory and Material Culture*, Oxford: Berg.

Haraway, D. J. (1991) *Simians, Cyborgs and Women. The Reinvention of Nature*, New York: Routledge.

Hegel, G. F. W. (1977) *Phenomenology of Spirit*, Oxford: Oxford University Press.

Heidegger, M. ([1927] 2010) *Being and Time*, Albany, NY: State University of New York Press.

Hertz, R. (1960) *Death and the Right Hand*, London: Cohen and West.

Higo, M. (2012) 'Surviving Death-Anxieties in Liquid Modern Times: Examining Zygmunt Bauman's Cultural Theory of Death and Dying', *Omega: Journal of Death and Dying*, 65(3): 221–238.

Hockey, J., Komaromy, C. and Woodthorpe, K. (eds.) (2010) *The Matter of Death. Space, Place and Materiality*, London: Palgrave Macmillan.

Holmberg, T. and Palm, F. (2008) 'The Body that Speaks the Gap: Feminist Theory and the Biological Question' in J. Bromseth, L. Käll Folkmarson and

K. Mattsson (eds.), *Body Claim(s)*, Uppsala: Centre for Gender Research: Crossroads of Knowledge.

Howarth, G. (2007) *Death & Dying. A Sociological Introduction*, Cambridge: Polity.

Husserl, E. (1995) *Cartesian Meditations. An Introduction to Phenomenology*, (10th impression) Dordrecht: Kluwer Academic Publishers.

Kellehear, A. (2007) *A Social History of Dying*, Cambridge: Cambridge University Press.

Klass, D., Silverman, P. R. and Nickman, S. L. (eds.) (1996) *Continuing Bonds: New Understandings of Grief*, Washington, DC: Taylor & Francis.

Králová, J. (2015) 'What is Social Death?', *Contemporary Social Science*, 10(3), 235–248.

Larsen, C. A. (2013) *The Rise and Fall of Social Cohesion: The Construction and De-construction of Social Trust in the US, UK, Sweden and Denmark*, Oxford: Oxford University Press.

Laqueur, T. (2015) *The Work of the Dead: A Cultural History of Mortal Remains*, New Jersey: Princeton University Press.

Lefebvre, H. (1984) *Everyday Life in the Modern World*, New Jersey: Transaction Publishers.

Lund, A. and Trondman, M. (2013) 'Förord till den svenska upplagan' in H. Larsen (ed.) *Den Nya Kultursociologin*, Lund: Studentlitteratur, 7–23.

Maddrell, A. and Sidaway, J. D. (2010) *Deathscapes: Spaces for Death, Dying Mourning and Remembrance*, Farnham: Ashgate Publishing Ltd.

McCormick, L. (2015) 'The Agency of Dead Musicians', *Contemporary Social Science*, 10(3), 323–335.

Meagher, D. K. and Balk, D. E. (eds.) (2013) *Handbook of Thanatology. The Essential Body of Knowledge for the Study of Death, Dying, and Bereavement*, New York: Routledge.

Mulkay, M. and Ernst, J. (1991) 'The Changing Profile of Social Death', *European Journal of Sociology*, 32(1), 172–172.

Niemeyer, R. A., Klass, D. and Dennis, M. R. (2014) 'A Social Constructionist Account of Grief: Loss and the Narration of Meaning', *Death Studies*, 38(8), 485–498.

Oksala, J. (2016) *Feminist Experiences. Foucauldian and Phenomenological Investigations*, Evanston, IL: Northwestern University Press.

Patterson, H. O. (1982) *Slavery and Social Death: A Comparative Study*, London: Harvard University Press.

Penfold-Mounce, R. (2015) 'Corpses, Popular Culture and Forensic Science: Public Obsession with Death', *Mortality*, 21(1): 19–35.

Penfold-Mounce, R. (2018) 'Posthumous Careers of Celebrities' in R. Penfold-Mounce (ed.) *Death, the Dead and Popular Culture*, Bingley: Emerald Publishing Limited: 9–39.

Rose, N. (1999) *The Power of Freedom: Reframing Political Thought*, Cambridge: Cambridge University Press.

Seale, C. (1998) *Constructing Death: The Sociology of Dying and Bereavement*, Cambridge: University Press.

Stanton Chapple, H., Bouton, B., Chow, A. Y., Gilbert, K. R., Kosminsky, P., Moore, J. and Whiting, P. (2017) 'The Body of Knowledge in Thanatology: An Outline', *Death Studies*, 41(2), 118–125.

Thompson, N., Allan, J., Carverhill, P. A., Cox, G. R., Davies, B., Doka, K., Granek, L., Harris, D., Ho, A., Klass, D., Small, N. and Wittkowski, J. (2016) 'The Case for a Sociology of Dying, Death, and Bereavement', *Death Studies*, 40(3), 172–181.

Unruh, D. R. (1983) 'Death and Personal History: Strategies of Identity Preservation', *Social Problems*, 30(3), 340–351.

Van Brussel, L. and Carpentier, N. (eds.) (2014) *The Social Construction of Death: Interdisciplinary Perspectives*, Basingstoke: Palgrave Macmillan.

Walter, T. (1999) *On Bereavement: The Culture of Grief*, Buckingham: Open University Press.

Walter, T. (2012) 'Why Different Countries Manage Death Differently: A Comparative Analysis of Modern Urban Societies', *The British Journal of Sociology*, 63(1), 123–145.

Walter, T. (2016) 'The Dead Who Become Angels: Bereavement and Vernacular Religion', *Omega: Journal of Death and Dying* 73(1), 3–28.

Woodthorpe, K. and Rumble, H. (2016) 'Funerals and Families: Locating Death as a Relational Issue', *The British Journal of Sociology*, 67(2), 242–259.

Yalom, I. D. (2008). *Staring at the Sun. Overcoming the Terror of Death*, Hoboken: Wiley.

Žižek, S. (1999) *The Ticklish Subject: The Absent Centre of Political Ontology*, London: Verso.

Part I

Places of Absence-Presence

2

Materializing Loss and Facing the Absence-Presence of the Dead

Annika Jonsson

Introduction

"Some days," Laura (age 53) says with a thoughtful expression on her face, "Pamela's flat was like a black hole, sucking me in although I was petrified." Pamela, a close friend of Laura, died of cancer a few years ago, and her flat, to some degree the whole neighborhood, remains a source of anxiety. Laura, being neither family nor a partner, was not asked to help when Pamela's home was taken care of and this, she feels, explains her unexpectedly strong reaction to the place afterward. Their intertwined lives were severed when the intimate and awful experience of losing Pamela ended with Laura being abruptly pushed to the side. Pamela's brother handed her some mementos when they had finished—a couple of Pamela's drawings and favorite vinyl records—but after almost 30 years of friendship, this only belittled the bond between them. Defining herself as a down-to-earth Scot, Laura initially had a hard time comprehending

A. Jonsson (✉)
Department of Social and Psychological Studies, Karlstad University, Karlstad, Sweden
e-mail: annika.jonsson@kau.se

© The Author(s) 2019
T. Holmberg et al. (eds.), *Death Matters*,
https://doi.org/10.1007/978-3-030-11485-5_2

why she felt so strongly about it. When she realized a new tenant had moved in, that added to the problem:

> It was Pamela's place. She lived there, she worked there, it was her place and when I was there, it felt like my place too. And then he turned up and it was like, 'how can he be there, it's not like the flat's empty?' That's how I reacted and it felt like a perfectly natural reaction.

Today, three years later, she says that the sadness is "clearer," but she still will not venture into that particular part of town without a very good reason. And she still feels very uncomfortable just thinking about Pamela's old home. How are we to make sense of this story?

Based on an interview study conducted in Sweden and the United Kingdom 2013–2017, this chapter explores how places and objects can be central to people's experience of losing a significant other, like in Laura's case above. Out of 34 interviews, five (three carried out in Sweden and two in the United Kingdom) have been selected for a deeper exploration of how bereaved individuals relate to material features they associate with the deceased.[1] It is well known that memorialization is quite often performed somewhere special and that bereaved persons tend to keep things they associate with the deceased person (Gibson, 2008; Hallam et al., 1999; Jonsson & Walter, 2017; Maddrell & Sidaway, 2010; Valentine, 2008). In these five cases, however, the interviewees' experiences are fundamentally bound to objects and places. Apart from this, these interviewees also express more anxiety and other negative emotions than the others do, but it is unclear whether this is significant or a mere coincidence. This aspect of the interviews nevertheless demands theoretical attention, and a conceptual framework will be elaborated below.

This framework is based on a cultural sociological understanding, according to which humans are not primarily governed by rational reasoning. Jeffrey Alexander (2003) asserts that people act on feelings and gut instinct, rather than on conscious thought. For this reason, social phenomena are imbued with emotions—a fact that sociology has traditionally failed to conceptualize or even admit (Smart, 2007). The landscape of loss is of course satiated with emotions, and the interviewees' experiences are primarily conveyed in terms of feelings. Alexander, however, reminds us that emotional responses are not arbitrary—they are shaped by social structures: "The secret to the compulsive power of social structures is that they have an inside. They are not only external to actors but internal to them. They are meaningful" (2003: 4). Meaning is assigned in accordance with what symbolic and material resources are available to actors in different contexts (Swidler, 1986). The interviewees' narratives are deeply personal, but in line with this argument, they also reflect how events, relationships and so on are perceived as significant and meaningful in a certain cultural context.

In addition to taking a cultural sociological approach to emotion and meaning making, this chapter examines how the interviewees' loss unfolds through a process of materialization. This process entails, as will be made clear throughout the text, assigning meaning and developing emotions in relation to matters associated with the deceased. It is set in motion when bereaved individuals encounter objects and places that they strongly relate to the deceased and, as a consequence, come to view as part of the now missing person or as essential to their relationship. Christine Valentine (2008: 114) analyzes how the participants in her study "materialised their loss" through "more formal ritualised social practices and the spaces and objects associated with these." What is materialized is both the presence and the absence of the deceased person—the presence that was and the absence that, in many ways, is. During a funeral service, for example, a body in a casket or the ashes in an urn are a salient reminder of the person and the person that is no more. It should be noted that the materialization investigated in this chapter unravels in mundane, everyday life, outside any kind of formalized, social arrangements. The reason for this can partly be found in the research design, which privileges ordinary life, and partly in the fact that the interviewees themselves gravitated toward this dimension.

According to Margaret Gibson (2008), the objects of the dead can be meaningful for mourners in different ways. Often the purpose is to extract the person's presence, but it can also be because they allow for shared grieving or because, as with clothes, they seem impossible to discard in a respectful way. Different notions about what happens after death may of course suggest different mental trajectories in this respect, but as Abby Day (2013) asserts, this does not erase the significance of the (lost) relationship. Indeed, she suggests that afterlife beliefs tend to be established on a relational foundation (see also Jonsson & Aronsson, 2015). This explains, for instance, why persons who claim to be atheists may still express that their deceased are in a better place. Donald Winnicott (1953) uses the concept of "transitional object," that is, objects connecting one experience with another, when discussing how children transition from a psychic to an external reality. This is, according to Winnicott, a non-pathological feature of human psychology—it helps us come to terms with, for instance, the loss of significant others. Vamik D. Volkan (1972), on the other hand, argues that "linking objects," that is, the things people hold on to, risk trapping them in the past and preventing them from moving on. Presumably, similar positions exist when it comes to places infused by the presence (and absence) of the deceased. In addition to cemeteries and other official places where the dead reside, people may feel the presence of the deceased in more personal places, for example, vacation spots they visited together and houses where they used to live (Jonsson & Walter, 2017). Gibson refers to such places as "spaces of memory" (2008: 191).

It is easy to slip into the debate on healthy and unhealthy grief when discussing the topic of loss. From a psychological point of view, some of the reactions and experiences described by the interviewees could no doubt be labeled complicated or prolonged grief disorder. Complicated grief disorder supposedly occurs in circa seven percent of mourners and tends to be interpreted as a failure to understand what has happened and an inability to properly deal with the loss (Shear, 2012). Walter (2006), however, convincingly argues that the idea of complicated grief in fact is rather complicated in itself, and that it to some degree is an outcome of society's desire to discipline grieving members. There is no doubt in my mind that the participants in my study know fully well that the person is dead and that all of their thoughts and actions can be traced back to this very realization. Instead of evaluating their accounts in terms of the normal and abnormal, a different framework is used to explain why the loss made and continues to make such a mark on their lives. This framework is outlined in the next section. Needless to say, the loss of a significant other often has a profound impact on a person, but at times, like in Laura's case, it throws the bereaved into a vicious emotional maelstrom.

Although grief brings inner turmoil for most people, the five cases presented in this chapter stand out because of the degree of despair and anxiety.

Absence-Presence and Anxiety

As already touched upon, the dead are often experienced as both present and absent by the bereaved. For the past 20 years or so, scholars within Death Studies/Thanatology have theorized and validated the presence of the deceased in the lives of the living. Remembering and sensing that dead loved ones are still near can be a real comfort for the bereaved (Vickio, 1999). The concept of "continuing bonds" has been established as a means to label the relationships that people (feel that they) maintain with their deceased (see Klass et al., 1996; Klass & Steffen, 2018). These relationships are built on vivid memories, conversations about and with the deceased, private and public rituals and so on (Hallam et al., 1999; Hallam & Hockey, 2001; Jonsson, 2015; Klass & Goss, 1999; Klass & Walter, 2001; Mathijssen, 2017; Valentine, 2008; Walter, 1999).

Sometimes the relationships are perceived (by the living) as a connection between two separate subjects, and at times the deceased is understood as primarily internalized within the self. As Arnar Árnason (2012) asserts, this doubleness can create ambivalence and conflict, if one is expected to act in contradiction to one's experiences. He provides the example of a Japanese widow who detested performing the daily rituals at her husband's household shrine and the yearly rites at the O'Bon festival, as these rituals implied he was out there somewhere and could be reached, rather than right here, with her. Jane Ribbens McCarthy and Raia Prokhovnik (2014) remark that the mind/body divide in Western culture creates an unnecessary confusion because the body is viewed as the site of personhood. The deceased thus becomes something of a paradox. Deceased individuals cannot really exist in their disembodied state, so when the living sense or imagine them, they are turned into spirits or ghosts. There is, to conclude, quite an elaborate framework concerning how, why and with what consequences deceased individuals are present in life here and now.

The most clear-cut, schematic description of the whereabouts of the dead (as well as the living) is provided by Elizabeth Hallam, Jenny Hockey and Glennys Howarth (1999: 3). They differentiate between four modes of existence/non-existence: a person can be (1) socially and biologically alive, (2) socially and biologically dead, (3) socially dead/biologically alive and, finally, (4) socially alive/biologically dead. Here we are honing in on the fourth dimension, where the dead person is both present and absent. Avril Maddrell (2013: 5) uses the concept absence-presence and stresses that:

> Rather than being the consciousness of what is absent, it is the now absent deceased having continuity of presence, being given presence through the experiential and relational tension between the physical absence (not being there) and emotional presence (a sense of still being there), i.e. absence-presence is greater than the sum of the parts. Absence is not merely a 'presence' in and of itself, but rather the absent is evoked, made present, in and through enfolded blendings of the visual, material, haptic, aural, olfactory, emotional-affective and spiritual planes, prompting memories and invoking a literal sense of continued 'presence', despite bodily and cognitive absence.

Maddrell alludes to the fact that relating to the now dead person is a process that propels the bereaved into a complex reality, where the familiar becomes unfamiliar and vice versa. As an absence-presence, the deceased may turn into a truly unsettling element in the lives of the living. Valentine (2008) makes clear that some amount of absence-presence is both inescapable and bearable for most (see also Hallam & Hockey, 2001), so the question, then, is why this ambivalence in some cases pervades too much of daily life and causes utter emotional chaos.

For the five interviewees presented below, the absence-presence of their dead created (is still creating, for some of them) a vortex of anxiety. To Laura, Pamela's flat, despite still being just that, turned into something else after her death—a foreign space and then a space occupied by a stranger. It seems as if the person and the place somehow merged in Laura's experience, resulting in a contorted absence-presence of Pamela, which drew her in and repelled her at the same time. Something very familiar suddenly felt very unfamiliar as well, in a manner that elicits

Sigmund Freud's (1919) notion of the uncanny. According to Dylan Trigg, the uncanny "leaves us in a state of disquiet, unnerved precisely because we lack the conceptual scheme to put the uncanny in its rightful 'place'" (2012: 28). He suggests that the places most conducive to the uncanny are the places that we cherish, and the truth of this is apparent in Laura's account. Avery Gordon (2008: 8), examining what she terms ghostly matter, asserts that social injustice and disruption at the level of society or in personal networks are reasons why the past sometimes becomes a troubling feature of the present, why an absent person sometimes gains a horrifying presence. A ghost is a figure, symbolizing that which has gone wrong. This too echoes Laura's experience of being pushed to the side and made practically irrelevant when Pamela's flat was cleared out. From this perspective, she was haunted by (the memory of) Pamela, whom she was, in a way, separated from due to social conventions.

To sum up, the absence-presence of the deceased is a complex phenomenon that, when powerful, invites us to use concepts like the uncanny and haunting in order to capture it. In this chapter, absence-presence is analyzed in the context of how people materialize loss by assigning meaning to places and objects they associate with the deceased. Emotions are at the very center of this process, which means that the act of assigning ought not be seen as conscious or intentional. Instead, this emotive practice should be viewed in relation to what material and symbolic resources are available to actors, and how social structure/convention, in the end, regulates thoughts and actions (cf. Swidler, 1986; Alexander, 2003; Gordon, 2008).

Materializing Loss: Five Examples

Below the five interviewees are presented and their narratives analyzed using the conceptual framework. Their names have been altered and names of places omitted, as pseudonymization was promised to all participants in the study.

Anna-Karin, 44

Anna-Karin's parents divorced when she was eight or nine, and after that, she and her sister visited their father every other weekend in his new flat. She says that she does not remember much of it—they played in the nearby park and went to restaurants and the town zoo. She had an ambiguous relationship with her father during her childhood. On the one hand, he was the free-spirited, fun parent who allowed them to do things their mother would not; on the other hand, he was away a lot and she did not really know him. As the years went by and friends and hobbies started to take up her time, their relationship deteriorated. For a long time, they only saw each other on birthdays and some holidays, even though Anna-Karin moved to the same city after finishing high school. Her father met a new woman and they lived together for roughly 20 years, before she left him. Then things took a turn for the worse. Anna-Karin's father started drinking too much and seemed to lose his sense of direction. The last year of his life, Anna-Karin had the feeling that he was trying to reconnect with her. He called more often and showed an interest in her life, even in her girlfriend—a topic he had previously tried to avoid as best he could. She visited him about once a month, mostly out of duty but also because she hoped that things would get better. One day he did not answer when she sent him a text message. She tried again a couple of times. She called him. Still no answer. Finally, she and her sister went to his place to see what was going on. They found him dead on the bedroom floor.

At the time of the interview, a year had passed since her father's death, and Anna-Karin, although feeling better, described how certain things kept resurfacing. Time and time again, she returned to the moment when she saw his phone on the kitchen table: "The realization that he would never send another text... It was such a profound thought. And it sounds weird, 'cause it's less important than the fact that we'd never sit down for a cup of coffee again, but for some reason it got to me." She also saw his watch on a shelf in the bathroom and yet again, she was struck by the reality of what had happened, "it was the same feeling, he'll never wear it again." As Gibson (2008: 188) notes, losing someone means that you have to come to terms with the fact that the person has disappeared and face "an irreversible absence." To Anna-Karin, her father's irreversible absence was effectively materialized through these particular objects, objects he used in his daily life.

At the same time, however, the watch and the phone manifested her father's presence, his person, as they suddenly became an elongation of him in a way that they had not been before. Gordon (2008) discusses "ghostly signals," referring to things like a chair that someone used to sit in, a piece of clothing that someone used to wear and so on. Gordon says that "these are the flashing half-signs ordinarily overlooked until that one day when they become animated by the *immense forces of atmosphere concealed in them*" (2008: 204, italics in original). This is an important aspect of the materialization of loss—how objects, in a sense, can be transformed into part-of-the-person. This transformation may certainly occur before death as well, but in Anna-Karin's case, the phone and the watch became ghostly signals when they were suddenly assigned new meaning (albeit for different reasons).

With some hesitation, Anna-Karin also talked about the stain on the floor, where her father or her father's body was discovered. Because he had been lying on the floor for a couple of days at room temperature, the decay of organic matter had begun, leaving a dark stain after he was removed. The putrefaction of a body is the most natural thing in the world from a biological point of view, but from the perspective of the mourner, this process may violate everything that is relationally sacred. Anna-Karin explained that she understood why the stain was there (and why it kept resurfacing in her mind) and that the real problem was what it symbolized: "It was there because we didn't have a very good relationship. If our relationship had been better, then it wouldn't have taken days and there would be no stain, perhaps he'd even be alive." The stain thus serves as a reminder of the forever flawed relationship between Anna-Karin and her father, and in that respect, it materializes her loss in a different and more haunting way than the other objects do (cf. Gordon, 2008). It was to remain the deepest source of anxiety for her during the year to come.

Josefin, 33

Josefin lost her father in an accident two years ago. He was on his way home from work when his bicycle was hit by a car. He died instantly, she was told by the police. She was also told that the driver of the car had done nothing wrong, it was her father who had not adhered to the traffic rules. There were, however, no witnesses, and Josefin and the rest of the family felt that the police had not really considered other options. What if the driver was responsible for the accident? In the interview, she described how this question tormented them in the beginning, and how she kept imagining the horrific event in detail. Her father was literally crushed, and this alone was a lot to handle. Sherwin B. Nuland notes that "dying is a messy business" (1995: 142), but some cases are arguably messier than others. Having to picture a loved one in a brutal accident is a gruesome first step to take as a mourner.

During the first year after the accident, it was difficult for Josefin to visit her mother, because her father's absence-presence was prominent in so many places throughout the house. His workshop in the garage was the toughest place. He liked carpentry and spent a lot of time there, restoring old furniture and building birdhouses and the like. While Josefin usually managed to avoid the garage as a physical space on her visits, she could not get away from her mother's talk about how troubled she was by it:

> He was in the process of sorting stuff out, there were small jars with screws and nuts and he'd written notes that said 'keep' or 'toss,' but of course nothing was ever tossed out. She (her mother) thought that was tough, seeing what he was doing, it was like he'd just stepped out of the room momentarily. But it's all gone now, there's just an empty desk.

It is no coincidence that his absence-presence was overwhelming in the workshop and that, consequently, her loss was materialized the most there—the place where he had been tinkering away with things on his own and where he was to be found and lost again in hundreds, if not thousands, of objects. While Anna-Karin materialized her loss through objects that could be removed from the scene (a watch and a phone) and still retain their meaning, Josefin did not mention any single item specifically, supposedly because it was all of them combined, in situ, that signaled her father's absence-presence. Once separated and handled elsewhere, they could be discarded.

It is significant that his absence-presence had to be, so to speak, cleared away. In the end, Josefin volunteered to, or was made to, take care of it. The place was too disturbing, to her but most notably to her mother. Gibson (2008: 188) notes that "the sense of being haunted both internally and externally can be comforting, even sought after." Conflating negative and positive experiences like this could potentially rob the concept of haunting of its analytical power. Likewise, we had better distinguish between remembrance, that is, intentional actions designed to bring back the deceased in different respects (Kasket, 2012; Shimazono & Kitts, 2013; Woodthorpe, 2010), and haunting. Haunting ought to be ontologized on experiential grounds, rather than intentional, or it risks losing its ability to capture the unexpected and uncontrollable. In Josefin's case, and here a parallel can perhaps be drawn to Anna-Karin, the suddenness of her father's death and the possibility of a crime clearly played a role in how her grief unfolded. The workshop—a space that he had created for himself (although other people were allowed to use it) and where he came to life in a special way—was the place from which he was absolutely erased, suddenly from one day to the next. It was, put differently, the place where the incongruence between before and after stood out the most for the rest of the family. This disruption, to abrupt to grasp emotionally, haunted them for some time and only started to ease its grip once Josefin felt compelled to enter the workshop to clean it out.

Laura, 53

As described in the introduction, Pamela's brother gave Laura a couple of her drawings and favorite vinyl records. These are now dutifully sitting on a shelf in her living room. They were clearly intended to become treasured mementos, but they are not. Instead, they remind Laura of the fact that, in the end, their relationship was not recognized as very important. Pamela felt like family to her, and she should have been there when her place was taken care of. Gibson (2008: 40) says that when a family member dies, the remaining members can use objects as a starting point when telling stories about the deceased and, in doing so, "reminding each other that their lives and identities are threaded together." Laura was not invited to be part of this process and experienced a form of disenfranchised grief (Doka, 1989), that is, grief that is not acknowledged in an appropriate way by others and/or society at large. Presumably, this is one of the reasons why she felt, and to some degree still feels, haunted, if you will, by the memory of Pamela. They were both mistreated in the end because their relationship was trivialized, and Laura feels a bit guilty for letting that happen. Had she been able to join the family in Pamela's flat, she would have had the chance to pick out objects that she assigned real meaning to and so materialize her loss on her own terms, much like Anna-Karin did with her father.

Laura is usually able to avoid the building where Pamela lived and where her absence-presence still lingers in a haunting way. In a few instances, she has been forced to enter that part of town and she describes how that would make her heart beat faster and how she would arrive "all sweaty and in a mess." From one perspective, it is not unlikely that the possibility to avoid Pamela's old flat charged the place even more. As Trigg (2012) notes, the uncanny is made manifest when we lack the conceptual scheme to put things in their rightful place, something that is particularly difficult when the unfamiliar forcefully invades cherished, taken-for-granted familiarity. By not purposefully confronting the disconcerting absence-presence of Pamela, Laura might have robbed herself of the chance to make sense of the loss and put things in order. Josefin, in comparison, had to go through such a process relatively soon after her father died owing to her mother's state of mind. When she finally approached the building sometime after Pamela's death, Laura was struck by a terrible anguish. On the next visit, she realized that there was a new tenant and her anxiety level rose even more. This goes to show that when loss is materialized such that places and persons are conflated, it can, depending on circumstances, put the bereaved in a situation where experienced realities collide.

Hanneke, 29

Hanneke lost her aunt, Veerle, when she was 20 years old, and this had a major impact on her. Veerle was something of an eccentric and led an unconventional life in a nearby town. "She had her own logic in a lot of ways," as Hanneke puts it. Hanneke and her family regularly spent weekends at her aunt's place, not least so that they could enjoy her big garden. Hanneke remembers the garden in great detail and talks about the small guesthouse, where they stayed during summer holidays. When Veerle died at the age of 60, the house was sold and demolished. Hanneke remarks, "when she died, the entire place died." In fact, the entire town where Veerle had lived "died" in Hanneke's eyes. Veerle was buried in the town cemetery, so Hanneke and her family now have to go there to visit her grave. Whenever they go, they carefully avoid going past the no-longer-there house. She says: "We always turn, 'cause I don't think we can bear driving past her house and it isn't there."

According to Emma Bell (2012), places and buildings can die and turn into corpses of a kind in the eyes of the people who used to go to them or work in them (see Olofsson, Chap. 4, this volume for a similar argument). Bell shows in her study how employees of a soon-to-be-shut-down industrial organization made sense of their loss by constructing a narrative of death in relation to the physical factory itself. No longer animated by (human) activity, places can become cadaverous features in land- or cityscapes. In Hanneke's case, the death of her aunt's house, apart from mirroring the death of her aunt, also marked the death of an era or a sort of wonderland. To Hanneke, Veerle, with all her animals and unusual ideas, symbolized an alternative way of doing things, a possibility to exist outside ordinary, human society. In *Death, Memory and Material Culture*, Elizabeth Hallam and Jenny Hockey (2001: 85) point to the importance of the material for maintaining continuing bonds between the living and the dead, "past presence and present absence are condensed into a spatially located object." Veerle's house, and to some extent the town, was the object where this condensation took place. When the house was bulldozed, it was as if the last material traces of Veerle were wiped out and converted into a pile of wood, concrete and pipes.

Although Hanneke was able to materialize her loss through loved objects she received from Veerle while she was still alive, she has conflated person and place, much like Josefin and Laura did, which makes it difficult to come to terms with the spatial absence-presence of her aunt. The fact that Veerle's house was torn down might constitute a special conundrum, as this tearing down, on a symbolic level, indicates the destruction of Veerle herself. While Josefin had the opportunity to disassemble her father's workshop, thereby painfully putting things in order, Hanneke lacks the material resources to do so. To compare her situation to Laura's, there is nothing left to approach or confront. As a consequence, Hanneke finds herself in limbo, avoiding something that materially speaking cannot be avoided, because it is no longer there. Gordon (2008: 8), however, states that haunting "describes how that which appears to be not there is often a seething presence," reminding us that absence is only absence to those who were not there, who do not know.

Olof, 86

Olof has spent many years of his life on a farm he bought with his wife. He has worked hard to be able to live off the land, and his wife's death a year ago was a tremendous blow. Even though he grieves over his wife, it is the death of his oldest son that seems to haunt him. The son, who died of cancer when he was only 34 years old, cared deeply for the farm and was the obvious heir of the estate. Olof remembers his son's projects as if it were yesterday—his son dug ditches, rebuilt the barn, engineered a handy car lift and much more. There are traces of him everywhere in the form of objects and various alterations and improvements. Just as in the case of Anna-Karin and her father's phone and watch, these are the "ghostly signals" (Gordon, 2008) he has to live with. The difference is that he encounters the absence-presence of his son on a daily basis whether he wants to or not—he lives his life in a space of memory (cf. Gibson, 2008). Unlike Josefin, he cannot really dissemble this space even if he would like to, not without ruining the farm.

It is not uncommon for grief to be accompanied by eerie events, as smells, music and the like may suddenly remind people of dead significant others (Hallam et al., 1999). To Olof, such occurrences have lost their experiential edge because he has been exposed to the absence-presence of his son for so many years, but he still feels that something went horribly wrong when he died. Memories, as Hallam and Hockey (2001: 105) assert, "stand as signals that the past has receded; they reveal a distance between the subject and past events." Contrary to this notion, Olof's account clearly shows how the then and the now coexist—he is very careful to provide the correct years and keep the linearity throughout the interview, at the same time as the past constantly bleeds into the present, mixing memories, emotions and experiences here and now. He wrestles with the fact that no one will take over the farm. His younger son has never showed an interest in that kind of life and his grandchildren are too small. The farm will, in a way, die with him (see Holmberg, Chap. 3, this volume for a similar argument).

In this sense, the death of his son was a twofold loss—it was the loss of a significant other as well as a dream for the future. Like Hanneke, then, he is mourning more than a person and the relationship with that person. Importantly, in the future he once imagined, he too would have a place, because someone would carry on his legacy. This phenomenon, referred to as "rippling" by Irvin D. Yalom (2009), means that people gain a sense of immortality. The discrepancy between what is and what should have been is conspicuous in Olof's account. The eerie, Gordon asserts, tends to seep in when we face "the always unsettled relationship between what we see and what we know" (2008: 194). When Olof takes his morning walk, he sees a thriving place. The farm has done well, even after he sold off the dairy cattle. What he knows is that the person who animated the place and made it (seem) permanent is gone. There is a sense of guilt in his narrative, and he even goes on to say "it should've been me." This guilt is not derived from a feeling that he did not do all that he could, but from the simple fact that his son was in his mid-30s when he died. Of course, living on a farm, Olof is well aware that neither life nor death follows a strict path, but this is beyond common-sense knowledge.

In sum, the narratives presented in this section demonstrate, in different ways, how bereavement is shaped by and also shapes the semiotic content of matter associated with the deceased. It seems clear that the materialization of loss can be a complex process that depends heavily on what role the now deceased person played in the life of the now bereaved, access to places and the right objects for the bereaved, as well as the cause of death.

Conclusions: Materialization and Absence-Presence of the Deceased

This chapter has explored how five people materialize loss, thereby facing the absence-presence of the deceased person they cared for. While people are alive, they animate the places and spaces they inhabit, and certain objects become part of them, of their subjectivity. Such places and objects can of course be deeply meaningful to friends, partners and family members all along, but they can also be given new meaning when the person dies. All of a sudden, a tea cup or an iPad might convey the person's personality and (non)existence in an almost shocking way. Objects and places imbued with meaning tend to bring us closer to dead significant others as memories and emotions related to the person are brought back or enhanced. The (experienced) presence of the person is usually accompanied by an absence, as we are also made aware of what is missing (which might, of course, be a relief depending on the nature of the relationship that was). Emotions, as a general rule, run deep when a significant other dies. What the interviewees have in common is that their grief is particularly marked by feelings of anxiety, disorientation and, in some cases, guilt. Arguably, such emotions are quite common among the bereaved, rather it is the strength and endurance of the emotions that are of importance.

The deceased persons enter the lives of the interviewees in the realm of the mundane—as a watch, a vinyl record, a jar with screws, a ditch. The analysis, however, reveals that objects have different status once they are assigned meaning. Josefin materialized the loss of her father in the many things found in his workshop, and it appeared to be their in situ position that made them meaningful in her eyes. Removed from the place, they lost their connection to her father, which shows that his absence-presence at the deepest level was tied to the workshop. Laura's account demonstrates the importance of having the opportunity to choose your own mementos, or in other words, of being able to develop a continued bond with the deceased (cf. Klass et al., 1996). The objects handed to her by Pamela's brother do not contain Pamela, so to speak, they merely mirror their disrupted relationship. How objects of the dead are retrieved is thus also crucial to what meaning can be assigned to them. Under certain circumstances, people may feel fine about simply receiving mementos, it all depends on the nature of the relationship that was and numerous other factors.

Like Josefin with her father, Olof experiences the absence-presence of his son in situ at the farm. No longer as affected by the ghostly signals (Gordon, 2008), he nevertheless lives his life in two worlds—the world that is and the world that should have been. Hanneke is going through something similar (although presumably not as intense), in that the alternative world created by her aunt Veerle died with her. The no-longer-there place where Veerle used to live is full of her presence, at the same time as it is, because of the demolished house, completely empty. This results in a disturbing absence-presence of Veerle that is hard for Hanneke to come to terms with. Similarly, Laura has to deal with the fact that Pamela's old place is now someone else's home, which means, symbolically, that Pamela cannot be there. It seems clear that when people regard places as part of the deceased person at the level of experience, this can lead to considerable distress. So-called person-in-place bonds, that is, continuing bonds where person and place are conflated, may alternatively offer bereaved persons the opportunity to be close to their deceased in a comforting way (Jonsson & Walter, 2017).

It is concluded that the interviewees are or were haunted by, or by the memories of, their dead significant others. To be haunted is to experience the deceased as a deeply unsettling absence-presence, here in the context of objects and place. Even though there are differences between the five cases presented, they all allude to the fact that absence and presence can be materialized simultaneously in ways that leave people terrified or in a state of deepest despair. Haunting occurs when the familiar and the unfamiliar collide and create an absence-presence that is impossible to make sense of, to put in order even the slightest bit. The argument here is not that all people need to confront houses or flats where dead significant others used to live, or that they should always help to sort out the belongings of the dead, even if this may indeed ease the discomfort for some. Rather, the argument is that we need to be able to analyze these kinds of experiences without resorting to pathologization. As these five cases clearly demonstrate, it is not, at the end of the day, these individuals who have somehow malfunctioned or failed to grasp reality, it is reality itself that is sometimes too ambiguous, fast and uncompromising. When analyzing the materialization of loss, then, we should keep in mind that depending on what kind of absence-presence individuals discover or are confronted with, they will be propelled into quite different scenarios. This needs to be acknowledged by researchers, clinicians and others alike, so that bereavement can be addressed without an assessment of the bereaved person per se.

Note

1. The interviewees were in the age range 29–86 years. Three of them were located through friends and colleagues, and I stumbled across two by chance. Four of the interviews took place in the interviewees' homes, and one was conducted at a café. Four of them were recorded and transcribed in full. In one case, notes were taken instead because the interviewee felt uneasy about how her voice would sound "on tape." The interviews followed the same pattern—they started with general talk about the interviewees' current life situation, moved on to the personality of the person that had died and the nature of their relationship, and ended with specific details about the death and the emotions involved. In three cases, a second interview was performed a couple of months after the first one, partly because the first interview had been cut short, but mostly because these persons expressed a need to talk more about what they had been through.

References

Alexander, J. (2003) *The Meanings of Social Life: A Cultural Sociology*, Oxford and New York: Oxford University Press.

Árnason, A. (2012) 'Individuals and Relationships: On the Possibilities and Impossibilities of Presence' in D. Davies and C. W. Park (eds.) *Emotion, Identity and Death: Mortality Across Disciplines*, Aldersot: Ashgate.

Bell, E. (2012) 'Ways of Seeing Organisational Death: A Critical Semiotic Analysis of Organizational Memorialisation', *Visual Studies*, 27(1), 4–17.

Day, A. (2013) *Believing in Belonging. Belief and Social Identity in the Modern World*, Oxford: Oxford University Press.

Doka, K. J. (ed.) (1989) *Disenfranchised Grief: Recognizing Hidden Sorrow*, Lexington, MA: Lexington Books.

Freud, S. (1919) 'The "Uncanny"' in *The Standard Edition of the Complete Psychological Works of Sigmund Freud, "An Infantile Neurosis" and Other Works, Vol. XVII (1917–1919)*, London: Hogarth.

Gibson, M. (2008) *Objects of the Dead: Mourning and Memory in Everyday Life*, Melbourne: Melbourne University.

Gordon, A. (2008) *Ghostly Matters: Haunting and the Sociological Imagination*, Minneapolis: University of Minnesota Press.

Hallam, E. and Hockey, J. (2001) *Death, Memory and Material Culture*, Oxford: Berg.

Hallam, E. Hockey, J. and Howarth, G. (1999) *Beyond the Body: Death and Social Identity*, London: Routledge.

Jonsson, A. (2015) 'Post-Mortem Social Death—Exploring the Absence of the Deceased', *Contemporary Social Science*, 10(3), 284–295.

Jonsson, A. and Aronsson, L. (2015) 'Afterlife Imagery in Sweden: The Role of Continuing Bonds', *Thanatos*, 4(2), 41–55.

Jonsson, A. and Walter, T. (2017) 'Continuing Bonds and Place', *Death Studies*, 41(7), 406–415.

Kasket, E. (2012) 'Continuing Bonds in the Age of Social Networking', *Bereavement Care*, 31(2), 62–69.

Klass, D., Silverman, P. R., and Nickman, S. L. (eds.) (1996) *Continuing Bonds: New Understandings of Grief*, Abingdon: Taylor & Francis.

Klass, D. and Goss, R. (1999) 'Spiritual Bonds to the Dead in a Cross-Cultural and Historical Perspective: Comparative Religion and Modern Grief', *Death Studies*, 23(6), 547–567.

Klass, D. and Steffen, E. M. (eds.) (2018) *Continuing Bonds in Bereavement*, New Directions for Research and Practice, London: Routledge.

Klass, D. and Walter, T. (2001) 'Processes of Grieving: How Bonds Are Continued' in M. Stroebe, R. Hansson, W. Stroebe, & H. Schut (eds.) *Handbook of Bereavement Research*, Washington, DC: American Psychological Association.

Maddrell, A. (2013) 'Living with the Deceased: Absence, Presence and Absence-Presence', *Cultural Geographies*, 20(4), 501–522.

Maddrell, A. and Sidaway, J. D. (2010) *Deathscapes: Spaces for Death, Dying Mourning and Remembrance*, Farnham: Ashgate Publishing, Ltd.

Mathijssen, B. (2017) 'Transforming Bonds: Ritualising Post-Mortem Relationships in the Netherlands', *Death Studies*, 23(3), 215–230.

Nuland, S. B. (1995) *How We Die: Reflections on Life's Final Chapter*, New York: Vintage Books.

Ribbens McCarthy, J. and Prokhovnik, R. (2014) 'Embodied Relationality and Caring After Death', *Body & Society*, 20(2), 18–43.

Shear, K. (2012) 'Grief and Mourning Gone Awry: Pathway and Course of Complicated Grief', *Dialogues in Clinical Neuroscience*, 14(2), 119–128.

Shimazono, S. and Kitts, M. (2013) 'Rituals of Death and Remembrance' in M. Jerryson, M. Juergensmeyer and M. Kitts (eds.) *The Oxford Handbook of Religion and Violence*, Oxford: Oxford University Press.

Smart, C. (2007) *Personal Life*, Cambridge: Polity Press.

Swidler, A. (1986) 'Culture in Action. Symbols and Strategies', *American Sociological Review*, 51(2), 273–286.

Trigg, D. (2012) *The Memory of Place. A Phenomenology of the Uncanny*, Athens: Ohio University Press.

Valentine, C. (2008) *Bereavement Narratives: Continuing Bonds in the Twenty-First Century*, London: Routledge.

Vickio, C. J. (1999) 'Together in Spirit: Keeping Our Relationships Alive When Loved Ones Die', *Death Studies*, 23(2), 161–175.

Volkan, V. (1972) 'The Linking Objects of Pathological Mourners', *Archives of General Psychiatry*, 27(2), 215–221.

Walter, T. (1999) *On Bereavement: The Culture of Grief*, Buckingham: Open University Press.

Walter, T. (2006) 'What Is Complicated Grief? A Social Constructionist Perspective', *Omega*, 52(1), 71–79.

Winnicott, D. W. (1953) 'Transitional Objects and Transitional Phenomena', *International Journal of Psycho-Analysis*, 34(2), 89–97.

Woodthorpe, K. (2010) 'Private Grief in Public Spaces: Interpreting Memorialisation in the Contemporary Cemetery' in J. Hockey, C. Komaromy and K. Woodthorpe (eds.) *The Matter of Death*, Basingstoke: Palgrave Macmillan.

Yalom, I. D. (2009) *Staring at the Sun. Overcoming the Terror of Death*, Hoboken: Wiley.

3

Mortmain: Manor Culture and Material Immortality

Tora Holmberg

Introduction

When considering the commitment, financial investments and work, one might ask what leads a minor fraction of the population to live in a castle or another major estate. One why-answer would be that the manor provides a resource for maintaining the cultural distinction that allows the landowning upper class to keep their privileges. But instead of seeking structural explanations for cultural practice, a cultural sociology seeks explanations from the inside, in the collective patterns of meaning making (Alexander & Smith, 2003: 12). Following this approach, the chapter asks how it comes that in an era of individualization, some people spend their whole lives caring for an inherited estate and its family tradition, sometimes with comparatively little monetary reward, in order to pass it on to future generations. I will approach this puzzle through the trope of "mortmain," a juridical arrangement with an ancient Western history. It means literally that land and other property use can be dictated to following gen-

T. Holmberg (✉)
Department of Sociology, Uppsala University, Uppsala, Sweden
e-mail: tora.holmberg@soc.uu.se

© The Author(s) 2019
T. Holmberg et al. (eds.), *Death Matters*,
https://doi.org/10.1007/978-3-030-11485-5_3

erations, many years after the death of the testator. However, mortmain is predominantly not a juridical but a cultural trope, as it manifests in symbolic as well as material structuring of meaning and practice.

Duke Charles Gordon-Lennox, owner of the castle Goodwood outside Portsmouth, West Sussex, serves as a telling example of the effects of such politics of inheritance. In the BBC series *British Aristocrats*, Charles tells the interviewer that "Goodwood is my life, it's part of my being, it cannot be changed" (SVT, 2012). Charles uses his profit-gaining side activities—fairs and car races—to finance what seem to be endless maintenance and improvement needs. The voiceover says: "The aristocrats call it mortmain, the dead hand of the past. We may see them as privileged, but they feel a great responsibility to carry on the family heritage." Carrying on the family heritage means, in practice, maintaining land and property. "Maintain" is in itself an ambiguous term, meaning both to support and to keep. What has been in history should be moved into the future, preferably in better condition than at the point of inheritance. In the TV episode, mortmain is said to condition Charles' practices; he is not free to do as he wishes with the Goodwood estate, even if he would like to. How can we understand the role of this "dead hand of the past," through which cultural practices is it performed, and with what effects? In this chapter, I am concerned with a certain element of manor culture, namely that of *förvaltning* (maintenance). This element centers around certain values like responsibility and sustainability, and material actors such as, apart from the manor and the land, portraits and other family collections. As "ghostly matters" (Gordon, 2008)—social figures affecting habituated practices—values and material actors allow people to navigate smoothly in their everyday life environments—in our case, the habitat of the landowning rural upper class.

This landowning rural upper class is here defined as a category of people who, like Charles Gordon-Lennox, inhabits old manors with considerable history and family traditions. This category of landowner may or may not have an aristocratic name or title—itself a symbolic marker of the upper class—but the common denominator is the way in which manor culture is shaped by former and future generations. Ultimately, this chapter explores intergenerational obligations and, by so doing, extends the analysis of class reproduction. The former generations act far beyond the juridical inheritance arrangements, through the manor and its emplaced family tradition and expectations, they influence present as well as future inhabitants. Thus, long-gone relatives and inherited goods, continue to impact on manor lifestyles, negotiating with changing conditions and ideals (Holmberg, 2017).

Through interviews with manor owners, this chapter demonstrates how the past becomes symbolically and materially manifest in everyday manor living, fostering a certain kind of intergenerational responsibility for the estate. The cultural sociological frame employed can be summarized as oriented toward the structuring of meaning though symbolic and material resources available in a specific historical and cultural setting (Swidler, 1986). I am attending to the ways in which the symbolic scripts of ghostly shadows of the past and the expectations for the future shape the everyday manor practices. The performance of these practices is understood in relation to cultural structuring of life and death, material arrangements and placemaking (cf. Alexander, 2004). The main point is that the everyday practices that take place at the manor are tightly knitted together with the historical place, its' temporal trajectories and the intergenerational meaning making.

At an early stage, I noticed that there seemed to be a consistent thread in interviews; namely, how the attachment to place plays out in explaining why all the hard work is ultimately worthwhile. Place attachment is a term often used in attempts to understand the dialectical process through which identity, home and belonging are constructed (de Blij, 2008; Duyvendak, 2011; Easthope, 2004). Consequently, the manor and various other material objects attached to the estate, at times gain a form of agency. How are we to understand this phenomenon? Heidegger argues in *Being and Time* (1962) that attachment to place is an integral part of being in the world. One cannot distinguish the being from either time or place. Different qualifications have later been made. Henri Lefebvre has developed Heidegger's concept of "dwelling" into a particular meaning, conceptualizing it in relation to the dialectics of time and space (1991). In other words, dwelling is a matter of being emplaced, as well as of memory, of longing, when not in place. Tuning in on dwelling means attending to the everyday practices, materialities and emotions that make us attached to a certain place. Of particular interest in this chapter is David Harvey's interpretation of the concept, according to which "dwelling is the capacity to achieve a spiritual unity between humans and things" (Harvey, 1996: 300–1). I argue below that when the manor is ascribed agency, it is not to be understood as an example of animistic thinking. These moments are rather exceptionally fitting illustrations of the term dwelling, in which the human and the material object come together in a "spiritual unity," situating being in time and place.

For the purposes of this chapter, the analyses are based on data from the project "Lifestyles at Swedish manors: Between tradition and change" (Holmberg, 2017, 2018). These data consist of hands-on house visits, including interviews with manor and castle owners in southern and central Sweden. The intent of the analytical approach is to, through understanding and writing the culture from within, capture how these owners' social world is built, how they understand it and by what symbolic and material means they navigate within it (Clifford & Marcus, 1986). All in all, I have made 14 visits (lasting from a few hours to a full day) and interviewed 22 men and women living at the estates I have visited. The owners were selected based on the criteria of a variability of age and gender, but a homogeneity in background (all but one with inherited manors and with a noble family background).[1]

"Manor" is here defined as a major estate, initially delegated by the king as noble privilege and thus possessing hundreds of years of emplaced history. It includes a number of houses and buildings, with an architecturally typical and dominant *corps de logi* (main building). This definition of a manor also applies to a castle; although in order to be called such, a member of royalty must actually have been a resident. Moreover, the manor incorporates considerable amounts of land, which allows for providing for the whole estate (Ulväng, 2008). The manors of the informants include between 800 and ≥10,000 acres of forests, fields and lakes, and the main buildings range from a few hundred square meters' living space to several thousand. It obviously takes a great deal of time and effort to manage such an estate, and the interviews circled around themes related to work, investments, life choices, home and family life. As the interviews were performed in Swedish, any quotes that appear in this chapter have been translated. Moreover, to ensure the confidentiality of participants, all names of people and manors are fictive, and details that may be identity-revealing are sometimes altered. In addition, I have also used journalistic and visual data to situate the manor lifestyles in the broader popular culture, mainly from Swedish coffee table magazines and television productions, which often cover at-home stories from the population my informants belong to.[2]

The background will be clarified in the research context laid out in the *Historical frame* section. The following two sections, *Maintaining the manor* and *Bringing life to the manor*, are the empirical ones, analyzing interviews, field notes and popular culture data, in order to answer how the hand of the dead works in everyday manor life. The sections show that the estate and its property, through certain symbolic and material structures, exercise influence over its' inhabitants. The culture sketched out in these sections revolves around values like responsibility and sustainability—values that are reinforced in interaction with the material aspects of the estate through the process of homemaking, of dwelling. Lastly, the *Material immortality* section provides a furthering of the analysis by discussing how mortmain can be understood in cultural sociological terms. Developing the frame on symbolic as well as material aspects of kinship, place and class reproduction, I close by suggesting "material immortality" as a frame for understanding the effects of mortmain in rural upper-class culture—the prospect to live on beyond ones' own death.

Historical Frame

Something that unites the landowning upper class in history is the nature of the estates and property, and the forms of habituated practices taking place there. Everyone knows who the land owner is, and he traditionally takes care of the workers and villagers while at the same time not sharing much socially with them. In the words of Digby Baltzell in his modern history of the American aristocracy, "upper class" is defined in terms of hierarchy (successful, top), social bonds (families, friendship, marriage) and lifestyle (distinctive, group solidarity), which together set the population aside from the majority of society (Baltzell, 1958: 7). Susanne Ostrander writes in a similar manner about the distinctiveness and exclusivity of the upper class, but moreover stresses the power aspects and relations based on social and cultural capital (1984: 5). Although certainly finding merit in these definitions, I rather stress a practice-oriented cultural sociological approach in which class, as system and identity, is performed through boundaries regarding symbolic structures, involving meaning, materiality, practice, and not least, values (Lamont & Fournier, 1992). It goes without saying that financial conditions and material objects are central to the structuring of social class. Quoting Michèle Lamont, class structures are built through cultural boundaries based on "money, morals, and manners" (1992).

There are of course nationally embedded, historically constructed contexts to take into account. In Sweden *Riddarhuset* (the House of knights), located in Stockholm, manifests the aristocracy as a remnant of the feudal period. As an interest organization and administrative common, Riddarhuset was established in 1617, in an age when the privileges of the nobility were growing and consolidating. At the same time, the legal foundations of the phenomenon of *fideicommissum*—meaning basically to commit something to someone's trust—were laid. The construct of the *fideicommissum* aimed at keeping estates and other property together, preventing the splits that accompany generational shifts. This way, property could be passed on via the male heir, most often the oldest son, from generation to generation, eternally. Avoiding the threat of splitting up the recently acquired privileges of the nobilities, the law prohibited disposal and thus helped preserving the "sacred whole" of the inherited estate (see Douglas, 1966).

Like Riddarhuset, the *fideicommissum* law dates from 1617, and states that, while the heir would inherit all of the estate and/or other property, he was not free to sell or share the inheritance but rather only to act as a commissioner.[3] Strictly speaking, he who was termed *fideicommissarius* did not own the property, but was expected to live on its returns. Although the legal construct was abandoned in the 1960s, there is still juridical space to make exceptions, which are approved by the Swedish government based on the existence of "prominent cultural heritage that is in need of conservation" (Regeringens proposition, 1999). Thus, there still exist around 20 manors and castles managed according to the 400 years of patriarchal rules that set aside constitutional law. Apart from the few *fideicommissum* exceptions that still exist, there are more widely accepted and timely inheritance and ownership solutions employed, also aimed at preventing the splitting of property: corporations, trusts and informal agreements among family members. In the present study the manors are run in all of the above forms, including a handful of *fideicommissum* estates.

Today, the aristocracy has lost all their formal privileges. Still, Riddarhuset remains a solid institution, keeping the nobility together and maintaining significant funds. As such, it manifests the aristocratic values of a class society of the past, challenging the equality and meritocracy embraced throughout modernity (see Holmqvist, 2015). One important cue to acknowledge in explaining this hard to bend remnant of the past is the persistence of its ideal of maintenance through its connections to place through dwelling and spiritual unity of past-present materiality that keep it going.

Maintaining the Manor

The structure of meaning used in interviews and elsewhere is built around the idea of keeping the whole, articulated as the pursuit to preserve and develop the manor for future generations. This strive constitutes a kind of moral compass that guides the interviewees' navigation in the world. The compass is based on values like modesty, dedication and responsibility, in which one's own priorities and choices are downplayed. Instead, it is all done in the interest of imagined future dwelling, oriented toward coming generations. The goal is to hand over the estate and property in better financial and material, self-maintaining, condition than before. As one of the interviewees, Oscar, states:

> I want to hand over a well-kept farm with well-kept buildings, forests, and land and the like, to the next generation. To someone who will continue to keep and maintain the estate.

When asked what he means by "maintain," a key term in virtually all interviews, Oscar replies: "Well, it's to, right, to keep and to let history live on, history meaning that, well, with respect for the old history, as I would have it." Respecting the old history and letting it live on through the successful management ("well-kept") of the cultural and natural heritage of the manor seems to be a matter of great concern. The profits gained by the labor of past generations should be carried into the future, for the benefit of coming ones. Thus, the fruits of the labor created in history are not to be consumed by the current owner, but rather to be transferred to coming generations. It is interesting to note how "history" is tightly attached to the manor that becomes a place where the past is housed. This way, contemporary (and future) manor life, incorporates and embodies respect to the unbroken lineage.

This ideal of keeping and maintaining is often asserted in moral terms, namely through the value of responsibility, illustrated nicely in the following quote from a lifestyle magazine. Christian, heir of the castle that has been in his family since 1659, has now, along with his wife Mette, recently renovated the 70 rooms in the main building:

> We're happy and proud of what we've done here, says Christian. We've fulfilled our responsibility to the building itself. We don't know anything about what the future will bring. But if we're allowed to wish, we hope one of our children will choose to live here and have a good life. (*Gods & Gårdar*, 2016a: 20)

The couple expresses that they are "happy and proud" of what they have accomplished, an expression that signals a fulfilled moral obligation, that of "responsibility." In fact, responsibility seems to be a key value for the maintenance culture. It is, like in the quote above, mainly articulated as being directed toward the estate, the manor, a responsibility often viewed as prioritized over the subject's own wishes. However, when speaking of their own children a subjective choice is ascribed to them. A similar story line is expressed by Claes, father of two:

And when you think, when we speak about the future, do you think your children will take over … from you? How important is that?
Well, but that's important, it is. Yes, since it's been in the family, right, for 200 years and there's been so damn much arguing and fights … about how

to deal with it, then it's part of the responsibility again, to make it live on, so to say. In a way it feels like you can't, if I were the one who broke it … like just 'nice, now I can split this up the way I like and sell a little and lead a life of luxury.' Then I would've somehow … I don't have the right, kind of; I would have torn up all my other relatives' … life choices.

Although Claes legally has the possibility to sell parts, or the whole, of the estate and consume the profit, morally he does not feel he has this choice. It would be like cheating his children of their 200-year heritage. This statement can be related to the analysis above, in which the children are ascribed more of a choice. While the informants themselves are prohibited to sell, the future generation is not chosen in the same way. In addition, it would also mean a betrayal of his ancestors to profit from their hard work and go against the mortmain ("I don't have the right"). Through this narrative, the interviewee's potential to break with tradition and give future generations more opportunities of choice is framed as morally wrong.

The articulated valuation of generations to come is not necessarily limited to one's own offspring. Madeleine, one of the two heiresses I interviewed, speaks of the handing over of resources in terms of sustainability:

What does it mean to you, maintenance?
That we maintain this means to me that we … care for the inheritance. That you take care of the resources we've … been given, to take over somehow. And hopefully improve them. It's part of the sustainability concept really, the idea that you're to leave something better for the next generation, so to say. Then you end up with development also, right, you can't just look for maintenance, I think. It's not just about statically holding this together, but there must partly be development too, I have difficulty seeing it as purely maintenance. But maintenance, to me, it's probably the historical aspect of it.

For Madeleine, it is important to "care for" the estate and develop it in order to leave something better behind. "We" is a somewhat ambivalent sign; it may refer to the interviewee's family, the local society, or even a global community. Similarly noteworthy is "sustainability," a key term in this excerpt, in fact in the whole interview, as it directs focus away from the manor and broadens the perspective to "tak[ing] care of the resources" in a wide sense. The collectivist value framed in contemporary parlance is in fact also salient in practice, since the property in Madeleine's hands has taken great steps toward sustainable forms of farming, wetlands and forestry, as well as the development of conservation areas. Thus, for her, maintenance is closely linked to sustainable development. Interestingly, it also connects the future of the land, through the "historical aspect." The moral conclusion is that the land one has been given should be cared for. Again, the dead hand of the past can be said to reach out through the land that is "given," stretching into the future of generations to come.

When I interviewed a middle-aged couple with adult children who all lived at the ancient manor, they told me the manor "came before them," both materially and morally: "Well, it's still the house that comes first, we just happen to live here for 20 or 30 years or whatever" (Interview, Einar and Charlotte). The commandment that the manor must be preserved and kept in the family is seldom expressed directly; it is rather an undercurrent in the socialization process, reproduced, for example, in narratives about the past. Fredrik explains:

> [The manor] would stay, so of course it builds, in a way, on what I sometimes humorously call that hereditary insanity, which makes it tremendously important that [the manor] remains, and that you fight for it. There is no one who says, who's expressed, that; but it's there and is present really through those stories you've been told by parents and grandparents, of how they've fought and often sacrificed themselves in order to make this work.

Fredrik says he cannot remember anyone actually telling him to take over, but rather that he just somehow knew this was the case. Most of the interviewees narrate in similar ways that already as small children they knew where they would live as adults; that they would inherit the manor. Like Fredrik, who ironically speaks of the "hereditary insanity," another interviewee speaks of how he was "brainwashed" into the task of taking over the family estate. It was, in his words, "decided already in 1694," but thankfully he has never regretted his (lack of) choice. It is sometimes "nice to have goals and structures" and to let go of anxiety about what to do with your life (Interview, Gustaf). A similar story is told in a lifestyle magazine, in which landowning entrepreneurs Erik and Anna are interviewed about their background. Erik states that for as long as he can remember he has known he would inherit the manor, a fact he never revolted against. "On the contrary," he says, "it was quite nice to have a fixed future. I've never had a need to realize myself in any other way" (*Gods & Gårdar*, 2016b: 39). The common thread in these quotes seems to be how the meaning of insanity, brainwashing or just good old-fashioned socialization, places the choices somewhere else than with the subject himself.

To summarize, in the long perspective of the manor's history, inhabitants are temporary visitors who conserve and develop the property for the good of generations to come. The interviewees are portrayed as down-prioritizing their own needs and wishes, putting the will of the estate first. Moreover, this upgrading of one's heritage also gives the owner a clear goal and meaning in life. This ideal can be seen as an expression of the old patriarchal moral duty, formulated as *noblesse oblige* (Mitford, 1956), a social contract with the surrounding society, articulating that the privileges you have been given come with certain responsibilities. Through the maintenance culture, it is not just the house that decides, but also earlier generations. Like other modern parents they do not dictate their children's choices, but one can suspect that the symbolic and material structuring of everyday life provides functions in similar ways. Mortmain serves as a guarantee to preserve the values attached to diligent ideals and collectivist contracts, from generation to generation.

Bringing Life to the Manor

This section continues the above analysis of the maintenance script, and asks how one keeps ancient property "alive," and how the tension between seventeenth-century traditions and the contemporary manor life is materialized and negotiated. This question is answered by looking at the ways the house is portrayed in terms of home, and highlighting the role of material actors such as family portraits. These portraits and other inherited property influence the lives of present inhabitants.

First, in order to situate the dead hand of the past and its role among the living, let us unpack the reoccurring metaphor of keeping a manor alive through inhabiting it and using it in certain ways. Gustaf, quoted above, lives in a castle in southern Sweden, claims that maintenance also means using all the buildings:

> We oversee that they're cared for in a way that allows nature and culture to thrive, and we do this when we use all the buildings. Every old stone house should be used; if not, they deteriorate and they lose their soul. The castle should be used; we should live in the whole castle.
> **And how?**
> They should be used, or they'll lose their soul, it won't be a happy house if you—as I know many have done, when you renovate a part in one of the wings and then the other's empty, it dies rather quickly.

The soul or spirit of a house is a common cultural trope, but one that takes on particular meaning in this context. One could say that the older the building, the more soul it has. For the manor to be kept alive, it needs to be actively inhabited. In consequence, keeping a place like this alive and not risking its death (when empty "it dies") is a maintenance strategy that clearly means a great deal of work. Guests are regularly invited, hunts organized, fresh flowers set out and, not least, the many hundreds, sometimes thousands, of square meters are kept clean and heated, which involves significant labor—sometimes performed by the owners themselves, sometimes by employees—and monetary expense. Thus, the bodies of the inhabitants and guests vitalize the manor. However, it is not simply that the estate needs to be used in order to prevent it from dying. It actually needs to be actively used as a family home and not just for other purposes. The following quote from Henry illustrates this theme:

> **What do you really mean by maintaining?**
> Well, it's to … to keep, and to let history live on. If I say history, well, with respect for the old history. Perhaps not; one could build a golf course, but say you build a huge golf course and a luxury hotel and the like—then it becomes something else. There are many, we've seen conference establish-ments where this feeling disappears. […] But to maintain, to feel, well, the

strokes of history and … many people come here and when they, as they also live in large houses, they say, 'oh, it's so amazing, you feel like this is such a friendly place.' And it's not just that we ourselves are being friendly; really it's in the house, and you can read in old writings and that sort of thing that there's a certain harmony here.

Henry, who lives with his family in an old manor which history is typically well documented in "old writings," points out that maintenance also means creating a kind of good spirit ("friendly," "harmony"). A prerequisite for keeping this atmosphere, brought about through the "strokes of history," is that you actually live in the manor, and not turn it into a commercial endeavor. Although it is somewhat paradoxical, the refusal to overly commercialize, and instead continue making it a "friendly place" and a home, reduces the financial frames for maintaining the substantial residence. Nevertheless, active use of the manor as a home is the prerequisite for harmony, in a continuous process of homemaking, of dwelling. In the quotes above, the meaning of home is clearly understood in terms of positive feelings, brought about by the continuous interaction between past and present inhabitants and the house.

As the informants experience some kind of interaction between themselves and the manors they take care of, one might argue that the houses and other artifacts acquire the role of actors in their narratives. As such, material objects might from time to time enact the dead hand of the past. As a typical example, the oil paintings work in such a way in the narratives involving one of the informants; Carl, who is in his 40s, lives with his wife, Hannah, and their two children in a distinguished castle in central Sweden:

The entrance and the hall are spacious and dark; the floor is cold. I'm taken on a tour around some of the halls on the second floor. Erik tells me in a well-rehearsed manner about the castle's history from the 17th century and onward, his family's background and how they acquired [the manor]. He shows me the portraits of all his ancestors—male and female—and proudly tells me about the careful and costly reconstructions he's done, furniture that has been inherited for ages, porcelain batteries, and other antiquities. (Field notes, 12 January, 2016)

When Carl shows me around the interior of the castle, the portraits in dark colors, framed in gold, speak of earlier generations. But they also speak directly *to* the viewer: looking down from above, the aunt, the grandfather, and his grandfather in turn, make one feel rather small and insignificant. The portraits signify the connections between the inhabitants and the place, the manor, in very material ways, connecting Carl and his family to his ancient history. As such, they function as important turning points in the telling of his, and the castle's, story. Carl's ancestors are said to be a mixture of stubborn military officers and strong ladies, while the more recent generations are represented by conscientious and strenuous entrepreneurs who worked hard to secure the castle's survival. Carl tells me his parents and grandparents led a simple and hardworking life, since the estate never really carried its own costs. To Carl, the portraits are reminders of relatively harsh times and the actors who came before him, and are to be thanked for the improved life conditions he and his family enjoy.

Another telling example of the agency of portraits is that of Einar and Charlotte, quoted above. They live in the ancient manor Einar inherited in the 1970s:

C: That old lady [portrait on the wall], I talk to her a lot; she's wise […] you have to sit down like this and ask the question, and then the answers come.

E: I've gotten the question a couple of times when people see these paintings, that, 'don't you feel pressure from the old ones'? And the answer is never; we do our best, and we like it, and we're absolutely certain they're very happy and that they think this in-law [nodding at Charlotte] is damn good. That's the way it is.

Einar, who is actually not from the old aristocracy but rather from a rural bourgeois family, and Charlotte, who used to be a city girl, talk here of how they actually communicate with the dead, and receive support through these conversations. The ancestors are portrayed in prominent places high on the wall, looking down upon the mortals who, at the moment, live at the estate. Although this story is told with some humor, the message is that the old relatives and former inhabitants reach out through the portraits and give their approval of Einar and Charlotte's conduct as well as character ("they're very happy," "they think this in-law is damn good"). Like in traditional education environments, for example, the role of the portraits is to reassure the current inhabitants that they are performing well, that their virtues are acceptable, and that they are fulfilling the values of the symbolic structure. Knowing about the ancestors and the history of the estate makes them legitimate members of the family lineage, in spiritual unity between human and thing (Harvey, 1996).

Many of us have photographs of beloved and deceased family members placed in various locations in our home, but few have oil portraits of dead relatives over a period of 300 years hanging on the walls of our dining rooms and salons. As pointed out by Pierre Bourdieu, displaying art in different ways not only reveals a taste acquired through one's position in the social space, but also works as providing class distinction (1984). Taste and our disposition toward certain objects, however, entail an active process involving both the subject and object of taste (Hennion, 2007). As pieces of their time, the portraits, painted with thick brushstrokes and framed in gold, along with the embroideries on the walls and the antique furniture, act as reminders of continuity and place-boundedness, making the antiquity of the manor and the family come together and entangle.

Conclusions: Material Immortality

In the introduction of this chapter, I asked how we are to understand that a privileged person like Duke Charles Gordon-Lennox claims that he is not free to do as he wishes with the large estate he owns and, in principle, could sell off in order to be able to spend the rest of his life on his car racing hobby. To put it plainly, the puzzle is that in theory Charles could do away with this property, which obviously costs more money than it generates, but instead strongly experiences that he is prohibited from doing this. One clue is mortmain, and how it can be understood as a cultural script that simultaneously constrains and enables action (cf. Alexander et al., 2011). I went on to ask whether and how this invisible hand of the dead works within the manor culture of the Swedish landowning upper class, and with what effects it operates. The empirical sections analyzed how maintaining property centers around certain moral values, such as responsibility and sustainability, and how the past, present and future are seen as interwoven temporalities bound up with the course of the manor. In this long perspective the needs of the estate come first, and one's own wishes either coincide with these needs or are downplayed in a potential clash of interests. Individuality, a value attached to the modern imperatives of will and choice, is not a highly regarded currency within this culture. Moreover, keeping the manor "alive" through home-making practices and caring for its "soul" is part of the manor culture. Buildings, family portraits and other antiquities bound to the manor, create what could be termed a "continuing bond" (Gibson, 2009; Valentine, 2008; see also Jonsson, Chap. 2, this volume) with earlier generations. Ancestors, with their work and life choices, play an important role in the socialization process through which the interviewees claim they always knew they would take over the responsibility. In addition, material objects make impressions on everyday practice, confirming moral character and choices, and generally making the work at the manor meaningful.

The human and non-human actors unite and produce the manor culture with its prohibition to sell or split property, and the self-sacrificing, hardworking subjectivity that is promoted. There is a subtext to the narratives, an inner voice dictating the demands to keep and maintain the manor at any cost. To hand in and sell, would be a disgrace. Noteworthy, in addition to the deceit it would be toward ancestors and following generations, it would be utterly disrespectful to the estate, as well as to the labor of past relatives. The human and non-human actors that attach the subject to a place, make one belong and feel at home. Moreover, the interviewees state that it is rather relieving to have the future laid out for you, and that it gives them comfort to know that what has been will continue long after their own death. Thus, mortmain not only involves perpetual ownership and a prohibition to sell, but also in effect unifies the dead, the living and the not yet born with the place in question—the manor. Moral boundaries also matters to the reproduction of class inequality (Lamont & Fournier, 1992). As such, the manor culture provides an invisible hand of class reproduction at the intersection of ancient stability and societal change.

The analysis shows how influences from the past become manifest through the meaning of maintenance; to support as well as to keep. In narratives on housing choices, homing practices and aspirations for the future, the interaction of human/non-human actors is clearly an important dimension. This interaction needs to be considered if one wishes to make sense of the attraction and influence that past generations, the manor and its land is said to exercise. While others speak of place attachment as the way in which individual subjects or collectives come to identify with and belong to a certain location (de Blij, 2008; Easthope, 2004), this chapter also demonstrates a reversed place attachment, that is, one in which the place *imposes itself* to the subject rather than the other way around, thus pointing at the dialectics between human and thing. Moreover, the attachment we are focusing on here is not only a relationship between the manor and its inhabitants, but with long gone as well as future generations. Following Heidegger, then, one can say that while being is material-symbolically tied to place, the temporalities that operate follow an intergenerational lineage.

With the backdrop of the cultural sociological perspective applied in this chapter, I argue that the investigated case of mortmain in manor culture is a manifestation of what I term "material immortality." As humans, a more or less conscious fear we have is that no one will remember us; that our lives will have been useless and will pass without leaving an imprint. Norbert Elias reminds us that historical continuity and the transmission of knowledge and collective memory between generations are of central concern to sociologists. The only thing that survives when we die is the imprint we have made on other people's lives, "what stays in their memories" (Elias, 1985: 67). Thanatologist Edwin Shneidman writes on the subject:

> Is there a fate worse than death? Yes! It is to be *oblivionated*, to fall into a vast anonymous maw as though one had never lived, to have absolutely no effective engram in the memory bank of a single human being, to have had a totally unimpactful life, to be thrown into a pauper's grave with only a biodegradable tattoo, to suffer a death without a future. (Shneidman, 2008: 154, italics in original)

Avoiding the hopeless prospect of a "death without a future," one can invest in the "post-self"—the "extension beyond the date of one's tombstone" (Shneidman, 2008: 152)—in various ways. This can be done, for example, through raising children who will remember you (what is sometimes called biological immortality), writing a will that stipulates the future behaviors of the bereaved, or achieving something extraordinary that will live on (e.g. art, innovation or a scientific breakthrough). The manor enables material immortality—eternal life for one's heirs as long as the estate is maintained and stays alive.

Mortmain provides excellent conditions for cultivating post-selves; the manor is soaked with post-selfish manifestations. However, it also provides opportunities for the not yet dead to invest in his or her post-self, through providing for children and others of coming generations and by leaving a specific imprint in the long history of the noble setting. This may include receiving posthumous recognition for being the one who renovated the castle, installed renewable energy sources, or opened an art gallery in the former stables. This material immortality, this second order life of generations lost, is guaranteed through the maintenance that is a central script to manor culture. The anachronistic figure of mortmain provides the opportunity for material immortality in, and of, manor culture.

Notes

1. Contact was first made via e-mail, and second through a phone call to confirm interest and make an appointment. Written and oral information about the project and its ethical concerns—foremost the principles of consent, possibility to withdraw and confidentiality—was given via e-mail and again at the actual meeting. There is a gender imbalance in the selected population for the study: 8 of the 22 interviewees, but only 2 of the 14 owners, are women. Although the selection is in no statistical sense representative of the wider population, it is certainly a recognizable characteristic that most heads of these manors are male.
2. I have analyzed 3 years of the bestselling magazine *Gods & Gårdar* (2014–16, 36 issues) and selected specific issues of *Antik & Auktion* and *Lantliv*

dealing with manor living. I have also analyzed popular TV documentaries such as British Aristocrats (SVT, 2012) and Slottsliv (3 seasons, TV8), but for this specific chapter this is mainly used as background research. It is worth noting that quotes used from these sources do not overlap with the informants of my study.

3. Properties other than estates could also become, or be included in, a *fideicommissum* (Regeringens proposition, 1999).

References

Alexander, J. C. (2004) 'Cultural Pragmatics: Social Performance Between Ritual and Strategy', *Sociological Theory*, 22(4), 527–573.

Alexander, J. C. and Smith, P. (2003) 'The Strong Program in Cultural Sociology' in J. C. Alexander (ed.) *The Meanings of Social Life*, Oxford: Oxford University Press.

Alexander, J. C., Lund, A. and Trondman, M. (2011) *Kulturell Sociologi. Program, Teori och Praktik*, Göteborg: Daidalos.

Baltzell, E. D. (1958) *Philadelphia Gentlemen. The Making of National Upper Class*, Glencoe, IL: Free Press.

de Blij, H. (2008) *The Power of Place. Geography, Destiny, and Globalization's Rough Landscape*, Oxford: Oxford University Press.

Bourdieu, P. (1984) *Distinction. A Social Critique of the Judgement of Taste*, Cambridge, MA: Harvard University Press.

Clifford, J. and Marcus, G. E. (eds.) (1986) *Writing Culture. The Poetics and Politics of Ethnography*, Berkeley, CA: University of California Press.

Douglas, M. (1966) *Purity and Danger. An Analysis of Concepts of Pollution and Taboo*, London: Routledge and Kegan Paul.

Duyvendak, J. W. (2011) *The Politics of Home. Belonging and Nostalgia in Europe and the United States*, New York: Palgrave Macmillan.

Easthope, H. (2004) 'A Place Called Home', *Housing, Theory & Society*, 21(3), 128–138.

Elias, N. (1985) *The Loneliness of the Dying*, London: Bloomsbury Publishing.

Gibson, M. (2009) *Objects of the Dead*, Melbourne: Melbourne University Press.

Gods & Gårdar. (2016a) Bonnier Tidskrifter AB, February, no. 2.

Gods & Gårdar. (2016b) Bonnier Tidskrifter AB, July, no. 7.

Gordon, A. (2008) *Ghostly Matters: Haunting and the Sociological Imagination*, Minneapolis: University of Minnesota Press.

Harvey, D. (1996) *Justice, Nature and the Geography of Difference*, Massachusetts: Blackwell Publishers.

Heidegger, M. (1962) *Being and Time*, London: SCM Press.

Hennion, A. (2007) 'Those Things that Hold Us Together: Taste and Sociology', *Cultural Sociology*, 1(1), 97–114.

Holmberg, T. (2017) 'Herrgårdens Värde. Förvaltning som Livsstil', *Bebyggelsehistorisk Tidskrift*, 35(74), 100–115.

Holmberg, T. (2018) 'Eliters Boende på Slott och Herrgårdar' in B. E. Eriksson, M. Holmqvist, and L. Sohl (eds.) *Eliter i Sverige*, Lund: Studentlitteratur.

Holmqvist, M. (2015) *Djursholm*, Stockholm: Atlantis.

Lamont, M. (1992) *Money, Morals, & Manners. The Culture of the French and the American Upper-Middle Class*, Chicago: University of Chicago Press.

Lamont, M. and Fournier, M. (1992) *Cultivating Differences, Symbolic Boundaries and the Making of Inequality*, Chicago: University of Chicago Press.

Lefebvre, H. (1991) *The Production of Space*, Oxford: Basil Blackwell.

Mitford, N. (ed.) (1956) *Noblesse Oblige: An Enquiry into the Identifiable Characteristics of the English Aristocracy*, New York: Harper.

Ostrander, S. A. (1984) *Women of the Upper Class*, Philadelphia: Temple University Press.

Regeringens Proposition. (1999) 'Kulturarv—Kulturmiljöer och Kulturföremål': 1998/99:114.

Shneidman, E. (2008) *A Commonsense Book of Death. Reflections at Ninety of a Lifelong Thanatologist*, New York: Rowman & Littlefield.

SVT. (2012) 'Brittiska aristokrater', *BBC*.

Swidler, A. (1986) 'Culture in Action. Symbols and Strategies', *American Sociological Review*, 51(2), 273–286.

Ulväng, G. (2008) *Herrgårdarnas Historia. Arbete, Liv och Bebyggelse på Uppländska Herrgårdar*, Halmstad: Hallgren & Björklund.

Valentine, C. (2008) *Bereavement Narratives. Continuing Bonds in the Twenty-First Century*, London: Routledge.

4

The Death of Place: Exploring Discourse and Materiality in Debates on Rural Development

Introduction

What determines whether or not something is alive? This deceivingly simple question, this chapter argues, is actually the most complicated one. The question becomes even more complex when one moves beyond the sphere of mere biological life and asks what it means, for example, for a place or a community to be alive. Seeking to provide a tentative answer, this chapter approaches metaphors of life and death through the prism of the abandoned place. Walking between the signifier and the signified, this chapter problematizes the notions of life and death in political debates on the deindustrialization and depopulation of rural communities in present-day Sweden. Fraught with dystopian and utopian images, the Swedish case is apt, because the debates ubiquitously draw on metaphors of the living and the dead when describing socioeconomic processes or development.

T. Olofsson (✉)
Department of Sociology, Uppsala University, Uppsala, Sweden
e-mail: tobias.olofsson@soc.uu.se

© The Author(s) 2019
T. Holmberg et al. (eds.), *Death Matters*,
https://doi.org/10.1007/978-3-030-11485-5_4

This chapter consists of three parts. The first part approaches the use of such metaphors in an attempt to understand what qualities are used to signify death in these debates. The chapter then moves to the signifiers, turning the relation between metaphor and place on its head and analyzing the metaphors from a perspective grounded in the materiality of the seemingly dead place. By moving between these two perspectives, this chapter aims to understand both the power and the limitations of the metaphors used in these particular debates. It begins this investigation by providing an account of recent developments in rural Sweden as well as of the use of images of life and death in political debates related to these large-scale trends. The first section concludes with a discussion of how death as a phenomenon is made contingent through open-ended discursive constructions of what it means for something to be dead. The second part draws on these contingencies in order to problematize the notion of death and what is used to signify the deadness of a place in contemporary debates. Discussing how the use of economically oriented discourses narrows the potential meanings of death, as well as life, in rural communities, this chapter's third part moves from the abstract levels of political debate and large-scale societal trends to experiences of the concrete material reality of abandoned and seemingly dead places. Arguing that death, even in relation to long-abandoned sites, is contingent on what is perceived to signify deadness, this chapter ends with a discussion of the narrowness of the conceptualizations of dead and dying places in contemporary political debate.

A Living Countryside! Trends and Debates Concerning Depopulation in Sweden

Human history is a history of the birth, life and death of cultures and communities that have emerged, flourished and perished over the years. Having perished, however, many long-lost communities and cultures still linger in the traces left by them in memory, scholarship and landscape, both in distant history and on shorter temporal horizons. Like many other Western rural communities, rural Sweden has recently seen dramatic developments in terms of falling employment, urban commuting and migration (Amcoff, 2001). The most telling aspect of this can be found in the urbanization that has taken place over the past 200 years. Through these processes, the Swedish population has shifted from a relatively small urban population of about 10 percent in 1800 (Statistics Sweden, 1993) to a large urban prevalence of about 85 percent in 2015 (Svanström, 2015).

Transformations such as the depopulation of rural regions and communities, however, do not constitute a phenomenon that is isolated to recent history, but instead similar trends can be traced throughout history, for example, to the mercantilist trade-focused urbanization policies put forth by the seventeenth-century Swedish king Gustavus Adolphus (Heckscher, 1954). Like today, urbanization and its related phenomena were subject to protest and debate. At that point, the peasants protested by writing letters to the crown, asking permission to move out of the cities and back to their farms. Today, activists and the concerned public petition legislatures asking for solutions to problems associated with urbanization, centralization and rural depopulation. Some of the recent protests have been memorialized through different catch phrases such as *Vi flytt' int'!* ("We won't move!"), coined in the early 1970s (Egan Sjölander & Payne, 2011), and *Hela landet ska leva!* ("The whole country shall live!"). The latter statement, which is also in contemporary use, evokes an imaginary of life and death in relation to the development and transformation of Swedish rurality.

Slogans concerning the need or ambition to keep rural areas alive as well as the need to maintain a "living countryside" feature in debates on different levels, from opinion pieces and letters to local newspapers to debates and propositions in parliament. Examples include discussions on how a more loosely regulated Swedish alcohol market would benefit rural communities by giving local producers the right to sell their products directly to consumers instead of going through the publicly owned alcohol monopoly *Systembolaget* (The Riksdag Administration, 2016b; Yngwe & Forsberg, 2017). Other discussions drawing on the same imaginary of how to ensure the life of the countryside include debates on how raising the legal number of firearms license holders can own would benefit hunters and thereby rural communities (The Riksdag Administration, 2016a), and on the potential benefits of relaxing construction and land-use legislations to make land in rural areas more attractive (The Riksdag Administration, 2017). The motions made by members of parliament cover everything from substantial de-regulation to the more trivial, but all have made use of life and death metaphors in relation to keeping the countryside alive, that is, keeping it from dying. But what does it mean for a place or a region to be alive?[1]

As mentioned above, the general question of what is dead or alive is contingent. Death is, in itself, a concept that is weighed down by a wide array of meanings. Just as darkness can be conceived of as the absence of light, death may—in its most basic conceptualization—be conceived of as the absence of life, or as "the possibility of no-longer-being-able-to-be-there"; death, in other words, is "the possibility of the absolute impossibility of Dasein" (Heidegger, 2013: 294; see also Neuman, Chap. 6, this volume). But when is something devoid of life? Raising this question in relation to constructions of human death, Nico Carpentier and Leen van Brussel highlight the existence of a wide range of conceptualizations of death: from the clinical death characterized by a steep reduction in body temperature and loss of heartbeat and respiratory functions, through the lack of brain activity, to the separation of body and soul, as in Christian discourses on death (Carpentier & Van Brussel, 2012: 103).

The issue of the meaning of living and dying is furthermore complicated by how that which in one sense may be dead might live on in the form of different technologies of memorialization such as commemorative street names (Azaryahu, 1996; Buben, 2015). Zygmunt Bauman (1992) called some such technologies "immortality strategies," observing that someone who is remembered after their death is, to certain extent, immortal (see Holmberg, Chap. 3, this volume). In other words, through memorialization, what is dead may remain alive. Because the self is "strewn all over the social landscape" and "not absolutely concentrated in one biological locale" (Abbott, 2016: 7; see also Schutz, 1962), parts of the deceased self may remain alive in the form of the memories and experiences of others. Issues of immortalization, however, are not as problematic or pressing from the perspective of the deceased as they are from that of the living—there is, after all, a lot of truth to Monty Python's old assertion that "you can still hear Beethoven, but Beethoven can't still hear you" (Palin & Monty Python, 1980). The perception of death may therefore be the perception of two different things. The first is the existential perception of one's own death or, to follow Martin Heidegger (2013), the being toward death. Here, the perception of death is the experience of being aware of one's own end. The second way in which death may be experienced is the perception of the death of other humans, animals, objects and places.

This chapter concerns itself with aspects of the second mode of perception, in general, and aspects of the perception of deadness as a quality of place, in particular. In line with the notion that death is contingent on what mode of being alive is used to assess the lack of life, and that what is dead may still be partially alive through memorialization, the death of a place is defined here, in effect, by what is taken as a measure of life. In order to grasp the death-life binary in relation to place, it is therefore necessary to understand not only what it means for something to be denoted as dead, but also the particular character of the life that is said to have ended. In order to accomplish this, the chapter will now move on to account for a recent example in the form of a government report on the preservation of rural communities in Sweden. Having done so, this chapter will then move on to the object to which deadness is ascribed, the goal being to explore the potential implications and limitations of claims regarding the death of a place.

Socioeconomic Discourses on the Life and Death of Places

Contemporary debates on the decline of the Swedish countryside are intimately tied to the communities occupying these places. In the discourses employed in these discussions, a dying place becomes a location where, from the perspective of community members, the conditions under which the community is to be reproduced are growing worse with time. The death of the countryside or of rural communities thereby becomes the "absence of a living cultivated landscape, absence of service and social welfare, absence of persons living and working in the area and the absence of a belief in the future" (Lundgren, 2013: 28). Here, the death of rural communities stands in stark contrast to the life of urban areas.

In a study of how metaphors around death are used in discourses concerning northern rural communities in Sweden, Anna Sofia Lundgren (2013) shows how death, as a concept, is used by informants discussing the present and the imagined future of their communities. In the informants' experiences, their communities are approaching death at the hands of politicians. Here, the cause of these rural communities dwindling away is said to be unfavorable policies. The survival of these rural communities is, in other words, conditioned on policy intervention. It is believed that if the politicians do not do something to save the community, it is sure to soon perish. As argued above, such statements are not limited to those living in these rural communities, but also feature in debates on national legislation. A range of possible interventions were recently discussed and put forward by a Parliamentary Committee on Rural Communities (*Parlamentariska Landsbygdskommittén*). The committee was tasked by the Swedish government with formulating suggestions for "a coherent national policy for long-term sustainable development in Sweden's rural communities" (Swedish Government Official Reports, 2017). The resulting report, issued by The Ministry of Enterprise and Innovation and The Parliamentary Committee on Rural Communities, identifies a series of problems and potential resolutions. The framing of these sustainment problems of rural communities first and foremost focuses on socioeconomic qualities, and the report is steeped in economic discourse. Throughout the report, the ambition is to ensure that rural communities be "given the same conditions to develop as other parts of Sweden." The committee furthermore discusses the need to counter current negative trends that have resulted in a "failure to exploit business potential" as well as "greater discrepancies between access to public services in different parts of the country" (Swedish Government Official Reports, 2017: 25). In the report, the countryside and rural communities appear as deceased parts of an organism, along the same lines as Emile Durkheim's metaphor for society (Durkheim, 2013). This organism, however, is portrayed as being plagued by different maladies, and various remedies are suggested to treat these (socioeconomic) ills.

The life-supporting interventions identified by the Parliamentary Committee on Rural Communities are, arguably, steeped in a particular set of conventions or local *epochés* (Schutz, 1944), in which a certain set of forms of worth (Boltanski & Thévenot, 2006) or grammars of worth (Centemeri, 2015) are granted prevalence. Seeking to contribute to "equal conditions for citizens to live and work in rural areas" or striving to increase "the capacity of rural areas to exploit opportunities for entrepreneurship," the report explores possibilities for rural communities to once again "contribute towards the positive development of the economy" (Swedish Government Official Reports, 2017: 26). By identifying the problems haunting rural communities today as lack of economization of opportunities and disconnection from the economy, the report defines the life and death of these places in terms of justice or fairness, economy and human activity. This, arguably, renders the maladies and remedies identified in the report—just as in the narratives provided in Lundgren's (2013) inquiry into the death of rural communities—somewhat narrow and fixed on maintaining or improving the current socioeconomic situation. The conceptualization of living, dying and dead places in the narratives analyzed by Lundgren and in the work by the Parliamentary Committee on Rural Communities is, therefore, limited to a certain set of discourses on dead places and linked to a particular set of signifiers, much like human death (see Carpentier & Van Brussel, 2012). Here as well, death appears to be a less straightforward phenomenon shaped by different discourses. Seeking to move beyond the discursive construction of the death of places, this chapter will now approach the problem of the contingent nature of such death from the opposite end. In doing so, I will analyze a set of seemingly[2] dead places.

In preparing this chapter, field walks have been carried out at 12 abandoned sites.[3] These include old industrial sites such as abandoned mines and iron-making sites, but also remains of domestic sites such as house foundations, Celtic fields and cairns, trapping pits and ruins (Table 4.1). During the field walks, the sites were also photographed for future visual analysis. Two of the sites are home to memorializing activities in the form of placards or museum events. The sites are located in Jämtland County except for an abandoned mine located in Uppsala County, both in Sweden.[4] Many of the sites were extensively overgrown.

Table 4.1 List of sites visited and photographed

Site	Type	Location
A	Closed-down mine	Dannemora, Östhammar Municipality
B	Peat extraction field and horse bedding factory	Bölesmyren, Berg Municipality
C	Iron-making site (furnace and slag heaps) of iron age or medieval date	Medvigge, Berg Municipality
D	Two charcoal pits	Östervigge, Berg Municipality
E	House foundation	Östervigge. Berg Municipality
F	Area with Celtic fields and cairns	Medvigge, Berg Municipality
G	Iron-making site (furnace and slag heaps) from Iron Age or Middles Ages	Västervigge, Berg Municipality
H	Trapping pit	Västervigge, Berg Municipality
I	Area with Celtic field, cairns and stone fence	Västervigge, Berg Municipality
J	Closed-down mine	Fröån, Åre Municipality
K	Ruins of slate constructions, farm buildings	Gråsjön, Åre Municipality

In the cases when vegetation and decay prevented the immediate identification of the site, the GPS coordinates provided by The Swedish National Heritage Board were used to pinpoint the site's location. Below I provide accounts from field walks at two of the sites visited for this project as well as references to the other sites. The analytical section focuses on these sites in particular to provide greater depth to the presentation, one being a modern and clearly visible site and the other an ancient site concealed under newer layers of life past and present. In the accounts that follow, I engage with the sites not only as objective entities but also as entities interpreted through the prism of the observer's temporal position and cognitions.[5] The interplay between place and observer presented below is, in other words, not only the interplay between the perceived and the perceiver, but also between the perceived materiality and the discourses internalized and recalled by the perceiver. Moving between different discourses, these interactions explore the contradictions of dead places by moving between the different signifiers that bring different sides of the signified to the fore, sometimes moving it closer to life than to death.

Left for Dead: Bundles of Life and Death in Abandoned Places

The Abandoned Peat Factory

On a cloudy afternoon in July 2017, I visited site B, an abandoned peat factory near Vigge, in Berg Municipality. The site is situated approximately three kilometers into a woodland area and is accessible only by a dirt road and an overgrown pathway. Having traversed the dirt road on a quad bike, I walked the 100 meters or so of the pathway. When approaching the site, I first came across a small bundle of planks and metal parts lying next to the path that leads to a large but distorted industrial complex. The site is dominated by young trees, the remains of a tall and tumbled wooden structure, a tangle of mechanical parts strewn among the moss and grass, and a still standing wooden structure that appears to have housed a conveyor belt where the peat was once transported into the factory where it was processed to become horse bedding.[6]

Upon closer inspection, I discovered that the site also features a series of concrete sleepers, the remains of which look like a small railway cart, and a series of wooden structures and rusty iron objects such as wheels and rods. In the nearby mire, 13 grooves measuring between 210 and 360 meters long, and 10 to 15 meters wide,[7] separated by narrow ridges covered in young pine trees and old wooden drying racks tell of the extractive operation that took place here during the first half of the twentieth century. Figure 4.1 shows one of these grooves as seen standing 10 meters onto one of the ridges.

The site lay silent, but for the continuous bussing of flies and gnats, as I began walking along the overgrown path looking at and photographing different objects and structures. The decaying wooden structures, the rusty wheelbases and pieces of machinery (depicted in Fig. 4.2), and the scarred mire all appeared before me as something that once was, but was

Fig. 4.1 Grove from previous peat extraction as seen from a ridge separating two groves

on the brink of being no more. The immediate impression was that death, in its most material sense, was highly present in the remains of the old industrial structures. This impression was even stronger at some of the other sites. The farmhouses at site K had moss and grass growing on them; the floors and ceilings had caved in. Also the iron-making sites, Celtic fields, and house foundations at sites C, E, F, G, H, I and L were barely identifiable, appearing only as discrete changes in the levels of earth with some stone formations or cairns giving hints of their former use; they gave the impression of death, decay and burials, because all that remained of these places lied buried somewhere beneath the thick moss, peat, roots and grass.

There was, however, another dimension to the decay of the old peat factory. Because I had previously been told about this site by close relatives who knew the place before it was abandoned, I found myself connecting to the site in a way I had not expected prior to this visit. As I stood among the remains of the factory building, I found myself

Fig. 4.2   Rusty and tangled-up machinery

rehearsing the stories my grandmother had told me of how she used to walk the crisscrossing paths through the forest carrying baskets of lunch sandwiches to the men working at the factory. Retelling the story to myself, I felt that I was able to, momentarily, bring the place back to life. Through this move, I found myself feeling closer to the site and to its history. I stood for a while imagining the life, the smells and the noises that once would have filled this now serene location. Seeing the machinery, wires and carts that lay strewn across the area, I remembered other stories of how the site, after the factory had closed down, had been stripped of all valuables. This also applied to the iron tracks upon which the peat was transported from the mire to the factory. When work ceased, the people working at the factory, I had been told, divided valuables and useful items between themselves, and left only what was too cumbersome to carry or too invaluable to bring from the site in the forest, down to the villages a few kilometers away. Knowing this history made the sense of death more acute, as the stories, when confronted with the decay and disarray of the site, amplified the lack of the life that once was, although plenty other forms of life were present at this "dead" industrial site.

The contingent nature of death discussed by Carpentier and van Brussels (2012) becomes apparent when one takes a step back and tries to see beyond the first impression of present-day decay and lifelessness. The site, with its slowly deteriorating remains, provides an opportunity for re-imagining—to try to see the site as it might have been in the (sometimes very distant) past of previous generations and to picture the social and economic activities they carried out there. This is not only true in the combination of decay, rubble and story that make up my present-day experience of the old peat factory. Also at the iron-making sites that I visited, the still visible piles of slag, appearing as small mounds, are intertwined in imaginaries of glowing furnaces, built, maintained and fed with ore and charcoal by people who are now long gone, although traces of a part of their lives still stand there, hidden from direct view, but nevertheless visible.

Plenty of hints of present-day activities could, however, be found at the sites or close by. The young trees growing across the site of the old peat factory provide one example of this as they—in their own right—were part of a growing reserve of raw materials for the present-day forestry industry, therefore contributing to a different form of (economic) life. Similar layers of disturbance of the old by the new could be seen at site D, where one of the old charcoal pits had been cut through by a present-day dirt road made for harvesters and other forestry machines. The most apparent form of juxtaposition of the present onto the historical was, however, found at the abandoned mine at site J, where visitors can attend guided tours and view the reconstructed nineteenth-century water wheel and flat rod system that drove the pumps pumping water out of the mine. Having done so, they can then choose to enjoy a cup of coffee and some local delicacies in a café built right on top of an old mine shaft. The appearance of death does not, therefore, seem to be wrought from the lack of life in general, but from the lack of certain forms or signs of life in particular, making the deadness of a place contingent upon the signifiers through which it is identified. These contingencies are further visible on the old iron-making site C.

The Veiled Iron-Making Site

Before my visit to the abandoned peat factory above, I visited another part of the same forest. Walking along an overgrown pathway one day in late June, I was looking for a place that had proven somewhat challenging to find. This was my second trip to visit site C, an iron-making site from the Iron Age or the Middle Ages. As I had failed to identify the place during my previous visit, I was now prepared with a detailed description of the site's location as well as the GPS coordinates provided by The Swedish National Heritage Board's Archaeological Sites and Monuments Database *Fornsök*. Located on a mire covered in debris from recent felling, the site was obscured under layers of materials and overgrown with moss and different types of grass, flowers and other plant life. After a while, however, I was able to successfully identify the two slag heaps on either side of a small depression where the furnace and bellows once stood. As I wandered around the site, I also discovered a tree stump upon which someone had placed a piece of slag (of about 10 × 4 × 3 centimeters and curved in a flat U-shape). Taking a closer look at the slag, I wondered whether it perhaps had been found by a logger at the time of the felling and whether he or she had placed it on the stump. It was an interesting experience, being able to touch and appreciate an object that directly referenced the furnace and the people who worked it many years ago (Fig. 4.3).

Standing at the site, the contingency of death came to my attention once more as I began imagining the long-dead persons who once worked the furnace, pumping air into and feeding it, smelting bog iron and throwing the slag onto the two heaps. I found myself wondering what to make of the place. Was it perhaps some kind of—perhaps unintentional—monument of memorialization standing there in the middle of the mire? The contrast between the barely visible furnace and its surroundings—debris from the felling, a hunting tower standing 50 meters

Fig. 4.3 Piece of slag on tree stump with cloudberry plant and felling in the background

away, the grass covered pathway and the cloudberry, blueberry and ling-onberry plants that covered the ground—was stark. When I let the imaginations of what the site might have looked like in the past go, the old furnace appeared to grow deader against the vivid canvas of the signifiers of economic, biological and social life that surrounded it.

What becomes apparent here is that one may speak of different dimensions of death. When traces of human activity begin decaying and are buried beneath the soil through the re-conquest effected by "nature," places die much like the humans who once worked or occupied them. But death here is not just about sites disappearing or being hidden from our gaze. Instead, it is interlinked with the cessation of use, for instance, the end of any socioeconomic or sociobiological practices, such as the smelting activities at sites C and G, the extraction of resources at sites A, B and J, or the abandonment of a site as in the cases of the Celtic farms and house foundations at E, F and I. But a dead place is not merely dead. Instead such a place holds a liminal position. Being perched somewhere in between, a dead place may also be alive, because death in terms of the cessation of human activity, arguably, resides in the hybridization of sites through which "nature" and "culture" are combined in any number of ways (see Latour, 1993). A place may, thus, be dead when seen from the perspective of any particular endeavor—such as the extraction of peat or the smelting of bog iron—but that does not mean that the place is completely dead. Instead, the death of a place, such as a peat extraction operation and horse bedding production site, becomes the prerequisite for the emergence of other forms of life. In the case of sites B and C, this meant the life of a place as woodland, an economic-biological entity that comes to life against a horizon of ecological habitats for flora and fauna as well as of an economized resource to be used in forestry industries. But what does this mean for today's struggling rural communities?

Bringing Dying Places Back to Life

Approaching these, seemingly, dead places, one soon realizes how death, seen as a quality of a place, is diffuse and unclear. Partially determined through material processes, such as the decay of wood and the re-conquest of a place by biological processes, the deadness of a place resides in the intersection between discourses—and what in these discourses signifies that something is alive, dead or dying—and what these qualities are applied to. There are, in other words, many ways in which a place can be described as being dead, but just as many ways in which it can be described as being alive, and the simplicity of the metaphor may hide a universe of life. When the relation between discourse and place is reversed, life emerges almost as shadow figures, or "phantasmagorias" (Benjamin, 2002), as statements regarding the deadness of a place fail to capture the complexity of the place itself. This does not come as a surprise, but may serve as a reminder that even the deadness of a place is, following

Carpentier and van Brussels (2012), contingent upon the discourses through which something is proclaimed dead, but also upon the perceiver and the purpose-at-hand in relation to which he or she assesses the place and its qualities (Schutz, 1962). Stating that a place is dead or dying, therefore, may provide a powerful imaginary of decay, while also limiting the scope of what should be counted as signs of life. What is apparent here is that places are born and die in many ways depending on the perspective from which one perceives them. What might appear dead at first glance may also seem alive if one were to take a step back and attempt to see beyond the immediate surface. Deadness as a quality becomes a matter of something being dead in relation to something else. The abandoned peat factory at site B is dead in relation to the economic practices that once took place there, but also alive in relation to the memory of said economic practices and in relation to present-day forestry.

This relational quality of the death of places has some bearing on the discussion of the life and death of rural communities. This chapter shows how parts of the rural landscape bear traces of lives long gone, but also that different forms of life come, go and co-exist simultaneously, as a site can be both the lingering remains of previous life at the same time as it is an area of resource regrowth for the forest industries. In this connection, one may argue that rural places will never fully die, or die a little all the time, as life takes different forms depending on the temporal and discursive location of those who valuate life and deadness. It may be that many of today's rural communities will dwindle away and be replaced by fly-in/fly-out or drive-in/drive-out economic practices,[8] but it does not have to be so. Instead, the death of rural communities—as well as the death of any place—is contingent on what one believes constitutes death. It may be that death arises from a lack of support for rural communities in policy and politics, as discussed by the informants in Lundgren's (2013) work on the death of communities in northern Sweden. Or perhaps demise follows from failures to "exploit business potential" and the emergence of "greater discrepancies between access to public services," as argued by The Ministry of Enterprise and Innovation and the Parliamentary Committee on Rural Communities (Swedish Government Official Reports, 2017: 25). At the end of the day, deadness must be wrought from something that is taken to signify a lack of life.

As the deadness of a place emerges in relation to conceptions of life, linking the death of a place and a community to a few signifiers, such as socioeconomic activity or politics, might be a much too narrow path for a living countryside to wander. This is, arguably, a complex question to which the answer has hitherto been sought by linking life (and thereby also death) to a narrow set of signifiers. This chapter has accounted for a range of such signifiers, including the "successful" exploitation of business potential or the availability of public services: signifiers linked to making rural communities functioning parts of the societal organism. But these signifiers represent only a few possible interpretations of what it means for a rural community, in its contemporary incarnation, to be alive. Having said this, it is important to note that the lack of socioeconomic activity and public services is, of course, a problematic issue that cannot be disregarded. This chapter does not seek to disprove these discourses, but to open up the discussion for additional perspectives. Is it enough for a place to be given a form of respiratory assistance through economic stimulation, or should life be approached as something more complex than merely missed opportunities to exploit resources and a lack of contributions to GDP? Karl Polanyi's (2001) classical study of the joint emergence of the modern market economy and state provides ample reason to doubt this. In his study, Polanyi outlines the contradictions inherent in claims made by liberal economists of his time, writing that:

> Some who would readily agree that life in a cultural void is no life at all nevertheless seem to expect that economic needs would automatically fill that void and make life appear livable under whatever conditions. This assumption is sharply contradicted by the result of anthropological research. (Polanyi, 2001: 165)

As there is little reason to suppose that anthropological research would bring about different results today, the somewhat unidimensional approach to the life and death of rural places found in the Parliamentary panel's report may be called into question. The "living countryside" is, after all, a complex bundle of qualities that come together to form the hybrids we see before us today.

Conclusions

The death of a place can be conceptualized and understood in many different ways. This chapter has highlighted this contingency in order to problematize the metaphorical use of death in contemporary debate on rural communities. In doing so, the analysis has outlined how "dead" places may potentially and simultaneously be "alive." This potentiality stems from how places may be connected to memories of past life as well as from the fact that even a seemingly dead place may be alive with other forms of (hybrid) life. For this reason, the answer to the question of whether a place is dead or alive resides in the framing of the question, and from which position and with what social stakes something is deemed to be dead. After all, a decaying wooden structure can both be the material representation of death and provide nourishment for new life. The important question is perhaps not where something lies along the continuum of life and death, but what constitutes a fulfilling life in relation to a place and community, and perhaps especially in relation to present-day rural communities and fly-in/fly-out economics.

Notes

1. A related question is perhaps what is really meant by the term "countryside," as what is often referred to as the Swedish countryside is actually a socioeconomically heterogeneous landscape (Hedlund, 2016).
2. I write "seemingly" as the deadness, following the discussion above, is contingent on what is made to characterize life-ness. What may seem dead from one point of view may be seen as full of life if one were to perceive it from another angle.
3. The sites are referred to by letters and include two closed-down mines (A and J), one peat extraction site and horse bedding factory (B), two iron-making sites from the Iron Age or Middles Ages, with remains of furnaces and slag heaps (C and G), one site with charcoal pits (D), two sites with house foundations (E and L), two areas of Celtic fields, cairns and stone fences (F and I), and a trapping pit (H).

4. Half of the sites were identified using newspaper articles, word of mouth or my own knowledge of the site, while the other half were identified using The Swedish National Heritage Board's Archaeological Sites and Monuments Database *Fornsök* available on the Board's website (raa.se).
5. See also Hans-Georg Gadamer (2012).
6. The fact that the factory produced horse bedding is featured in local memory of the site.
7. Measurements taken from The Swedish National Heritage Board's (2017) *Fornsök* database entry on the site.
8. For examples of such developments, see Martin Perry and James E. Rowe (2015) or Keith Storey (2001).

References

Abbott, A. D. (2016) *Processual Sociology*, Chicago: University of Chicago Press.

Amcoff, J. (2001) *Samtida Bosättning på Svensk Landsbygd* [*Contemporary Settlement in the Swedish Countryside*], Dissertation, Uppsala: Uppsala University.

Azaryahu, M. (1996) 'The Power of Commemorative Street Names', *Environment and Planning D: Society and Space*, 14(3), 311–330.

Bauman, Z. (1992) *Mortality, Immortality and Other Life Strategies*, Cambridge: Polity Press.

Benjamin, W. (2002) *The Arcades Project*, 1st paperback ed., Cambridge: Harvard University Press.

Boltanski, L. and Thévenot, L. (2006) *On Justification: Economies of Worth*, Princeton: Princeton University Press.

Buben, A. (2015) 'Technology of the Dead: Objects of Loving Remembrance or Replaceable Resources?', *Philosophical Papers*, 44(1), 15–37.

Carpentier, N. and Van Brussel, L. (2012) 'On the Contingency of Death: A Discourse-Theoretical Perspective on the Construction of Death', *Critical Discourse Studies*, 9(2), 99–115.

Centemeri, L. (2015) 'Reframing Problems of Incommensurability in Environmental Conflicts Through Pragmatic Sociology: From Value Pluralism to the Plurality of Modes of Engagement with the Environment', *Environmental Values*, 24(3), 299–320.

Durkheim, E. (2013) *The Division of Labour in Society*, Houndmills: Palgrave Macmillan.

Egan Sjölander, A. and Payne, J. G. (eds.) (2011) *Tracking Discourses: Politics, Identity and Social Change*, Lund: Nordic Academic Press.

Gadamer, H. G. (2012) 'Om Förståelsens Cirkel' in K. Marc-Wogau (ed.) *Filosofin Genom Tiderna*, Stockholm: Thales.

Heckscher, E. F. (1954) *An Economic History of Sweden*, Cambridge: Harvard University Press.

Hedlund, M. (2016) 'Mapping the Socioeconomic Landscape of Rural Sweden: Towards a Typology of Rural Areas', *Regional Studies*, 50(3), 460–474.

Heidegger, M. (2013) *Being and Time*, Malden: Blackwell.

Latour, B. (1993) *We Have Never Been Modern*, Cambridge: Harvard University Press.

Lundgren, A. S. (2013) 'Landsbygdsdöden', *Kulturella Perspektiv*, 2, 27–33.

Palin, M. and Monty Python. (1980) *Decomposing Composers*, Vol. Monty Python's Contractual Obligation Album, New York City: Arista Records.

Perry, M. and Rowe, J. E. (2015) 'Fly-in, Fly-out, Drive-in, Drive-Out: The Australian Mining Boom and Its Impacts on the Local Economy', *Local Economy*, 30(1), 139–148.

Polanyi, K. (2001) *The Great Transformation: The Political and Economic Origins of Our Time*, 2nd Beacon Paperback ed., Boston: Beacon Press.

Schutz, A. (1944) 'On Multiple Realities', *Philosophy and Phenomenological Research*, 5(4), 533–576.

Schutz, A. (1962) *Collected Papers. 1, The Problem of Social Reality*, The Hague: M. Nijhoff.

Statistics Sweden (ed.) (1993) *Markanvändningen i Sverige*, 2. utg, Stockholm and Örebro: Statistiska Centralbyrån and SCB förlag.

Storey, K. (2001) 'Fly-in/Fly-out and Fly-over: Mining and Regional Development in Western Australia', *Australian Geographer*, 32(2), 133–148.

Svanström, S. (2015) 'Urbanisering—Från Land till Stad', *Scb.Se*, https://www.scb.se/sv_/Hitta-statistik/Artiklar/Urbanisering%2D%2Dfran-land-till-stad/, data accessed 30 November 2017.

Swedish Government Official Reports. (2017) *För Sveriges Landsbygder—En Sammanhållen Politik för Arbete, Hållbar Tillväxt och Välfärd: Slutbetänkande av Parlamentariska Landsbygdskommittén*, Stockholm: Wolters Kluwer.

Swedish National Heritage Board. (2017) 'Riksantikvarieämbetet—Fornsök'. *RAÄ-Nummer Berg 233*, http://kulturarvsdata.se/raa/fmi/html/12000000139787, data accessed 8 September 2017.

The Riksdag Administration. (2017) 'Interpellation 2016/17: 414 Byggande På Jordbruksmark', http://www.riksdagen.se/sv/webb-tv/video/interpellationsdebatt/byggande-pa-jordbruksmark_H410414, data accessed 4 September 2017.

The Riksdag Administration. (2016a) 'Motion 2016/17:554 Antal Vapen i Vapengarderoben', http://www.riksdagen.se/sv/dokument-lagar/dokument/motion/tillat-fler-vapen-i-vapengarderoben_H402554, data accessed 4 September 2017.

The Riksdag Administration. (2016b) 'Motion 2016/17:2026 Skåne Som Pilotlän För Gårdsförsäljning', http://www.riksdagen.se/sv/dokument-lagar/dokument/motion/skane-som-pilotlan-for-gardsforsaljning_H4022026, data accessed 4 September 2017.

Yngwe, K. and Forsberg, H. (2017) 'C: Tillåt Gårdsförsäljning av Alkohol—För en Levande Landsbygd', *Sundsvalls Tidning*, August 22.

Part II

Disease/Bodies

5

Living and Dying with Bacteria: Paradoxical Figures of Death

Hedvig Gröndal

Introduction

The position and status of bacteria have changed. In conjunction with the development of bacteriology in the late nineteenth century, bacteria were primarily recognized as pathogens, attacking human bodies (cf. Paxson, 2008; Tomes, 1999). In recent decades, however, bacteria have emerged in science, popular science and the news media as crucial to our survival or even integral parts of the human organism (cf. Helmreich, 2016; Ingram, 2011). Quite paradoxically, this way of relating to bacteria also involves growing concerns about bacteria developing resistance against antibiotics. Antibiotic resistance is depicted as a road back to the Dark Ages, as an impending apocalypse in which bacteria retaliate against the human urge to control nature. Thus, the contemporary position of bacteria is inherently ambiguous, and in this chapter I explore how bacteria can contribute to a cultural sociological discussion on death. By exploring bacteria as a cultural sociological matter, this chapter furthers

H. Gröndal (✉)
Uppsala University, Uppsala, Sweden
e-mail: hedvig.grondal@soc.uu.se

© The Author(s) 2019
T. Holmberg et al. (eds.), *Death Matters*,
https://doi.org/10.1007/978-3-030-11485-5_5

our present understanding of death and its relation to life. I make use of scholarship on human-microbial relations from the humanities and social sciences, as well as accounts from the media, science and popular science.

Theoretically, this chapter draws on an understanding of bacteria as crucial actors in social relations, and of human-microbial relations as simultaneously discursive and material. Heterogeneous interrelated elements—such as cultural understandings of dirt and disease, bacteria, antibiotics, medical technologies—all take part in producing human-microbial relations in their specific form (cf. Latour, 1993a, b). My theoretical perspective is developed in the following two sections. I begin with a discussion of our shared cultural history with bacteria, focusing on how the status of bacteria—initially understood and managed primarily as deadly threats—has changed and become more ambiguous. Following this, I elaborate further on bacteria as crucial elements of, and inseparable from, human culture. Subsequently, I explore a case in which the life/death dialectics is particularly salient: gut bacteria, described as both necessary for human survival and as agents in decomposing dead bodies. Using accounts from the news media and science, I show how bacteria's multiple configurations shed light on the relation between life and death, and how the dividing line between them is drawn and redrawn. In the discussion, I argue that bacteria have the potential to both unsettle and settle life and death as certain states and as each other's opposites. I also suggest that bacteria can be conceptualized as paradoxical figures, enabling both opposing and symbiotic understandings of life and death—as excluding and feeding each other.

Cultural History of Bacteria

The Australian Nobel Prize-winning physician Sir Macfarlane Burnet described the development of antibiotics as "the end of one of the most important social revolutions in history–the virtual elimination of infectious disease as a significant factor in social life" (quoted in Bud, 2007: 33). When bacteriology developed in the nineteenth century, many bacterial infections were lethal.[1] Microbial actors intervened in social relations primarily as agents of infection and death. For example, Louis Pasteur's success in developing bacteriology was largely rooted in the ability to vaccinate against the greatly feared anthrax infection (cf. Latour, 1993a). If bacteria were agents of death, hygienic and antiseptic practices as well as vaccines were promoters of life.

When penicillin was introduced after the Second World War, small doses of the drug could suddenly cure previously lethal infections—such as pneumonia, rheumatic fever and syphilis (Bud, 2007: 3). As noted by Landecker (2016), antibiotics also had effects on reproduction by decreasing miscarriages and birth defects caused by venereal diseases such as gonorrhea and syphilis. Thus, with antibiotics (together with antiseptic practices as well as improvements in overall welfare—mainly better living conditions and nutrition), the illness panorama in the Western world changed rapidly and radically. A future where bacteria and infectious diseases were no longer significant health problems was thought to be within reach (cf. Singer, 2015). As recently as in the late 1970s, the United Nations declared that a worldwide "epidemiological transition" was about to occur, involving "a new era in which chronic diseases of old age would prevail over infection" (Cooper, 2006). Later on, antibiotics made advanced medical procedures possible; modern medical practices such as cancer treatment, transplantations and neonatal intensive care relied heavily on this new drug. Thus, antibiotics held the promise of the continuous advancement of health. As such, the drug became a symbol of scientific progress and "the golden age of medicine"—a sign of modernity itself (Brown & Nettleton, 2017; Bud, 2007).

Although bacteriology's germ theory of disease might appear to be universally true, notions of bacteria have not been constant. They have changed and will continue to change (cf. Tomes, 1999). Such a shift has become especially evident in recent years, when bacteria are no longer described solely as causing disease, but also as beneficial—even necessary for human survival. Paxson and Helmreich (2014: 167) write "the abundant microbe has moved from being a sign of peril to being also one of promise."[2] Hird's (2009: 127) characterization of bacteria as "the stuff of life" refers to research showing how bacteria have been essential to the evolution of all life on earth. As a telling example, bacteria are understood as extraterrestrial signs of life in contemporary astrobiology (Helmreich,

2015; cf. Paxson & Helmreich, 2014—who note that the very word "microbe" means "small life"). Importantly, the conception of microbes, in general, and bacteria, in particular, as life-givers is dependent on new technologies, which visualize microbes in novel ways—especially through genetic mapping. In this way, bacteria that cannot be identified using traditional culturing technologies can be exposed. Scholars suggest that the changed perception of bacteria is not only a matter of new technologies, but also connected to a broader environmental vision—involving a general move toward more "natural" and ecological ways of living and a conception of nature as threatened (cf. Paxson & Helmreich, 2014; Sangodeyi, 2014). Paxson and Helmreich also suggest that the traditional scientific view of bacteria as ill-natured extraneous alien pathogens can be tied to a modernist Cold War tendency to see enemies everywhere.[3]

Somewhat paradoxically, the reformulation of microbes as potential promoters of life has taken place simultaneously with increasing attention being paid to antimicrobial resistance in the scientific, public and political sphere. In the news media, antibiotic-resistant bacteria are described as "super bugs" and as bringers of the apocalypse (cf. Brown & Crawford, 2009; Brown & Nettleton, 2017; Nerlich & James, 2009). In the contemporary public discourse, antibiotics are no longer a symbol of scientific progression and control of nature (cf. Bud, 2007: 195), but rather a potential threat, materializing modern hubris. Antibiotic resistance is "nature's revenge" on human imperialism (cf. the journalist Cannon's influential book from 1996: *Superbugs: Nature's Revenge. Why Antibiotics Can Breed Disease*).

As shown above, the contemporary position of bacteria is inherently ambiguous (Brown & Nettleton, 2017: 495). Today, bacteria represent health and life, on the one hand, and the death of individuals as well as the ultimate danger to humanity, on the other. What are the consequences of this ambiguous position for the boundaries and relation between life and death? In order to examine this and contribute to a cultural sociological discussion—which takes bacteria into account—I make use of a perspective on bacterial and human cultures that views them as being co-produced through complex relations, as well as being discursive and material. In the following section, I will elaborate further on this interpretation.

The Coproduction of Bacterial and Human Cultures

The previous section, outlining the cultural history of bacteria, shows that our understanding and management of bacteria are highly cultural matters (Tomes, 1999; Paxson, 2012: 160). Paxson's quote (2014: 115)—"modern life has been antiseptic"—illustrates that such practices not only are antibacterial, but also have implications for how humans relate to each other and the world. The quote sums up the notion that antibiotics, sanitation and pasteurization have been crucial to modernity itself. Through these practices, the modern body—and society as a whole—has been protected against attacking alien germs, infection and death. Importantly, understandings of bacteria inhabit consequences for all aspects of life: medical, moral and social. Sangodeyi (2014: 27) suggests that when bacteriology was incorporated into everyday practices, disease came to be seen as individuals' or families' inability to maintain modern hygienic standards.[4] Cleanliness turned out to be the sign not only of the absence of disease, but also of social order and high moral standards. Tomes (1999) points out that avoidance of germs, from early on in life, is highly integrated into our everyday social practices, even today.

Hird (2009) gives another example of how human-bacterial relations need to be acknowledged for what they are: social and highly political:

Shifting our focus to a bacterial perspective, we can think about how much European colonization of the Americas, the Antipodes and Africa was precipitated through bacterial organization, communication and general liveliness: that bacteria colonized at least as much as humans ever did. […] What I am getting at here is a kind of on going mixed natural-cultural-social history with bacteria. (Hird, 2009: 56)

Hird illustrates that what we understand as a human history of colonization and imperialism was in fact a development that also involved bacterial forces, and bacteria have tended to act in favor of the colonizers. The example highlights the complexity of the intertwined human-microbial cultural history, involving human as well as bacterial agency.

Latour (1993a: 35) writes: "Society is not made up just of men, for everywhere microbes intervene and act. [...] We cannot form society with the social alone. We have to add the action of microbes." Latour illustrates how bacteria are inseparable from, and essential parts of, human culture. Along these lines, this chapter draws on the notion that nature and culture are inseparable from one another and are created together (cf. Haraway, 2003; Latour, 1993b). Although bacteria might appear to be purely natural objects, this is an overly simplified notion—bacteria are simultaneously natural and artificial. The way in which bacteria are understood and managed—as actors of life or of death—is culturally specific. It depends on specific knowledge, infections and technologies, but also on culturally specific ideas about how humans should relate to each other and the world. Importantly, bacteria may influence these practices in predictable as well as unpredictable ways (cf. Paxson & Helmreich, 2014: 168).

Not even scientifically controlled bacterial cultures—growing in laboratories on agar plates—are solely natural phenomena. When culturing bacteria, specific concentrations of antibiotics are used to prevent the growth of "irrelevant" microbes. Which bacteria are perceived as relevant or irrelevant to culture is not only a scientific matter, but involves taking into account how specific bacteria carry with them a history of commonly feared infections. To use another example, when estimating whether a specific bacterium is resistant to antibiotics, antibiotic resistance has to be defined: It is not a given phenomenon. The methods used to culture and measure antibiotic-resistant bacteria differ across contexts. This means that bacterial cultures are inseparable from the specific social and material context in which they are produced. However, this interdependence works both ways—the microbiologist is also reliant on bacterial agency to produce a successful bacterial culture—the bacterial culture might fail, the "wrong" bacterial species might grow or bacteria might resist being cultured altogether. In fact, it is estimated that only a small proportion of the total bacterial diversity can be grown in a laboratory (cf. Stewart, 2012).

When bacteria are handled—for example, cultured, measured, treated, carried, washed away or consumed—they do not remain the same. As a consequence of interaction with humans, technology and antibiotics, the biology of bacteria has changed (cf. Landecker, 2016). For example, the plurality of bacterial species in the human gut flora is thought to be decreasing due to our modern lifestyle, and vaccination and hygiene practices have eradicated a number of lethal infections, such as anthrax and polio. However, the most significant bacterial evolution occurring in interaction with human practices has been the development of antimicrobial resistance. Owing to the extensive and commercial use of antibiotics, bacteria have increasingly developed resistance to these substances. In addition, other human practices might be fueling the evolution and spread of resistant bacteria. For instance, specific tourism practices facilitate the spread of resistant bacteria. Discussing Spain, Bud (2007: 137) writes: "its germs have good access to humans"—meaning that the unusually high rate of antibiotic-resistant bacteria in the country and the large number of tourists promote the spread of such bacteria. Thus, antimicrobial-resistant bacteria can grow in healthy humans, who thus carry and spread the bacteria unknowingly. Researchers actually refer to the human microbiome as a "reservoir of antimicrobial resistance" (Penders et al., 2013: 1).[5]

These resistant bacteria make the complex relation and interconnectedness between bacterial and social practices particularly obvious. They prove that bacteria are not only dealt with culturally, but also influence cultural practices—sometimes in ways that cannot be foreseen (cf. Paxson & Helmreich, 2014: 167). Antimicrobial resistance can be characterized as a failed cultivation of bacteria, a cultivation that takes place partly inside our own bodies and often beyond our control and knowledge. It is—in some sense—uncertain who is cultivating whom (cf. Tsing's discussion [2012: 144] on domestication as "complex relations of dependency and interdependence"). In the next section, I draw on this understanding of bacteria and human-microbial relations when focusing on a specific case—gut bacteria—in order to explore microbes as a cultural sociological matter that can contribute to a cultural sociological discussion on death and life as well as their interrelation.

Homo Microbis, Life and Death

Mapping the bacteria living on and in the human body has led to conceptualizations of the human organism as a multispecies achievement. Helmreich (2015) describes the phenomenon of "microbiomania" in popular science and science studies, and the emergence of the human as *Homo microbis*, where the microbiome is the central metaphor for humanity. Helmreich (2015: 62) writes: "No longer merely the lineal descendants of previous generations of earlier hominoids, anthropoids, mammals, chordates, animals, and so on, humans are tangled mixtures, Frankensteins, of a welter of teeny microbial friends and enemies." Work by Hird (2009) can be used to exemplify such microbiomania. Given the co-evolution of humans and bacteria, Hird (2009: 26) (referring to Haraway, 2008) describes the human organism and bacteria as *symbionts all-the-way-down*—as inseparable from each other. Hird (2009: 26) writes that we, in our encounters with bacteria, need to recognize "that 'I' am bacteria, that bacteria are us."

Looking at the news media, Helmreich's statement about microbiomania is largely confirmed. In the BBC article "More than half of your body is not human" (Gallagher, 2018), a microbiologist is cited saying: "your body isn't just you." A similar, slightly older, example from the Swedish news media is an article titled "You are more bacteria than human" (*Du är mer bakterie än människa*) (Boys, 2012). Both articles state that human cells and genes are outnumbered by bacterial cells and genes. Moreover, the articles describe how microbes previously considered pathogenic have been found to live in and on the human body without causing infection.

The inseparability and interdependence of humans and bacteria are perhaps best illustrated by popular representations of the gut flora: the community of microbes residing in the digestive tract of humans and animals. This flora is often described as something that needs to be carefully nurtured through hygienic practices, specific (probiotic) food and avoidance of antibiotics. Microbiologist Martin Blaser, author of the popular science book *Missing Microbes*, is described in the Swedish news media as "the man who wants to protect our inner bacteria against the attacks of the modern society" (Lindblad, 2016a). Blaser argues that our "modern lifestyle" is detrimental to our resident bacteria, and the root cause of diseases such as obesity, juvenile diabetes and asthma. Here, the presence of microbes is seen as crucial to good health, and practices that were once considered salubrious are instead described as downright harmful.

Related news stories, mirroring a similar reconceptualization of human-microbial relations, depict the gut flora as "shaping" the human brain (Gustafsson, 2016) and bacteria as "ruling our lives" (Lindblad, 2016b). In these stories, the gut flora is not only essential to human well-being, but fundamentally formative to our personalities and the choices we make. The consequence is, again, that the gut flora has to be meticulously managed through proper food and avoidance of antibiotics.

These examples show how being human is discussed as a multispecies achievement—humans are "super organisms," "a symbiont all the way down" (cf. Hird, 2009), a "zoo of microbes,"[6] and an "eco-system" (The Scientist, 2014).[7] Here, the microbes living on and in the human body are in need of attentive care if they are to achieve optimal co-existence, and lead a long healthy life. But what are the cultural sociological implications of Homo microbis for conceptualizations of, and boundaries between, life and death?

Decomposition as a Site of Life and Death

In 2015, a Guardian article stated: "Far from being 'dead,' […], a rotting corpse is teeming with life" (Costandi, 2015). The text describes that when a human dies and the immune system stops working, previously protective bacteria—in particular the gut flora—spread freely throughout the dead body. "Left unchecked, our gut bacteria begin to digest the intestines, and then the surrounding tissues, from the inside out, using the chemical cocktail that leaks out of damaged cells as a food source." In the early stages of decomposition, the bacteria fuel (and are fueled by) the decomposition process. They break down tissues and transform them into gas, liquids and salts.

Homo microbis and the human organism as a multispecies achievement not only raise questions about what is it means to be human (cf. Helmreich, 2015; Hird, 2009; Holmberg, 2005), but also about who, and *what*, actually vanishes when a person dies. As Brice (2014: 171) argues, in relation to the life of yeast in wineries: "In a more-than-human world killing becomes difficult to confine to a single unwanted organism or species" (Brice, 2014: 171). Not only killing, but also the entire life-death binary is based on the notion of the individual (human) subject—this binary is insufficient if we wish to understand the (non-)death of the Homo microbis.

Though the enlacement of the human and bacterial world might shake up our dichotomous understanding of life and death, recent research complicates the matter even further. Microbial life, thriving in corpses, can be employed as a resource in defining the exact time of death of a human. Finley et al. state:

> Microorganisms are ubiquitous in the environment and occupy nearly every habitat, even those of animals, including humans. These microorganisms that inhabit larger host organisms make up complex multispecies communities that change rapidly when the host organism dies and have been referred to as epinecrotic [microbial communities residing in and/or moving on the surface of decomposing remains] microbial communities of decomposing animal carcasses. (Finley et al., 2015: 623)

The quote describes microbes as "ubiquitous" and as parts of "complex multispecies communities," constituted in tandem with their animal host during both its life span and its demise. This reasoning is familiar from the discussion on Homo microbis. Here, however, bacterial animation in the corpse is utilized as a "microbial clock." This "clock" is constituted both by the human microbiome, which changes rapidly when the human organism dies, and by microbes from the corpse's surroundings (Finley et al., 2015: 627; cf. Metcalf et al., 2013, 2016). Although scientific consensus has been univocal for quite some time—bacteria do constitute the major driving force in decomposition of mammals—it is only in recent years that mapping microbial activity in corpses has become a distinct research field. These studies are performed in facilities nicknamed "body farms," where processes of decay are studied in human donors' bodies, and sometimes in non-human animals, often pigs. Dead bodies are left to rot in a variety of milieus, and they are examined during different stages of the decomposition process (Mossop, 2014).[8] Whereas in forensics the stages of putrefaction have traditionally been identified through the presence and activity of different insects—for example, blowflies and beetles—microbial communities are now increasingly considered to provide relevant clues as to the death of the human host. The expectation is that the microbial clock will offer an even more precise estimation of the time of death than previous forensic methods have (Finley et al., 2015). In particular, it is predicted that this research will be fruitful when bodies are found for which the cause of death is uncertain, making it essential as forensic evidence in criminal cases. Researchers hope that the microbial clock will complement other clues, like cell phone calls and testimonies (cf. Hyde et al., 2015).

Conceiving of the human body as an ecosystem, where bacteria are inseparable from the human anatomy, may convolute taken-for-granted boundaries between life and death. The description of "death" in the *Oxford Dictionary* ("The end of life. The cessation of life") does not seem to be completely accurate. In fact, the dead body is a site where renewed and vital activity flourishes. The corpse is "teeming with life"—life that can indeed be considered part of the human while living. On the one hand, the microbial clock confirms that life and death are opposites and that their frontiers can be defined exactly. On the other hand, the microbial flora constituting this very method is the consequence of the human body being a multispecies achievement—a "zoo of microbes"—potentially challenging the very notion of the human organism as a separate and individual entity.

Conclusions: Bacteria as Paradoxical Figures of Life and Death

In this chapter, I have explored how bacteria can contribute to a cultural sociological discussion about death. I have argued for understanding bacteria and human-microbial relations as fundamental parts of—and inseparable from—human culture. Our understanding of bacteria, and the way they relate to human practices, has consequences for how we relate to each other and the world. I have especially highlighted the implications of bacteria's ambiguous position for how we understand death and life: their boundaries and relation. I have shown how bacteria both challenge and confirm life and death as distinct states and as opposites. Below, I will elaborate on how this chapter relates to previous research and how bacteria can be conceptualized in relation to death.

Just as death is ubiquitously but also ambiguously present (cf. Holmberg, Jonsson, & Palm, Chap. 1, this volume), bacteria seem to appear everywhere, but are also notoriously hard to grasp. They are incorporated into our most mundane everyday social practices, but their ability to develop resistance gives them the Herculean potential to transform—or terminate—the world as we know it. Rather than being merely a medical matter, bacteria are constitutive of culture—active in life as well as in death. Invisible to the human eye, they proliferate everywhere around, on and inside us—bacteria are detectable only through the signs and traces they leave in and on our bodies, or via certain technologies and techniques. The very constitution of existing bacteria is dependent on these technologies, and for this reason, bacteria have a position as both artificial and natural objects (Paxson & Helmreich, 2014).

My account of our shared cultural history with bacteria started from a narrative in which bacteria are the actors of disease and death—actors that could be managed or eliminated through antiseptic practices, but especially by antibiotics. Seen through the recent scientific and popular scientific discourse, however, bacteria are not only invasive and alien threats, but also prerequisites for health. Bacteria are ambiguously positioned in the contemporary discourse as actors of life and of death simultaneously, changing their position and their manner in ways that are difficult to predict or even grasp. In the case explored above, I have especially reflected on the duality of the beneficial gut flora. In order to function, the human digestive system is dependent on bacteria, and based on this affinity the human organism is sometimes described as a multispecies achievement. However, these friendly gut bacteria—together with external bacteria, fungi, insects and invertebrates—are also important participants in breaking down our bodies after we have died. Together, they dissolve our anatomy and supply building blocks for the perpetuation of human existence. The gut flora shifts from being made up of health-maintaining helpers to containing unscrupulous gravediggers only to become the conceivers of new life. Bacteria act as a paradoxical undead point of existence that keeps insisting on itself beyond individual death, much like the HIV virus in bareback culture (cf. Palm, Chap. 7, this volume). However, when employed as a "microbial clock," the same bacteria can be used to confirm the definitive death of the individual, drawing a distinct line between the living and the dead.

Research on death and culture that challenges the definition of—and relation between—death and life is not new. In the field of death studies, Hallam et al. (1999) develop a discussion on the possibility of being "socially dead" while "biologically alive," and vice versa, in relation to certain physical conditions. Hallam et al. (1999: 12) problematize prevailing conceptualizations by arguing that some phenomena challenge the "assumed opposition between 'life' and 'death', which is characteristic of contemporary western societies." However, the discussion on bacteria in this chapter might be applicable if we wish to further problematize the notion of "biological death." Thus, the sociological discussion of bacteria as a cultural matter goes beyond studying solely the "social" or "cultural" dimension of death. Furthermore, what seems to be a purely biological death is always both social and natural, as are bacterial cultures. As we can see, "biological death" is contingent, uncertain and a subject for cultural sociological research on death and dying.

Such an argument resonates with previous research. For example, Lock (2003) has shown how scientific controversies concerning "brain dead" persons, or using her term "living cadavers," center on whether or not these individuals are actually biologically dead. She shows how the category of "brain death" inhabits the capacity to move the actual site of death from the heart to the brain. This is dependent on certain technologies that make it possible to keep people alive even when their heart stops beating, and to measure activity in the brain. Another example, from a very different context, is Hayden's (2003) study showing how brine shrimps, which have the baffling ability to "survive death,"[9] are used in biology and pathology to "illustrate the porous boundary between life and death." Landecker's (2000) discussion on laboratory cultivation of a human cell line is also worth mentioning. Using serial culture, and given the appropriate conditions, somatic cells from a biopsy can go on dividing and growing endlessly—even though the patient is long gone. Landecker pursues the notion that these immortalized cell lines create a paradoxical tension with regard to conventional views on death and dying.

New developments in bioscience challenge, and can potentially reconfigure, boundaries as well as the meaning of the human body, birth, illness and life itself. This has been the subject of a large body of research conducted during the past few decades (cf. Franklin & Lock, 2003; Rose, 2007; Tamminen, 2012; Webster, 2012). For example, Webster (2012: 1) states that novel relations to life, originating from biotechnologies and new biological artifacts, lead to questioning "the boundaries between human and animal, organic and nonorganic, living and the suspension of living (*and the meaning of death itself*)" (Webster, 2012: 2, my italics). When life changes, so does death. Moreover, genetic mapping of the human microbiome and the Homo microbis relies on advances in the biosciences. Due to their slippery nature, bacteria might be conceptualized as "boundary walkers" (Holmberg & Ideland, 2009; cf. Haraway, 1997). Bacteria are objects that migrate on and across the margins of social and natural, health and illness, self and non-self, life and death. In doing so, they challenge and reconfigure these categories and dichotomies. However, and importantly, bacteria can also confirm such boundaries. In this sense, they can be compared to autoimmune diseases that "manifest the paradoxical and sometimes deadly proposition that the body/self both is and is not itself" (Cohen, 2004: 8). In line with Cohen's argument concerning the contradictory character of autoimmunity, it becomes meaningful to contemplate bacteria in the same manner (cf. Brown & Nettleton, 2017). Bacteria are capable of coincidentally unsettling and destabilizing the boundaries between life and death, dismantling their status as opposing phenomena. Consequently, they can be viewed as paradoxical figures, enabling us to understand life and death as both opposites and symbiotic—states that simultaneously exclude and sustain each other.

Notes

1. These bacterial infections are still the cause of many deaths in certain parts of the world.
2. Sangodeyi (2014: 7) points out, however, that "microbes have always been spoken of in an 'idiom of promise'." For example, Pasteur empathized that

microbes were necessary for the health of human beings. In bacteriology, the focus has nevertheless been on pathogens (Sangodeyi, 2014: 23).

3. See also Cooper (2006: 115), who instead argues that the view of microbes as potentially beneficial for the human organism is related to a conception of the enemy as being everywhere: around us and even inside us. Thus, humanity is engaged in an unpredictable guerrilla war where all boundaries are unsafe.

4. Important to note, however, is how this notion was not only a product of bacteriology, but also aligned with previous religious beliefs in an "invisible world" of forces that could determine life and death (Tomes, 1999: 7).

5. See also for example van Schaik (2015).

6. Helmreich (2015: 65, quoting Sagan who in turn quotes Dorion Clair Folsom).

7. See also Nerlich and Hellsten's (2009) analysis of metaphors concerning the microbiome in science and popular science.

8. For information about Body Farms, see National Geographic's video: http://video.nationalgeographic.com/video/body-farm-sci, accessed 10 May 2018.

9. The brine shrimp is a suspended animator—it is capable of inducing a temporary cessation of bodily functions to achieve a hypometabolic state.

References

Boys, K. (2012) 'Du är Mer Bakterie än Människa', *Dagens Nyheter*, 17 June 2012.

Brice, J. (2014) 'Killing in More-than-Human Spaces: Pasteurisation, Fungi, and the Metabolic Lives of Wine', *Environmental Humanities*, 4(1), 171–194.

Brown, B. and Crawford, P. (2009) '"Post Antibiotic Apocalypse": Discourses of Mutation in Narratives of MRSA', *Sociology of Health & Illness*, 31(4), 508–524.

Brown, N. and Nettleton, S. (2017) '"There Is Worse to Come": The Biopolitics of Traumatism in Antimicrobial Resistance (AMR)', *The Sociological Review*, 65(3), 493–508.

Bud, R. (2007) *Penicillin: Triumph and Tragedy*, Oxford: Oxford University Press.

Cohen, E. (2004) 'My Self as an Other: On Autoimmunity and "Other" Paradoxes', *Medical Humanities*, 30(1), 7–11.

Cooper, M. (2006) 'Pre-Empting Emergence: The Biological Turn in the War on Terror', *Theory, Culture & Society*, 23(4), 113–135.

Costandi, M. (2015, May) 'Life After Death: The Science of Human Decomposition', *The Guardian*, https://www.theguardian.com/science/neurophilosophy-/2015/may/05/life-after-death, accessed 10 May 2018.

Finley, S. J., Benbow, M. E. and Javan, G. T. (2015) 'Microbial Communities Associated with Human Decomposition and Their Potential Use as Postmortem Clocks', *International Journal of Legal Medicine*, 129(3), 623–632.

Franklin, S. and Lock, M. (2003) 'Animation and Cessation: The Remaking of Life and Death' in S. Franklin and M. Lock (eds.) *Remaking Life and Death: Toward an Anthropology of the Biosciences*, Santa Fe: School of American Research Press.

Gallagher, J. (2018, April 10) 'More than Half Your Body Is Not Human', *BBC News*, http://www.bbc.com/news/health-43674270, accessed 15 June 2018.

Gustafsson, P. (2016, November 1) 'Bakterier Formar Vår Hjärna', *Sveriges Radio*, http://sverigesradio.se/sida/avsnitt/800453?programid=412, accessed 10 May 2018.

Hallam, E., Hockey, J. L. and Howarth, G. (1999) *Beyond the Body: Death and Social Identity*, London: Routledge.

Haraway, D. J. (1997) *Modest_Witness@Second_Millennium. FemaleMana_Meets_OncoMouse!*, London: Routledge.

Haraway, D. J. (2003) *The Companion Species Manifesto: Dogs, People and Significant Otherness*, Chicago: Prickly Paradigm.

Haraway, D. J. (2008) *When Species Meet*, Minneapolis: University of Minnesota Press.

Hayden, C. (2003) 'Suspended Animation: A Brine Shrimp Essay' in S. Franklin and M. Lock (eds.) *Remaking Life & Death: Toward an Anthropology of the Biosciences*, Santa Fe: School of American Research Press.

Helmreich, S. (2016) *Sounding the Limits of Life: Essays in the Anthropology of Biology and Beyond*, Princeton: Princeton University Press.

Hird, M. J. (2009) *The Origins of Sociable Life: Evolution After Science Studies*, Basingstoke: Palgrave Macmillan.

Holmberg, T. (2005) *Vetenskap på Gränsen*, Lund: Arkiv förlag.

Holmberg, T. and Ideland, M. (2009) 'Transgenic Silences: The Rhetoric of Comparisons and Transgenic Mice as "Ordinary Treasures"', *BioSocieties*, 4(2–3), 165–181.

Hyde, E. R., Haarmann, D. P., Petrosino, J. F., Lynne, A. M. and Bucheli, S. R. (2015) 'Initial Insights into Bacterial Succession During Human Decomposition', *International Journal of Legal Medicine*, 129(3), 661–671.

Ingram, M. (2011) 'Fermentation, Rot and Other Human-Microbial Performances' in M. J. Goldman, P. Nadasdy and M. Turner (eds.) *Knowing Nature: Conversations at the Intersection of Political Ecology and Science Studies*, Chicago: The University of Chicago Press.

Landecker, H. (2000) 'Immortality, In Vito', in P. Brodwin (ed.) *Biotechnology and Culture. Bodies, Anxieties, Ethics*, Bloomington and Indianapolis: Indiana University Press.

Landecker, H. (2016) 'Antibiotic Resistance and the Biology of History', *Body & Society*, 22(4), 19–52.

Latour, B. (1993a) *The Pasteurization of France*, Cambridge: Harvard University Press.

Latour, B. (1993b) *We Have Never Been Modern*, Cambridge: Harvard University Press.

Lindblad, T. (2016a, November 29) 'Brist på Bakterier Kan Göra Oss Sjuka', *Sveriges Radio*, http://sverigesradio.se/sida/avsnitt/813364?programid=412, accessed 10 May 2018.

Lindblad, T. (2016b, September 19) 'Bakterierna Styr Svåra Liv', *Sveriges Radio*, http://sverigesradio.se/sida/avsnitt/780424?programid=412, accessed 10 May 2018.

Lock, M. (2003) 'On Making Up the Good-as-Dead in a Utilitarian World' in S. Franklin and M. Lock (eds.) *Remaking Life and Death: Toward an Anthropology of the Biosciences*, Santa Fe: School of American Research Press.

Metcalf, J. L., Wegener Parfrey, L., Gonzalez, A., Lauber, C. L., Knights, D., Ackermann, G., Humphrey, G. C., Gebert, M. J., Van Treuren, W., Berg-Lyons, D., Keepers, K., Guo, Y., Bullard, J., Fierer, N., Carter, D. O. and Knight, R. (2013) 'A Microbial Clock Provides an Accurate Estimate of the Postmortem Interval in a Mouse Model System', *eLife*, 2: e01104.

Metcalf, J. L., Carter, D. O. and Knight, R. (2016) 'Microbiology of Death', *Current Biology*, 26(13), R561–R563.

Mossop, B. (2014, July 10) 'From Ancient DNA to Decay: An Interview with Jessica Metcalf', *eLife*, https://elifesciences.org/interviews/ff613808/jessica-metcalf, accessed 10 May 2018.

Nerlich, B. and Hellsten, I. (2009) 'Beyond the Human Genome: Microbes, Metaphors and What It Means to Be Human in an Interconnected Post-Genomic World', *New Genetics and Society*, 28(1), 19–36.

Nerlich, B. and James, R. (2009) '"The Post-Antibiotic Apocalypse" and the "War on Superbugs": Catastrophe Discourse in Microbiology, its Rhetorical Form and Political Function', *Public Understanding of Science*, 18(5), 574–590.

Paxson, H. (2008) 'Post-Pasteurian Cultures: The Microbiopolitics of Raw-Milk Cheese in the United States', *Cultural Anthropology*, 23(1), 15–47.

Paxson, H. (2012) *The Life of Cheese*, Berkeley: University of California Press.

Paxson, H. (2014) 'Microbiopolitics' in E. Kirksey (ed.) *The Multispecies Saloon*, Durham and London: Duke University Press.

Paxson, H. and Helmreich, S. (2014) 'The Perils and Promises of Microbial Abundance: Novel Natures and Model Ecosystems, From Artisanal Cheese to Alien Seas', *Social Studies of Science*, 44(2), 165–193.

Penders, J., Stobberingh, E. E., Savelkoul, P. H. M. and Wolffs, P. F. G. (2013) 'The Human Microbiome as a Reservoir of Antimicrobial Resistance', *Frontiers in Microbiology*, 87(4), 1–7.

Rose, N. (2007) *The Politics of Life Itself: Biomedicine, Power, and Subjectivity in the Twenty-First Century*, Princeton: Princeton University Press.

Sangodeyi, F. I. (2014) *The Making of the Microbial Body, 1900s–2012*, Doctoral Dissertation, Cambridge: Harvard University.

Singer, M. (2015) *Anthropology of Infectious Disease*, New York: Routledge.

Stewart, E. J. (2012) 'Growing Unculturable Bacteria', *Journal of Bacteriology*, 194(16), 4151–4160.

Tamminen, S. (2012) 'Still Life? Frozen Gametes, National Gene Banks and Re-Configuration of Animality' in N. Vermeulen, S. Tamminen and A. Webster (eds.) *Bio-Objects: Life in the 21st Century*, New York: Routledge.

The Scientist. (2014, August 1) 'The Body's Eco-System', *The Scientist*, https://www.the-scientist.com/features/the-bodys-ecosystem-37085, accessed 10 May 2018.

Tomes, N. (1999) *The Gospel of Germs: Men, Women, and the Microbe in American Life*, Cambridge: Harvard University Press.

Tsing, A. (2012) 'Unruly Edges: Mushrooms as Companion Species. For Donna Haraway', *Environmental Humanities*, 1(1), 141–154.

van Schaik, W. (2015) 'The Human Gut Resistome', *Phil. Trans. R. Soc. B*, 370(1670), 1–9.

Webster, A. (2012) 'Introduction. Bio-objects: Exploring the Boundaries of Life' in N. Vermeulen, S. Tamminen and A. Webster (eds.) *Bio-Objects: Life in the 21st Century*, New York: Routledge.

6

On Anorexia Nervosa and the Embodied Being-Toward-Death

Nicklas Neuman

Introduction

It is a banal fact that an individual who does not eat will eventually die from starvation. The reasons for starvation are many, as are the existential experiences of starving. Anorexia nervosa (hereafter AN) is one cause of deadly starvation. It is a deadly disease that seizes the life of the person suffering from it. It is a disease of deterioration—biological, psychological, social, and existential—that, as this chapter will show, has a multifaceted relation to life and death.

I have chosen to study recovery stories about AN found in a sample of articles using qualitative interviews, and I demonstrate how death comes to matter by zooming in on how life and death are described as both embodied and existential experiences by those who have suffered from AN. I do this by re-analyzing narratives from the articles, all written by scholars in health science disciplines, for example, caring science and

N. Neuman (✉)
Department of Food Studies, Nutrition and Dietetics, Uppsala University,
Uppsala, Sweden
e-mail: nicklas.neuman@ikv.uu.se

© The Author(s) 2019
T. Holmberg et al. (eds.), *Death Matters*,
https://doi.org/10.1007/978-3-030-11485-5_6

107

clinical psychology. Theoretically, I draw on Heidegger's (2010 [1927]) existentialist concept of death combined with Merleau-Ponty's (2012 [1945]) phenomenology of embodied perception.

The reason I include discussions about life in the stories—not only death explicitly—is that I, in line with the theoretical framing of this book, treat the concept of life as indistinguishable from its relation to death. No death can ever have meaning unless it is related to a life. Moreover, the recovery stories highlight notions of life and death for the disorder itself, not only the individual suffering from it, as AN is described as having a life of its own that places the sufferer's self under siege. The end of the disorder is thus not only important to the individual's survival, but also framed as an existential prerequisite for the re-birth of a "true self."

Anorexia Nervosa and Death

In the most recent version of the American Psychiatric Association's *Diagnostic and Statistical Manual of Mental Disorders* (*DSM-5*) (APA, 2013), the standard international handbook on mental diagnoses, the criteria for AN are as follows:

A. Restriction of energy intake relative to requirements, leading to a significantly low body weight in the context of age, sex, developmental trajectory, and physical health. Significantly low weight is defined as a weight that is less than minimally normal or, for children and adolescents, less than that minimally expected.
B. Intense fear of gaining weight or becoming fat, or persistent behavior that interferes with weight gain, even though at a significantly low weight.
C. Disturbance in the way in which one's body weight or shape is experienced, undue influence of body weight or shape on self-evaluation, or persistent lack of recognition of the seriousness of the current low body weight. (APA, 2013: 338–9)

Moreover, the disorder is divided into two subtypes: the restricting type, characterized primarily "by dieting, fasting and/or excessive exercise," and the binge eating/purging type, in which the individual engages in "binge eating and purging behavior (i.e., self-induced vomiting or the misuses of laxatives, diuretics or enemas)" (APA, 2013: 339). The criteria differ in significant ways from those of the previous manual, the *DSM-IV*. For example, the latter included a fourth criterion (Criterion D), deleted in *DSM-5*, which, "[i]n postmenarcheal females," included "amenorrhea, i.e., the absence of at least three consecutive menstrual cycles. (A woman is considered to have amenorrhea if her periods occur only following hormone, e.g., estrogen, administration)" (APA, 1994: 545). Moreover, Criterion A was detailed and focused on *weight*, even quantified, instead of restrictions of energy intake:

> Refusal to maintain body weight at or above a minimally normal weight for age and height (e.g., weight loss leading to maintenance of body weight less than 85% of that expected; or failure to make expected weight gain during period of growth, leading to body weight less than 85% of that expected). (APA, 1994: 544)

These changes from one edition to another demonstrate how AN, like many other psychiatric disorders, is largely a disorder for which the shared understanding of the patient and the criteria clearly bear markers of our culture.

Moreover, due to progress in research seeking to isolate heritability from environmental factors, we can also safely say that genetic predispositions play a great, maybe even the leading, role in the etiology of AN. However, methodological problems (such as underpowered sample sizes in twin studies) make it difficult to provide exact estimates (Baker et al., 2017; Bulik et al., 2007). The interconnectedness of suffering, defined as involving both psychiatric and somatic diagnoses, and the interaction between genes and environment provide a prime example of the ineffectiveness of distinguishing mind from body and biology from culture. AN is experienced in the body and through the body, *as* body, but in relation to a culture that frames the disorder in certain ways (as gendered, associated with perfectionism, self-sacrifice, and so on).

As pointed out in the diagnostic manuals, AN is a disorder in which suffering is severe, the co-morbidities many, and mortality rates high. Mortality rates are not only significantly higher than those for the other clinical categories of eating disorders—such as bulimia nervosa (BN), binge eating disorder (BED), and unspecified feeding and eating disorders (UFED)—but also very high in comparison to psychiatric disorders in general. This includes both deaths that are directly associated with the biological effects of the disorder and indirectly through suicide (Keshaviah et al., 2014). It is in fact a deadly disorder. However, given that we are social animals, death is more to us than just the on-off switch for bodily functions. Death, as well as illness, is understood relationally and is attached to social and cultural meanings that change over time and across contexts. As I will go on to argue in the following, AN, as a deadly disease, is an existential possibility perceived through the body.

Death and Embodiment in Existentialist Phenomenology

As the subtitle of this section suggests, my theoretical strategy is to approach death from the standpoint of existentialist phenomenology. This is not very original, but already an established part of feminist theories of embodiment (Schott, 2010) and the sociology of death (Thompson & Cox, 2017). My main contribution is empirical. It is not an analysis of dying itself, as is common in the sociology of death (e.g., Exley, 2004; Walter, 2008). The focus is rather on recovery stories, where existential and biological death are acknowledged, including stories of a deadly disease as an embodied being-in-the-world. And as I will describe in detail in the following section, I analyze this based on studies in health and caring sciences, where the initial purpose was never sociological, but clinical. As such, this chapter can hopefully contribute both to the sociology of death and to clinical research on AN as well as other eating disorders.

In *Being and Time*, Heidegger (2010 [1927]) argued that our very existence is in fact a constant being-toward-death. He defined death as "the possibility of the absolute impossibility of Dasein [his concept of 'being there' that encapsulates the condition of existence]" (Heidegger, 2010: 241). By this he meant, in brief, that death is a constant possibility that reminds us of the potential end of our being-in-the-world. Not a specific moment, but a being. Death is Dasein toward its end, and our mortality defines us as human beings. The "full existential and ontological concept" of death, as this end of Dasein, is defined as "*the ownmost, nonrelational, certain, and, as such, indefinite and insuperable possibility of Dasein*" (Heidegger, 2010: 248, italics in original). Non-relationality refers to an understanding of death as something that is experienced only by the individual himself/herself, impossible to understand in relation to others' deaths; nobody can step in and die or take death away from her/him. Death is faced alone. This certainty means that death, as an inevitable possibility, shapes how we experience and give meaning to the world. That it is indefinite represents the fact that we never know for sure how, when, or why death will occur. Insuperability, finally, highlights the fact that death cannot be surpassed or overcome.

Because death as a condition is not experienced in daily life, that is, one cannot know what it is like to die (except in the precise moment of death), it is only experienced as a possibility, as its "*ownmost* potentiality-of-being" (Heidegger, 2010: 248, italics in original). However, Heidegger distinguishes between the existential condition of death and the causes of death. A serious illness will reduce the functions of the body, perhaps to the extent that the ill person will die, but this is not death as an existential condition. Instead, he termed this biological process "demise," which is different from the existential process of "dying." Dying, in contrast, is the process of losing one's existence. I urge the reader to keep this distinction between demise and dying in mind, as it has proven to be highly relevant to the present empirical analysis. The reason death is so central to *Being and Time* is that Heidegger sees this as the potentiality that shapes the way we experience our existence in the world and how we live, and that affects the potential for us to lead authentic lives. We will die sooner or later. To Heidegger, this fundamental fact of life lies at the core of our very existence.

It is true that death is the end existentially. It is, however, not the end sociologically. Heidegger hinted at the sociological significance of death when he discussed our relationships to others' death. "The 'deceased,' as distinct from the dead body, has been torn away from 'those remaining behind' and is the object of 'being taken care of' ['Besorgens'] in funeral rites, burial, and the cult of graves" (Heidegger, 2010: 229). However, "[t]he deceased has abandoned our '*world*' and left it behind. Nonetheless, it is *in terms of this world* that those remaining can still be with him" (Heidegger, 2010: 230, italics in original). Heidegger does not go further than to acknowledge our experience of and care for the deceased, however. Instead, he rejects the notion that this experience can ever truly grasp "the way of being we have in mind, namely, coming-to-an-end" (Heidegger, 2010: 230). Sociologically, however, death is not an end in the sense of a finite moment for the actor. Taking a Heideggerian perspective, I would thus view death as indeed being a constant potentiality for being, albeit not only existentially for ourselves, but also in relation to other social actors. A dead person is still attributed meaning. She/he also continues to play a part materially (the body has to be taken care of, there are funeral costs to be paid, objects associated with the dead person might be saved, etc.) as well as in people's memory (e.g., Holmberg, Chap. 3, this volume; Jonsson, Chap. 2, this volume). Her Dasein has ended, but "she" (as a subject) has not.

Whereas Heidegger's notion of the existential condition of death is of relevance to our understanding of AN, later phenomenological thinkers have pointed to a shortcoming in his theorization of human perception and the body's centrality of being. Clearly, the concept of demise makes visible the recognition that bodily sensations play a part in the potentiality of death. Furthermore, in the parts of *Being and Time* where Heidegger discusses the spatiality of Dasein, or when he writes about the experience of other people's death (seeing the end of a Dasein from the outside), corporeality is acknowledged as well. Still, it would seem, he did not consider embodiment central to the existential condition of being. And this is crucial, at least when existentialist phenomenology is to be applied to the empirical case of AN, in which the body is both an obsession and something that is strongly experienced through the sensations of hunger, pain, fatigue, and frozenness. This calls for a more profound existentialist phenomenology of embodiment.

In *Phenomenology of Perception*, Merleau-Ponty (2012 [1945]) brought the lived body and the perceived world into existentialist phenomenology. It is through the body that we perceive and remember. We do not *have* bodies, we *are* bodies, and we make our entrance into the world *as* bodies. Two examples he investigated were anosognosia and the phantom limb. The first is a condition in which a person is unaware of, or denies, a bodily dysfunction, such as a paralyzed limb, and the second is a condition in which a limb that has been lost physically (e.g., blown off in combat) is still experienced. These conditions, he argued, can be explained neither as purely physiological nor as purely psychological. Reduced to physiology, they would be interpreted as "the mere suppression or the mere persistence of interoceptive stimulations," and reduced to psychology, "the phantom limb becomes a memory, a positive judgment, or a perception; anosognosia becomes a forgetting, a negative judgment, or a non-perception" (Merleau-Ponty, 2012: 82).

Furthermore, Merleau-Ponty did not only put these two phenomena outside the scope of physiology or psychology, but he also rejected a *mixed* explanation of the two. They can, however, be understood from the point of view of being-in-the-world (Merleau-Ponty, 2012: 84). Furthermore:

> [F]or a living being, having a body means being united with a definite milieu, merging with certain projects, and being perpetually engaged therein. Moreover, given that it is true that I am conscious of my body through the world and if my body is the unperceived term at the center of the world toward which every object turns its face, then it is true for the same reason that my body is the pivot of the world. I know that objects have several faces because I can move around them, and in this sense I am conscious of the world by means of my body. (Merleau-Ponty, 2012: 84)

The reason I mention his examples of anosognosia and the phantom limb is, once again, their relevance to understanding AN. Here we encounter a medical condition that, at least during certain stages, involves both experiences of what is actually not present—a fat or even "insufficiently" slim body—and unawareness or denial of something that is—a dysfunctional mind (i.e., "dysfunctional" in the sense of a pathological relationship to eating and the body). I would like to clarify that even though I, following Merleau-Ponty, take the mind/body split to be a false dichotomy, and thus consider everything that we do, think, and feel to be

Table 6.1 Papers analyzed

Author(s)	Year	n
Björk & Ahlström	2008	14
Björk et al.	2012	15
Darcy et al.	2010	20
Federici & Kaplan	2008	15
Granek	2007	5
Jenkins & Ogden	2012	15
Lamoureux & Bottorff	2005	9
Linville et al.	2012	22
Nilsson & Hägglöf	2006	58
Nordbø et al.	2012	36
Nordbø et al.	2006	18[a]
Offord et al.	2006	7
Patching & Lawler	2009	20
Pettersen & Rosenvinge	2002	48
Pettersen et al.	2016	15[b]
Redenbach & Lawler	2003	5
Tan et al.	2003	17
Tierney	2008	10
Wallin et al.	2014	15[b]
Total n (each individual counted only once)		**316**

[a]These 18 individuals were also included in Nordbø et al. (2012)
[b]These 15 individuals were also included in Björk et al. (2012)

processes in the body, I will use the terminology of the literature with which I am in dialogue (see Table 6.1). This means a division between, for example, psychiatric and somatic disorders, where AN is defined as belonging to the former (APA, 2013).

To sum up, we know that people who suffer from, and have suffered from, AN are at greater risk of early death, biologically speaking, compared to the average population. We also know that the mortality risk increases with the severity of the disorder. Being-toward-death, our ownmost existential condition, is stronger for the sufferer regardless of whether she/he perceives it as such. Given that we accept Merleau-Ponty's notion that our being-in-the-world is perceived through the body, we can reasonably assume that AN is a strongly experienced being-toward-death, meaning that the world is experienced through very strong—and agonizing—bodily sensations. My question, based on a parallel reading of *Being and Time* and *Phenomenology of Perception*, is therefore how AN come to be narrated as an embodied being-toward-death.

Approaching Recovery Stories

For this chapter, I have collected a sample of qualitative interview studies published in peer-reviewed scientific journals. I have not conducted an exhaustive review or a meta-synthesis (for a meta-synthesis about recovery from AN, see Duncan et al., 2015). Instead, the search criteria included a broad set of stories that would allow me to analyze life and death. My criteria for inclusion were that the papers (1) focused on recovery stories, (2) used qualitative interviews as a method (exclusively or in combination with other methods), (3) included individuals suffering from AN as the only or main group of interviewees, and (4) were judged as having been written in a "health sciences" paradigm. By "health sciences," I mean disciplines and scientific perspectives in which the purpose of the research is to provide preventive and clinical knowledge about the patient group. As it turned out, this was mostly caring sciences and clinical psychology. I have also chosen relatively recent studies, published after 2000, in order to capture up-to-date literature that frames the disorder in a manner closest to the contemporary scientific understanding.

When collecting relevant papers, I departed from those I had read previously and then "snowballed" through their reference lists. Following this, I searched for "anorexia qualitative interviews recovery" on Google Scholar and selected another set of publications that met my inclusion criteria. Lastly, I also found papers through recommendations at the webpages (e.g., a column to the right on the webpage entitled "People also read" with relevant publications for the same readership). In deciding when to stop looking for more articles, I adhered to the redundancy criteria suggested by Yvonna S. Lincoln and Egon G. Guba (1985). This means that data collection continues until the researcher notices that the same phenomena tend to repeat themselves, and new data thus become redundant. In the findings presented below, I use some of these articles to maneuver in my argumentation. Thus, all are not presented explicitly, but have contributed to the analysis. In the end, the selection amounted to 19 analyzed papers (see Table 6.1).

Given my methodological approach, I have been an analyst of already analyzed material. I did not interview, transcribe, or explore the data in their "raw" form. I am therefore limited in what I can say by the fact that I am analyzing quotes chosen and already analyzed by other researchers. Furthermore, the papers differ in their methodological or theoretical approaches and research questions asked. Hence, targeting a diverse set of papers from one specific perspective, as I have done here, is not unproblematic. However, the fact that similar patterns and conclusions emerged in several studies independent of each other could be seen as a strength, given that the authors were from different contexts and started from more or less different perspectives. My analysis is presented below.

Anorexia and the Fear of Death

In this first theme, I demonstrate how death as demise—biological death—was described as something the individuals suffering from AN recognized, and sometimes even as a crucial aspect of recovery. Unsurprisingly, most studies focused on aspects of life that, according to the participants themselves, had been beneficial for their recovery. In some, experiencing the risk of death was explicitly mentioned. For example, in an Australian study, five persons formerly suffering from both AN and bulimia nervosa identified fear of death and desire for an improved life as catalysts for recovery (Redenbach & Lawler, 2003). Some of them "were frightened of dying," the authors write, and "[t]heir fear of death provided them with the impetus to change their behaviour" (Redenbach & Lawler, 2003: 153). Moreover, as expressed in the quotes below, the disorder exhausted them and felt like self-torture.

> [A]nd they mentioned in the article women being hospitalised and possibly dying and I thought oh god how can I keep doing this to myself … and I wasn't necessarily getting any happier for it, you know. (Redenbach & Lawler, 2003: 153)

> I was reaching a point where I was getting tired, I was just tired of this. I was tired of my thinking, I was tired of myself, just tired of all of this…. I never ever want to go back there. (Redenbach & Lawler, 2003: 154)

As I will develop further below, the different stories in the studies often consist of accounts of a self that is hurt or repressed. Or as in the last quote, the disorder is referred to as a place, and she "never ever want[s] to go back there." Another study, published by Canadian researchers, also identified a fear of death resulting from learning about the dangers of the disorder (Lamoureux & Bottorff, 2005). They write about "Diana," a woman who, "like others who delved into the literature, began to recognize for the first time the potential of dying from the disorder" and who, when quoted, talked about approaching her 30s and telling herself that "I am not going to go through the next 30 years of my life like this…. I won't live through it" (Lamoureux & Bottorff, 2005: 175). Here, we find evidence for the existence of a demise (in Heidegger's terminology) and, in Diana's quote, a manifested recognition of her being-toward-death, that is, a de facto existence that was moving toward death.

In a study from Sweden, the fear of death was also explicitly mentioned by the researchers, but only presented quantitatively as a percentage of responses with "[u]nexpected commentaries or events" consisting of "significant experiences that sometimes had to do with life and death, usually thinking that continued starvation would lead to death" or the death and illness of a friend (Nilsson & Hägglöf, 2006: 307–8). According to Heidegger, the experience of the death and illness of a friend is an untrue one, because death is seen as fundamentally non-relational. It works as a reminder, and the potentiality of it is manifested in front of us. But, he argued, we cannot grasp it fully. Nevertheless, this observation of death or of a sick friend's demise is claimed to have affected the women's road toward recovery and is therefore relational in a sociological sense. And as I argued above, the sociological significance of the dead person does not end simply because the Dasein does. A dead person is no longer a being, at least not to Heidegger, but she/he matters sociologically. In this case, the dead or demising people to whom the interviewees related were not met face to face. They appeared in text or as friends, but still seemed to have induced a fear of death that sparked a stronger quest for recovery.

Whereas acknowledgment of the risk of death associated with the disease can partly be interpreted clinically as a wake-up call for recovery, the language of a place and of "doing this to myself" also suggests something existential. There is an "I" in another place, detached from the self and abused. The next two sections will analyze this in more depth, looking at how the body is portrayed as being a hostage of the disease as well as how the disease is framed both as friend and enemy.

The Body as Hostage

In addition to explicit acknowledgments of death as demise, several stories centered on an embodied experience of the disorder. The disorder is a lived embodied experience, but also described as being located in the mind and separated from the body. One example is from a study on patients' reluctance to recover with 36 Norwegian women who had been in AN treatment for a varied amount of time (0.5–14 years, 5.1 years on average) (Nordbø et al., 2012). Rarely did the embodied perception of the disorder become clearer than in a quote from this study, in an interview with "Heidi":

Heidi:	...something happens when I eat. It feels as my thighs immediately expand. I know it isn't possible but...
Interviewer:	But that is how you feel.
Heidi:	Yeah, physically. It is difficult. ...I feel rotten and become very restless. Others have noted that my legs actually are shaking, something I wasn't aware of myself (Nordbø et al., 2012: 64).

Here, Heidi describes how her life is almost held hostage by a bodily sensation of what the food does to her. She feels her thighs expanding immediately after ingesting food; her legs are the limbs through which her life-world is perceived. Others, she continued, have noticed something completely different, a bodily reaction that she is unaware of. This embodied perception became an obstacle to recovery, to living the life she wanted to live.

Similar references to the body emerged in Tabita Björk and Gerd Ahlström (2008), drawing on interviews with 14 Swedish women, in which the themes identified centered on perceptions of a new life after the disorder. One theme about cooperating with the body consisted of stories having to do "with valuing one's health and giving it priority, which is shown by listening to the signals of the body and taking care of it" (Björk & Ahlström, 2008: 934). This is what "Helen" had to say:

> A very big difference is that I'm aware of my body. I hear signals. When I was ill I thought my head was completely separated from my body. I couldn't hear what it wanted—or I didn't listen. I was never aware of being tired or thirsty or hungry. There was something lacking in my basic instinct for survival. Now we're more of a piece, me and my body. We work as a team, quite simply, and I listen to how my body's feeling. (Björk & Ahlström, 2008: 935)

The authors use the quote as an example of the content of their identified theme about cooperating with the body without conducting further analysis, but there is undoubtedly room for further theorizing. For example, the idea that Helen suddenly became aware of a body that previously felt detached from her mind illustrates Merleau-Ponty's discussions about anosognosia and the phantom limb, where he characterizes them as neither purely physiological nor purely psychological conditions. As with his interpretation of anosognosia, this story is also about denial, or at least suppression, of a bodily dysfunction. But whereas anosognosia is normally about a particular body part, AN concerns the whole body. Whereas something was lacking in Helen's "basic instinct for survival," an embodied disposition away from what might cause death, she and her body—suddenly a "we"—work as a "team," suggesting that she previously experienced the two as distinct entities. However, Helen's sense of a mind detached from the body below her neck is in fact not a mind detached from, but a mind that is *part of,* the system that we call a "body." Thus, it would be inadequate to explain her expressed lack of thirst, hunger, or tiredness as either solely physiological or solely psychological. Rather, it constitutes an existential condition of her being-in-the-world.

The stories share similarities with Sontag's (1978) writing on the metaphors of cancer and tuberculosis. While tuberculosis, located in the lungs, "is, metaphorically, a disease of the soul," cancer, "as a disease that can strike anywhere, is a disease of the body. Far from revealing anything spiritual, it reveals that the body is, all too woefully, just the body" (Sontag, 1978: 18). AN is both a "disease of the soul"—in the existential sense of being-in-the-world—and a disease that strikes everywhere. Signals from "the body" are listened to and acknowledged, once again united with the self that was under siege by the disease. Moreover, Svenaeus (2013), writing from a phenomenological perspective, has discussed how the body becomes alienated and uncanny for the anorexic. She (Svenaeus only discusses females) starts to take notice of her body, through the gaze of others and her own gaze. She starves it, exercises it obsessively, and embodies her sense of self. In the most severe cases, this continues until it ends in death. However, because neither Sontag nor Svenaeus focuses explicitly on clinical recovery stories, they do not capture the role of the body as I have demonstrated here, that is, how the alienated and uncanny body is yet again unified with and familiar to the person suffering from AN. Furthermore, as I develop below, the disease itself is granted agency as both a friend and an enemy.

The Life and Death of the Disorder—Friend and Enemy

In this last section, I demonstrate how the disorder itself is described as having a life. In other words, the disorder is perceived as a kind of entity that has lived "inside" the persons with AN. The disease is not only described as a maleficent intruder, but also as a source of security one can lean against. Regardless of which it is, the disease must be exorcised if the person is to survive, both existentially and biologically.

First, in a Norwegian study about reluctance to recover, the analysis identified a theme centered on the sense of there being positive value in having the disorder (Nordbø et al., 2012). Participants were said to perceive benefits because "AN could evoke positive feelings such as the feeling of security or the feeling that there is meaning and purpose in life" (Nordbø et al., 2012: 64). However, in addition to being a purpose in life, or something that could provide infinitesimal sensations of pleasure (feeling "high" or successful through the starvation), the disorder was described in such a way that it was almost granted agency, as a friend who gives one a sense of security.

Ann: I feel this diagnosis is a sort of net beneath me. If I fail or make a fool of myself, it catches me, the anorexia catches me. So if anything goes wrong I could use the anorexia to show that I'm good at something, that I manage something, or have control. So I'm afraid to completely recover because then I won't have any safety net (Nordbø et al., 2012: 64).

Grete: Now I could blame the anorexia. I would lose having something to blame. I don't know. …I believe I'm gaining more than I'm losing (Nordbø et al., 2012: 65).

Here, the disorder is framed as an entity that "catches" Ann if she falls, and it is the only thing that Grete can blame for how she feels. AN is described as having a life of its own, it seems, and if the disorder were to disappear, neither Ann nor Grete would know what to do. Expressed this way, it is framed as an almost destructive relationship they fear to leave, even though they know they have to (otherwise they would not have been in treatment).

Returning to Heidi from the preceding section, she expressed having few reasons to live: "To have something to live for has been actualized now in this period as I try to change and recover. Because, what am I going to live for then" (Nordbø et al., 2012: 63). That aspect had been very difficult for her, "that's why I haven't managed to give up my eating disorder" (Nordbø et al., 2012: 63). A life without AN seemed to be a life without any meaning and purpose. The authors interpreted this as a sense of "feeling stuck," similar to what I described above as being held hostage. When AN becomes a "friend," then it is the only thing that provides any sense of purpose or control. Living with it is safer than living without it, despite the fact that living with it can result in death.

As would be anticipated from the statistical gender skewness of the disorder, most participants in the studies were women, although not all. Three papers were based on a sample of 15 men from Sweden and Norway with different eating disorders (Björk et al., 2012; Pettersen et al., 2016; Wallin et al., 2014). In an interview with "Alexander," the narrative of becoming free from something that restricts you is repeated:

It's freedom to make my own decisions and … listen to myself. When you're sick you listen to yourself, although in the wrong way. You listen to your sickness instead, and when you feel better you don't listen to yourself in the same way. (Björk et al., 2012: 466)

Again, this story reveals a self that is manipulated or even ruled by the disorder—an "I" that is listening to "yourself" in different ways depending on its strength. This conception of the disorder as an entity, mostly as an enemy but sometimes as one's only source of security, returns again and again, whether from male or female interviewees. One last example comes from an Australian study on life histories of recovery from disordered eating (Redenbach & Lawler, 2003: 154): "I looked at myself in the mirror," said one participant who was not named in the article, "and thought if I had the willpower to do this much damage to myself I have the willpower to get better. I just decided I wanted to be a new me—one without an eating disorder." This quote implies that the body reflects the disorder; that thing in the mirror made the interviewed woman realize that, if she could accomplish such damage, with all it requires in terms of life restriction, then surely she must be strong enough to become "a new me" without an eating disorder.

The stories presented above allude to an existential relationship with the disorder. This has also been discussed by Svenaeus (2013: 89), who argues that "the uncanny nature of the anorexic body might foster a kind of personalization of the illness in which the anorexia is perceived as a creature with its own voice." In Halse et al. (2008), one of the families of an anorexic girl even personified the disorder as "the bitch," something they suggested served as an emotional resource for the family to fight someone they hated within the daughter they loved. In addition, the stories also share striking similarities with those of the recovering alcoholics studied by Denzin (1993). Denzin argues that participants in Alcoholics Anonymous go through a process in which an alcoholic self—a self that is also experienced through the body, given the detrimental effects of alcoholism on the whole human organism—becomes a new sober self. Understood in this way, the lived experience of AN seems to be one of having an unwanted guest in one's body, almost like a poltergeist that must be driven out.

Conclusions

The analyses presented in this chapter reveal how AN is associated with biological demise and the life of the body in the recovery stories, but equally portrayed as a disorder "inside the body," with a life of its own. It thus appears as though the self is detached from the body, but it is nonetheless from the body that the person's life and the life of the disorder are perceived. For a deadly disorder like AN, the recovery process—analyzed through a lens that sees life and death as relational—becomes a struggle for survival between the disorder as an entity and the self.

Death is explicitly present but also expressed existentially in the sense of a "me" before and after the disorder. While Heidegger's being-toward-death is ontological—death as part of the being and not one particular empirical occasion—a sociological exploration gives further insights into the situations in which death is more or less acknowledged or feared. The studies reveal that the participants in fact recognize this risk very well, at least in a stage where they begin to accept the idea of recovering.

Moreover, my analysis also highlights the existential and embodied relationship to different forms of death: to dying and demise, to the person and to the disorder itself. This relationship to the disorder was one of abuse and control, an enemy, but for some also one of security, something to live for and something that comprised a purpose. A general interpretation of stories such as these is that the body and the mind are understood separately, while bodily signals have been repressed and denied, but finally liberated when recovery begins taking shape. "Helen" recognized AN as a disorder that held her so completely hostage that her survival instinct had faded (Björk & Ahlström, 2008).

This might reflect a broader medical discourse, a way for those suffering from AN to speak of their disorder "as anorexics do." By this I mean an established way of thinking and talking about the disorder that becomes internalized in their own ways of thinking and talking about it, similar to Hacking's (1999) suggestions that autism is an interactive category—an empirical category that is bound to be affected by how the medical and scientific communities talk about it. Thus, if this explanation were correct, the story of the anorexic would reproduce itself.

We must also entertain the possibility that this is precisely how the interviewees perceive(d) it—that the disorder in fact does make persons with AN feel as if they are no longer their "true self," and that they actually feel there is a person "somewhere in there" that the disorder is defeating. As Merleau-Ponty argued about anosognosia and the phantom limb, AN also does not seem to be reducible to a purely physiological or purely psychological phenomenon, or to a "mix" of the two. Instead, it is existentially and bodily perceived as a being-in-the-world. The disorder has a grip on one's constant being, even to the extent that it is granted an existence of its own.

However, the actual causes and experiences are not the questions under investigation in this chapter. Instead, I have explored how the embodied being-toward-death is expressed in stories of recovery from AN. I demonstrate accounts of fear of biological death combined with an existential relationship to a disease that is holding the self as hostage and is granted agency as both friend and enemy (see e.g., Gröndal, Chap. 5, this volume). As such, and as I have argued above, when recovery from AN is narrated, death is recognized in its biological form, as demise, and at the same time as an embodied perception of being-in-the-world. It is also a deadly medical condition, an existential condition, and a cultural phenomenon.

References

APA. (1994) *Diagnostic and Statistical Manual of Mental Disorders: DSM-IV*, 4th edn., Washington, DC: American Psychiatric Association.

APA. (2013) *Diagnostic and Statistical Manual of Mental Disorders: DSM-5*, 5th edn., Washington, DC: American Psychiatric Association.

Baker, J. H., Schaumberg, K. and Munn-Chernoff, M. A. (2017) 'Genetics of Anorexia Nervosa', *Current Psychiatry Reports*, 19(11), 84.

Björk, T. and Ahlström, G. (2008) 'The Patient's Perception of Having Recovered from an Eating Disorder', *Health Care for Women International*, 29(8–9), 926–944, https://doi.org/10.1080/07399330802269543.

Björk, T., Wallin, K. and Pettersen, G. (2012) 'Male Experiences of Life After Recovery from an Eating Disorder', *Eating Disorders*, 20(5), 460–468.

Bulik, C. M., Slof-Op't Landt, M. C. T., van Furth, E. F. and Sullivan, P. F. (2007). 'The Genetics of Anorexia Nervosa', *Annual Review of Nutrition*, 27(1), 263–275.

Darcy, A. M., Katz, S., Fitzpatrick, K. K., Forsberg, S., Utzinger, L. and Lock, J. (2010) 'All Better? How Former Anorexia Nervosa Patients Define Recovery and Engaged in Treatment', *European Eating Disorders Review*, 18(4), 260–270.

Denzin, N. K. (1993) *The Alcoholic Society: Addiction and Recovery of the Self*, New Brunswick, NJ: Transaction Publishers.

Duncan, T. K., Sebar, B. and Lee, J. (2015) 'Reclamation of Power and Self: A Meta-Synthesis Exploring the Process of Recovery From Anorexia Nervosa', *Advances in Eating Disorders*, 3(2), 177–190.

Exley, C. (2004) 'The Sociology of Dying, Death and Bereavement', *Sociology of Health & Illness*, 26(1), 110–122.

Federici, A. and Kaplan, A. S. (2008) 'The Patient's Account of Relapse and Recovery in Anorexia Nervosa: A Qualitative Study', *European Eating Disorders Review*, 16(1), 1–10.

Granek, L. (2007) '"You're a Whole Lot of Person": Understanding the Journey Through Anorexia to Recovery: A Qualitative Study', *The Humanistic Psychologist*, 35(4), 363–385.

Hacking, I. (1999) *The Social Construction of What?*, Cambridge, MA: Harvard University Press.

Halse, C., Honey, A. and Boughtwood, D. (2008) *Inside Anorexia: The Experiences of Girls and Their Families*, London: Jessica Kingsley Publishers.

Heidegger, M. (2010 [1927]) *Being and Time* (Trans J. Stambaugh), Albany, NY: State University of New York Press.

Jenkins, J. and Ogden, J. (2012) 'Becoming "Whole" Again: A Qualitative Study of Women's Views of Recovering from Anorexia Nervosa', *European Eating Disorders Review*, 20(1), e23–e31.

Keshaviah, A., Edkins, K., Hastings, E. R., Krishna, M., Franko, D. L. and Herzog, D. B. (2014) 'Re-Examining Premature Mortality in Anorexia Nervosa: A Meta-Analysis Redux', *Comprehensive Psychiatry*, 55(8), 1773–1784.

Lamoureux, M. M. H. and Bottorff, J. L. (2005) '"Becoming the Real Me:" Recovering from Anorexia Nervosa', *Health Care for Women International*, 26(2), 170–188.

Lincoln, Y. S. and Guba, E. G. (1985) *Naturalistic Inquiry*, Beverly Hills: Sage.

Linville, D., Brown, T., Sturm, K. and McDougal, T. (2012) 'Eating Disorders and Social Support: Perspectives of Recovered Individuals', *Eating Disorders*, 20(3), 216–231.

Merleau-Ponty, M. (2012 [1945]) *Phenomenology of Perception* (Trans D. A. Landes), London: Routledge.

Nilsson, K. and Hägglöf, B. (2006) 'Patient Perspectives of Recovery in Adolescent Onset Anorexia Nervosa', *Eating Disorders*, 14(4), 305–311.

Nordbø, R. H. S., Espeset, E. M. S., Gulliksen, K. S., Skårderud, F., Geller, J. and Holte, A. (2012) 'Reluctance to Recover in Anorexia Nervosa', *European Eating Disorders Review*, 20(1), 60–67.

Nordbø, R. H. S., Espeset, E. M. S., Gulliksen, K. S., Skårderud, F. and Holte, A. (2006) 'The Meaning of Self-Starvation: Qualitative Study of Patients' Perception of Anorexia Nervosa', *International Journal of Eating Disorders*, 39(7), 556–564.

Offord, A., Turner, H. and Cooper, M. (2006) 'Adolescent Inpatient Treatment for Anorexia Nervosa: A Qualitative Study Exploring Young Adults' Retrospective Views of Treatment and Discharge', *European Eating Disorders Review*, 14(6), 377–387.

Patching, J. and Lawler, J. (2009) 'Understanding Women's Experiences of Developing an Eating Disorder and Recovering: A Life-History Approach', *Nursing Inquiry*, 16(1), 10–21.

Pettersen, G. and Rosenvinge, J. H. (2002) 'Improvement and Recovery from Eating Disorders: A Patient Perspective', *Eating Disorders*, 10(1), 61–71.

Pettersen, G., Wallin, K. and Björk, T. (2016) 'How Do Males Recover from Eating Disorders? An Interview Study', *BMJ Open*, 6(8). https://doi.org/10.1136/bmjopen-2015-010760.

Redenbach, J. and Lawler, J. (2003) 'Recovery from Disordered Eating: What Life Histories Reveal', *Contemporary Nurse*, 15(1–2), 148–156.

Schott, R. M. (ed.) (2010) *Birth, Death, and Femininity: Philosophies of Embodiment*, Bloomington: Indiana University Press.

Sontag, S. (1978) *Illness as Metaphor*, New York: Farrar, Straus & Giroux.

Svenaeus, F. (2013) 'Anorexia Nervosa and the Body Uncanny: A Phenomenological Approach', *Philosophy, Psychiatry, and Psychology*, 20(1), 81–91.

Tan, J. O. A., Hope, T. and Stewart, A. (2003) 'Anorexia Nervosa and Personal Identity: The Accounts of Patients and their Parents', *International Journal of Law and Psychiatry*, 26(5), 533–548.

Thompson, N. and Cox, G. R. (2017) *Handbook of the Sociology of Death, Grief, and Bereavement: A Guide to Theory and Practice*, New York: Routledge.

Tierney, S. (2008) 'The Individual Within a Condition: A Qualitative Study of Young People's Reflections on Being Treated for Anorexia Nervosa', *Journal of the American Psychiatric Nurses Association*, 13(6), 368–375.

Wallin, K., Pettersen, G., Björk, T. and Råstam, M. (2014) 'A Qualitative Study of Males' Perceptions About Causes of Eating Disorder', *Psychology*, 5(15), 1813–1820.

Walter, T. (2008) 'The Sociology of Death', *Sociology Compass*, 2(1), 317–336.

7

Viral Desires: Enjoyment and Death in the Contemporary Discourse on Barebacking

Fredrik Palm

Introduction

Ever since the outbreak of AIDS, anonymous sexual practice has been closely associated with the risk of disease and death. Casual sex among gay men in particular has been the target of considerable public and medical attention, and this attention has not infrequently been shaped by neoconservative moral rhetoric (Bersani, 2010). However, the threat of AIDS has also had a more productive role in the gay community, indirectly resulting in a strengthening of collective bonds. A sense of community emerged as a response to fears of disease and death, and early on, these feelings of solidarity were informed by a kind of *protective doctrine* that emphasized safe sex practices and an understanding of homosexual intimate relations modeled on heterosexual coupledom. From this time on, gay men were expected to adopt a cautious attitude toward sex in line with the ruling discourses on health and intimacy, and failing to do so was seen by many as a threat not only to the individual lives of gays,

F. Palm (✉)
Department of Sociology, Uppsala University, Uppsala, Sweden
e-mail: fredrik.palm@soc.uu.se

© The Author(s) 2019
T. Holmberg et al. (eds.), *Death Matters*,
https://doi.org/10.1007/978-3-030-11485-5_7

but more importantly to the gay community itself. Promiscuity had been translated into a specific care of self and others among gays (Crimp, 1988: 253–4).

Of course, there were sexual practices that did not fit this restrictive way of living, one symbolically important example being *barebacking*. Originally, the term simply referred to unprotected sexual encounters in general. Today, however, it is mostly used to denote unprotected anal intercourse in male same-sex practices, as well as more organized practices and cultures that explicitly reject the protective doctrine. The arguably most debated bareback practice that came to attract attention early on (and still does) was that of "bug chasing," in which HIV-negative men (*bug chasers*) actively seek out sex with HIV-positive men (*gift givers*). As a phenomenon, bug chasing was publically recognized in the mid-1990s. Until then, barebacking had largely been associated with a quite individual attitude: "what I don't know, can't hurt me" (Gauthier & Forsyth, 1999). As such, it was typically regarded as an expression of ignorance of the dangers associated with HIV among gay men. However, the emergence of web-based communities openly promoting bug chasing challenged this idea of barebacking. Bug chasers clearly did not ignore the dangers involved in anonymous sexual encounters (Garcia, 2013: 1032). On the contrary, infection, or *seroconversion* (i.e., the process of being infected), was at the heart of bug chasing insofar as it explicitly involved interaction between HIV-negative bug chasers and HIV-positive gift givers (Dean, 2009; Gauthier & Forsyth, 1999). Rather than being something to avoid, the HIV virus seemed to be constitutive of the desire that structured bug chasing. Bug chasers seemed to crave infection, or at least something associated with it. Unsurprisingly, the very notion of such a desire sparked discussions about how to understand the bug chasing culture, not least how it relates to death, and this is a discussion that is still very much alive.

The protective doctrine is premised on the assumption of a natural association between the HIV virus, AIDS as a disease and death, and this premise understandably informed the early alarmist sex panic discourse surrounding AIDS (Kagan, 2015). This is also reflected in the research on barebacking, where a number of empirical studies argue that death plays an important role in the bug chasing experience. For instance, Graydon's study of 17 publicly accessible "Giftgivers newsgroups" reported a pattern in these communities of reveling in the assumed consequences of HIV, and he argued that this attitude among gift givers risked affirming rather than challenging typical anti-gay narratives (Graydon, 2007: 283). Others have stressed how bug chasing offers a "line of flight" from fears and anxieties about being infected (Hammond et al., 2016). In contrast, some commentators conceive of such fears as part of the sexual health discourse that is thought to regulate modern intimacy (Dean, 2009; Robinson, 2014). According to such a view, the link between HIV and death must be seen as part of the larger bio-political regulation of life (Foucault, 1998).

Part of this repressive bio-politics is the imperative to use a condom that has been propagated by the health discourse. Indeed, it has been suggested that the condom embodies a rationalized order of "sexual dispassion" insofar as it imposes an artificial obstacle on intimacy (Garcia, 2013: 1039), not merely decreasing sexual satisfaction but more importantly relegating gay sex to a kind of "desexualized quarantine" (Gonzalez, 2010: 102). Thus, conceived as a materialization of the Weberian rationalization and dis-enchantment of contemporary sexuality (Robinson, 2014), latex in this perspective appears as the ruin of gay intimacy (Gauthier & Forsyth, 1999: 91). The figure of the condom in this sense works as a veritable latex cage that embodies the spirit of capitalism in Weber's sense, thus depriving sexuality of its magic.

Coming out of this cage of fear and sexual dis-enchantment, bug chasing has in contrast been celebrated for its re-evaluation of sexual risks and intensities, but also for its ability to produce new forms of solidarity among gay men. Some researchers have claimed that seroconversion could be seen as freeing individuals from "decades of fear-based prevention campaigns" (Hammond et al., 2016: 272), and some findings suggest that bug chasers often report that their fear of death is surpassed by fears of social exclusion (Gauthier & Forsyth, 1999: 93). In this sense, researchers have challenged the suggested link between bug chasing and death, and instead point to the social role of the virus. According to such claims, bug chasing would then be structured around a positive desire to belong to the community of barebackers. And as the virus is then transformed from a social stigma into a mark of distinction, this would explain the attraction of being infected and carrying the virus. Infection promises membership in an exclusive brotherhood in which the so-called HIV-positive "poz boyz" are idealized and "revered as fighters of a holy war" (Gauthier & Forsyth, 1999: 91; see also Grov, 2004: 341).

The discourse on barebacking is hence divided over the question of death's role in barebacking. On the one hand, we have those who insist that the link between death and bug chasing is vital to understanding barebacking. On the other hand, we have those who play down the centrality of death and at least partly uncouple barebacking from death, instead turning to other explanations. This raises interesting sociological questions, as it points to how death matters and becomes a discursive stake in contemporary discourses on sexuality and subjectivity. In the particular debate described above, the link between sexuality and death represents a political liability that must be managed carefully. It is thus no coincidence that advocates of barebacking have tried to explain bareback sex in ways that do not primarily involve death.

This chapter studies this discursive uncoupling as it occurs in the arguably most important work on bug chasing to date in queer studies, self-proclaimed barebacker and Professor of English Tim Dean's *Unlimited Intimacy: Reflections on the Subculture of Barebacking* (2009). With his "defining, full-length study" (Garcia, 2013), Dean offers the most sustained effort hitherto to describe the desire that organizes barebacking, in general, and bug chasing, in particular. Through an elaborate analysis of various dimensions and contexts of bug chasing (media discourse, bareback porn, documentaries, biographical material, etc.), he offers a rigorous account of bareback desire as one of unreserved intimacy and solidarity among anonymous gay men.

In this respect, Dean's work does not only offer an account that outlines barebacking relationality as a radical alternative to sexual normativity. It also provides us with a text that is tarrying with death as a problem of sexual politics. Dean states early on that bareback culture is not "all about death" (Dean, 2009: 6), and this claim indicates how a certain distance between barebacking and death becomes key in his critique of heteronormativity. In contrast to such distance, however, he bases his account on theoretical assumptions about a less contingent relation between desire, pleasure and death. In this vein, he links death to sexuality in general in an attempt to close the gap between the morbid desire of barebacking and heteronormative intimacy, arguing that all desire is constitutively linked to a certain fascination with death. But as this chapter will argue, this generalized understanding of sexuality as always and already linked with death sits uneasily with Dean's more exceptionalist and idealizing notion of bareback desire as an ethical act aimed at solidarity. The next section outlines the fundamental theoretical tension in his text between his notion of bareback desire and the psychoanalytical notion that enjoyment is originally split, arguing that the former idealizes barebacking. The subsequent sections analyze how this general tendency toward idealization structures two crucial discussions in his work: that characterizing bareback desire as unlimited desire and that concerning how this desire relates to risk.

Enjoyment in Queer Theory and Psychoanalysis

Theoretically, Dean's project is firmly rooted in Lacanian psychoanalysis and queer theory, both of which support his critique of conventional intimacy. In particular, they are important for his rejection of idealized understandings of sexuality, and his baseline notion that phenomena such as power, violence and death are inherent in sexual experience. Like influential queer thinkers such as Leo Bersani, Lee Edelman and Judith Butler, Dean turns to psychoanalysis to rethink anonymous sexual relations as potentially radical forms of relationality that might interrupt the dominance of the heterosexual norms and institutions surrounding intimate life. In this context, psychoanalysis allows him to challenge heteronormative ways of reducing sex to some kind of obscure natural sex and to formulate a more complex account of sexual desire.

Dean uses a number of notions to describe sexuality. The following account will touch on these notions. The basic discussion is organized around Freud's theory of erotic pleasure (Eros) and the so-called *Lust im Unlust* (pleasure in displeasure), which he primarily introduces in *Beyond the Pleasure Principle* and ties to the death drive (Thanatos). In queer thinking, however, these concepts are often filtered through the Lacanian framework and rendered in a somewhat simplified manner as *desire* and *enjoyment*, respectively. On top of this, Dean draws on Jean Laplanche's account of the same conceptual pair as *satisfaction* and *enjoyment*, which Bersani, in particular, has used to approach sexuality. Although this plethora of concepts might be a great deal for the reader to digest, the crucial point of the following discussion is to outline the originally split structure of enjoyment as it features in psychoanalytical theory and to compare this with Dean's interpretation of bareback desire, then to see how these fit together. This section then considers how enjoyment allows Dean to account for the role of death in bareback desire, but also how this understanding relates to the notion of a desire for solidarity. It is argued that Dean ultimately privileges the latter idea that barebacking is motivated by a common desire for solidarity in bareback culture, and thus masks the link between death and desire that psychoanalysis assumes is constitutive of sexuality.

Following queer psychoanalytical accounts, Dean suggests that normative heterosexuality is structured according to an imaginary logic that misrecognizes sex insofar as it reduces it to mere sexual reproduction and pleasure. Heterosexual discourse reduces sex, cleansing it of its non-normative elements as if these were unnatural. In this vein, Bersani describes how, during the AIDS crisis, homosexuality was represented as an unnatural and uncontrollable threat to heterosexual life (Bersani, 2010: 9). The close discursive links that appeared between the HIV virus, death and homosexuality reinforced the sense of the threat that gay lifestyle posed to such life. Bersani argues that these links continue a long tradition of heteronormative marginalization and stigmatization of homosexual desire, and shows how gay sex is symbolically related to earlier threats posed to heterosexual desire, for instance, by the oversexualized figures of the nymphomaniac and the prostitute. According to Bersani, it was an underlying fear that such figures might stir male heterosexual desire out of control that resurfaced with AIDS. The epidemic threatened to corrupt the heterosexual good life. In the same vein, Dean assumes that heterosexuality reproduces itself through a systematic exclusion of sexual excess, like that of barebacking. But he also argues that a similar exclusion of excess structures the imaginary ideal of the "good" homosexual (Dean, 2009: 20).

Although today there is a sense in the gay community that "the barebacking moment" might have passed (Mowlabocus et al., 2014: 1476), Dean's work indicates that it is still relevant to discuss as a case of how tensions between ideal and actual practice are being negotiated in contemporary sexuality. According to Dean, barebacker intimacy interrupts current assumptions of good sex and debunks idealized views of sexuality. As one study of gay male discourses on barebacking in France pinpoints, the core of the debate on barebacking was the tension between the ideal of safe sex and actual sexual practices (Girard, 2016: 22). And if the protective doctrine assumes that gay solidarity rests on safe sex, Dean approaches the actual sex of barebacking as a form of care in its own right. In line with Bersani, he claims that homosexual anonymous practices involve a queer solidarity with others and the world that transcends the boundaries of subjectivity (Bersani, 2010). Barebacking establishes a kind of "bio-social kinship" of anonymous belonging, organized around disseminating and sharing the HIV virus (Dean, 2009: 92). Rather than engaging in egoistic unprotected intercourse, the barebacker surrenders to the collective of brothers in a radical appreciation of difference, heterogeneity and otherness.

It is important to note how Dean's critique of the imaginary ideals embedding gay sex communicates with Lacan's well-known problematization of the imaginary logic of the ego. Like idealized forms of sex in Dean's argument, the ego—according to Lacan—represents a reduction of the complex and contradictory structure of subjectivity to the concrete gestalt of the mirror image (Lacan, 2002: 3–7). According to Jean Laplanche, this imaginary reduction also structures what psychoanalysis coins *satisfaction*, which therefore can be described as a form of pleasure congruent with the ideal of the ego (Laplanche, 1976: 105; see also Lacan, 2002). It is thus a form of pleasure based on reduction and idealization, not only of subjectivity, but also of sexuality as such. Moreover, Lacanian psychoanalysis introduces the term *jouissance* (enjoyment) to indicate the excessive pleasure that such idealizations repress. Like subjectivity, enjoyment then marks complexities and tensions in sexuality usually not recognized in imaginary satisfaction. If subjectivity contains elements that disrupt the perfected ideal of the ego, then enjoyment contains something that seems to contradict the very essence of pleasure, namely pain. Unlike the gratifying and pleasing character of satisfaction, enjoyment in psychoanalysis represents an abysmal or masochist form of *pleasure in displeasure,* according to which "the subject then suffers in order to derive enjoyment" (Laplanche, 1976: 104). This is then a pleasure that introduces something which seems to go against the grain of what a good life and good sex mean. "Actual sex," in this sense, would then involve something that opposes simple pleasure and life, and it is for this reason Freud ultimately calls this force the death drive. Ultimately, the actuality of sex directs us to the limitations and mortality of the subject. For Dean, it is vital that barebacking as enjoyment disrupts the separatedness of the ego. It is likewise important that the desire for seroconversion materializes ego death through a fantasy of bodily disintegration (Dean, 2009: 22).

Although Dean's effort to develop an understanding of bareback desire builds on psychoanalytical ideas about sexual pleasure, there is a tension between the latter and the notion of barebacking desire as a particular form of desire aimed at solidarity. As will be further developed below, the structure of this desire of solidarity in fact replaces that of enjoyment insofar as it gives way to an exceptional desire in which the role of displeasure almost disappears. We see this most clearly in the way in which the notion of bareback desire obscures the role that the displeasure of death plays in it.

Before we approach this obscurity in Dean's text, we might note here how a Lacanian understanding of barebacking insists on the Freudian claim that the subject, while recognizing and accepting death consciously, denies death on an unconscious level. Thus, psychoanalysis shows how sexual fantasies are used to manage the threat of death and maintain a hidden belief in immortality. In desire, the prospect of death materializes itself in the subjective experience of *lack*, be it in the form of lacking a desired object or lacking sexual vitality on the part of the subject. For the subject, the experience of such a lack signals that life will inevitably come to an end. The unconscious sense of immortality is thus threatened through the experience of lack.

Now, this is where the work of sexual fantasy and excitement intervenes to undo this prospect of death. Providing a scene on which the subject can stage her own struggle with death, fantasy allows the subject to cancel out the trauma of mortality, and it is this connection to the dimension of death that gives sexuality its power to fascinate, excite and give rise to disgust. This is how sexual enjoyment is linked with and dependent on displeasure. In sexual excitement, the subject enjoys the encounter with trauma and displeasure, and temporarily triumphs over and cancels out that which threatens the subject (Palm, 2016: 131; Stoller, 1986: 55; see also Furst & Idevall, Chap. 11, this volume). In this psychoanalytic sense, sexual practice, fantasy and excitement would therefore serve as apparatuses that transform fear of particular dangers into enjoyment linked to the existential drama of death. As we will see below, it is this constitutive link between pleasure, displeasure and death that Dean's account of bareback desire masks. As a consequence, bareback desire is deprived of excitement, as understood by psychoanalysis.

If this chapter up to this point has dealt with Dean's tendency to idealize barebacking desire on a general level, the following two sections pay closer attention to more specific ways in which his account of bareback desire, one based on solidarity, masks the split nature of enjoyment. First, this is done in relation to his notion of barebacking as unlimited intimacy. Second, his account of risk is considered.

Unlimited Desire

This section turns to Dean's idea of bareback culture as an *unlimited intimacy* that, according to his account, contains a desire for brotherhood and solidarity that shatters the ego and interrupts modern assumptions of subjectivity (Dean, 2009: 25). Characteristic of this desire is that it rejects the conventional limits of life and sexuality. Its unlimited character represents a radical acknowledgment of finitude and death (Dean, 2009: 66). Barebackers are "fucking without limits because they don't want to live forever," and hence they transcend the conventional fear of individual death that marks heteronormative sexuality as well as the health discourse (Dean, 2009: 66). In this sense, the notion of unlimited intimacy is a counter-narrative to normative stories of barebacking. Below, two aspects of Dean's account of unlimited desire are attended to: (1) his tendency to blur individual stakes in his idealization of this communal desire and (2) his understanding of the structural role of the limit in barebacking.

Dean argues that barebacking as a whole is organized around a collective motif to breed the virus as a source of life, and that this collective drive produces solidarity that extends beyond individual life (Dean, 2009: 49). In line with Lacan, he argues that bug chasing, in particular, resignifies the virus and turns this previously negative signifier into an element of pride (Dean, 2009: 21). Through the creative work of fantasy, the HIV virus is produced as a value "to be incorporated inside one's body" (Dean, 2009: 53). Bug chasing replaces the narrative that portrays barebacking as inevitably causing sickness and death with a story about kinship (Dean, 2009: 69). However, this counter-narrative has a problematic tendency to idealize the collective and its desire, something we can observe in his claim that solidarity among barebackers is founded on a fantasy of permanence.

> HIV [...] allows men to bond with each other; as a shared substance, it permits those bonds to be conceived in kinship terms, thereby materializing a sense of brotherhood [...] From a bug chaser's perspective, then, becoming HIV positive involves fraternity more than disease. In a world of casual sex and transient relationships, seroconversion offers the fantasy of a world of permanence. (Dean, 2009: 78)

From a Lacanian point of view, this positive notion of a fantasy of permanence is problematic because it repeats the imaginary logic that Dean usually opposes. As a "structuring motif of bareback culture," this fantasy of transition does not merely mirror the core process of identification (Garcia, 2013: 1050n). It also seems that identification with the barebacker fraternity provides the subject with an imaginary ground that—just like the fantasy of the good homosexual—denies sexuality's links with death and allows the subject to retain his sense of being, somehow, immortal.

That an imaginary, idealizing logic is at work in Dean's text is given further support by his account of the particular desire of gift giving, an argument that clearly obscures the existence of individual stakes in barebacking desire. In this context, he abstracts the act of gifting away from its sexual function, reducing it to an act whose sole goal is to breed the virus and establish the fraternity of seroconverted barebackers. Drawing on Derrida's well-known analysis of the gift (Derrida, 1995), Dean frames seroconversion as an ethical gesture that donates something without the expectation of a return, claiming that the gift giver offers the virus self-lessly and that gift giving is to be regarded as an essentially altruistic act (Dean, 2009: 79). Yet Dean's conclusion obscures the role of excitement in gift giving and appears to contradict his own discussion of "the erotic pleasure of giving." It denies the possibility that gifting as enjoyment might depend on a sense of displeasure, namely the morbid pleasure derived by fascination with the displeasure caused in the other. But given that he cites an excerpt from the novel *The Sluts* to describe gift giving as simultaneously life giving and mortifying, it is in fact this distinctive erotic quality of murderous exploitation that emerges as the decisive element in the experience of a gift giver he accounts for.

> My thing was and is bareback sex—breeding, bug chasing, and so on. Yeah, I like the "I might be sentencing someone to death when I cum inside him" thing a lot. I love the gambling aspect of raw sex. I love the idea that having hot sex with a bottom could have a permanent, negative impact on his life. I love how barebacking makes having sex heavy and meaningful. (Cooper, 2005, cited in Dean, 2009: 84)

Although this excerpt is from a work of fiction, it draws attention to the erotic fantasy of seroconversion, and how such fantasy relies on gambling with the other's life and death. This is a sexual fantasy that does not halt at some abstract sense of shattering one's own ego, but claims to create meaningfulness based on a very concrete violation of the other. Such violence and power are systematically masked by the notions discussed here. If Dean's text downplays asymmetries between different positions and individuals in bareback culture, notions such as "unlimited intimacy," "solidarity" and "altruism" are all parts in a systematic canceling out of differences (differences in power, desire, etc.). On a structural level, this boils down to rendering barebacking enjoyment independent of structures of power and difference.

To move on to the second example of idealization in his text, the transgressive form of barebacking practice for Dean ultimately suggests that its desire is independent not only of differences and power, but furthermore of the limitations of life and sexuality as such.

> When barebackers take "No Limits" as their rallying cry, we see that they're emphasizing how sex can function as an arena in which the most basic barriers—including those of disgust and shame—may be negotiated or overcome. Freud claims not only that desire is capable of overcoming disgust but that "the sexual instinct in its strength *enjoys* overriding this disgust." Sexual desire might be described as that which can be satisfied only by exceeding a limit, specifically a boundary of one's own psychic constitution. It is not just culturally conventional boundaries but one's own real limits that must be defeated in order to achieve complete erotic enjoyment. The motto "No Limits!" thus entails the challenge of locating new limits to repel, as if an imperialism of desire. (Dean, 2009: 137)

Here, Dean points out the inherent link between enjoyment and the limit, insofar as he suggests that erotic enjoyment is achieved through the transgression of psychic and symbolic boundaries. In a perpetual "challenge of locating new limits to repel," enjoyment emerges precisely through its negative relation to symbolic boundaries. Yet this negative relation between enjoyment and symbolic limit is not really captured by the motto of "No Limits!" Together with his claims that bareback desire can be understood as a form of unlimited intimacy and a "fucking without limits," the motto suggests that bareback culture is a sexual arena that ultimately realizes a form of sexuality that is not dependent on the symbolic boundaries of shame and disgust. In contrast to this, most examples from Dean's book suggest that the bug chaser is never beyond such boundaries. More often than not, the bug chaser appears to be obsessed with transgression of boundaries, constantly fucking the very symbolic limit, rather than without or outside it.

In this sense, barebacking seems surprisingly conventional, at least if we consider the psychoanalytical claim that "masculine desire" typically emerges through transgressions of the law. If anything, bug chasing then seems to make explicit the fascination with danger, disgust and risk that, according to psychoanalysis, structures all sexuality. Now we will turn to this fascination with risks and its relation to bareback ethics, as Dean depicts them.

Barebacking as an Ethics of Risk Without Risk

Perhaps the tendency toward idealization—which was addressed above in relation to the structural role of limits and boundaries in barebacking desire—is expressed most clearly in Dean's outline of barebacking as an ethics of risk. As indicated above, his account is structured by a number of oppositions, most importantly those between self and other, and between heteronormative sex and bug chasing. To these, we can add a third: the opposition between safety and risk. Overall, Dean argues that current heteronormativity excludes, or seeks to exclude, sexual others such as the bug chaser. Against such exclusions he pits the psychoanalytical claim that risk is essential for desire and that in fact "there is no desire that does not have a risk built into it" (Dean, 2009: 67). From this follows that any notion of safe desire is deeply ideological, and traditional sexual norms that eliminate risk are therefore "pathological" because they are based on repression of vital dimensions of enjoyment (Dean, 2009: 67).

In contrast, Dean posits that the willingness to embrace the risk of being infected is an acknowledgment of risk (Dean, 2009: 68). The barebacker puts his existence at stake, and this potentially ego-shattering act opens subjectivity to the uncertainty entailed in being vulnerable to the other (Dean, 2009: 210). Therefore, it is not transgression that Dean claims bareback culture ultimately points to, but an ethical form of enjoyment that risks the ego and opens up to the other. Not all barebacking practices embody this ethical enjoyment. Rather there is, according to Dean, a radical potential in bug chasing. For instance, he notes that there are many barebackers who limit themselves to specific persons or character traits, or who single out a specific sexual activity. Such versions of bare-backing would not be in line with an ethics based on otherness, as they re-appropriate the other and "insulate the self from alterity" (Dean, 2009: 211). In contrast, radical enjoyment seeks otherness, and in it the other excites because he embodies something that appears to be unknown to the subject. This can be observed, according to Dean, in the procedure of cruising, a form of aimless searching that exposes the subject to the risk of intimacy with the other that transcends both the limitations of the ego and the risk of disease (Dean, 2009: 211). If ethical enjoyment is tanta-mount to the willingness to embrace risk, it is because risk relates the subject to otherness and interrupts intimacy based on identification with a certain ideal image. Unlike "good homosexuals," self-identified bare-backers are happy to be outlaws. Uninterested in a right-based discourse, they do not aim to become legally recognized. They only demand the right to "fuck whom and how they wish" (Dean, 2009: 9). Yet upon closer examination, Dean's central assumption that bareback culture embraces risk is highly ambiguous. In fact, the barebacker's embrace of risk appears to be one that liberates him from it.

> By embracing risk one eliminates risk, in the tautological sense that sero-conversion alleviates the perpetual worry about HIV infection [...] Paradoxically bareback culture institutionalizes risk as a permanent condi-tion of experience, embracing and erotizing it, while promulgating the idea that seroconversion renders moot one particular risk. (Dean, 2009: 69)

The quote suggests that risk is both integrated and excluded through seroconversion. Seroconversion undoes the threat of being infected, but at the same time, the sense of risk persists through a shared "fantasy of risk" among barebackers. Now, a crucial feature of this argument—that lies at the heart of his claim that barebacking culture is one of risk—is the smooth translation of *embracing the virus* into *embracing risk* as if these embraces were equivalent. This shift probably goes unnoticed, because common sense tells us HIV is deadly, and thus fatally risky. Of course embracing the virus implies a risk! But precisely here we need to ask our-selves what risk Dean is alluding to.

According to his account, it cannot, for instance, be the risk of sacrificing one's own life for the idolized fraternity of "poz boyz." Indeed, Dean explicitly rejects such a sacrificial reading of bug chasing as another example of heteronormative efforts to stigmatize barebacking (Dean, 2009: 58). Instead he suggests a more univocally positive reading, according to which the desire for solidarity and belonging orients the culture in general (Dean, 2009: 60). Moreover, he positions this desire in direct contradiction to a desire that would emerge through the subject's relation to his own death. Bareback intimacy is beyond such a relation, because it is based not on the primacy of the self, but on the other.

> [T]he notion of intimacy at stake in one barebacker's characterization of his erotic practice as "unlimited intimacy" cannot be anything but impersonal. This perspective on erotic impersonality qualifies as ethical by virtue of its registering the primacy not of the self but of the other, and by its willingness to engage intimacy less as a source of comfort than of risk. The risks of intimacy are more profound than the risks of disease, although we tend to use the latter as an alibi for shunning the former. In its refusal of the pernicious ideology of safety, bareback subculture infers that the pleasures of intimacy may be worth the risks. (Dean, 2009: 211)

So, yes, barebacking is ego-shattering, but this ego-shattering is not the actual aim of its desire. The real aim or cause of it is instead a risk associated with intimacy. And as Dean frames this risk, it emerges through the vulnerability of the self to otherness, here understood as an impersonal domain more original and ethical than that of subjectivity.

Again it is possible to link this idea of an ego-shattering and impersonal domain of otherness to death and disease, insofar as these could be said to concretely embody such otherness in the experience of the subject. But Dean is careful not to do this, and clearly posits the subjective risk of disease and death in contrast to this more profound other-risk of intimacy. If anything, the former seems ideological and imaginary, masking and obscuring the latter. And if the barebacker has embraced the risk of the virus, it is no longer a risk that puts the ego at stake. Death and disease are still there, but not part of the equation of desire. The risk of disease is worth taking in order to derive the pleasures of intimacy.

Although this notion of a transcendent desire does not lack in theoretical sophistication, it fails to appreciate the inherent risk between this other-intimacy and the mortality and boundaries of the subject. If Dean argues for a desire without a subject, he fails to clarify what risk or eroticization would mean in this new form of intimacy. What would the risk be and for whom? Wherein lies the arousing element of such desire? In fact, the idea of a completely impersonal intimacy appears to be almost asexual.

This asexual character of impersonal intimacy in fact mirrors Dean's notion of gift-giving desire as something altruistic, because as already argued it is difficult to discern any erotic potential in altruism if eroticism must include something the subject can sense as displeasure. For instance, it is easy to understand how the risk of shattering the ego could work as displeasure. Exposing one's vulnerability to the point of risking one's life clearly contains a danger of subjective destitution that could operate as a traumatic instance, an encounter from which the subject could then derive excitement. Such excitement could then be repeated as long as the subject can fantasize that the sexual act he is taking part in communicates with this danger. But as soon as seroconversion occurs, the table is turned. The sexual act will no longer imply the same risk, and thus we must ask what erotic element the seroconverted has access to. If he has indeed embraced the virus in terms of having incorporated it into his body, it seems unlikely that he will be able to maintain the sense of risk previously attached to the virus, as he has already given up his life for the brotherhood. Without a subject about to lose itself as ego, there seems to be no risk, no danger and consequently no enjoyment. The gift-giving act would appear to be bereft of enjoyment. It appears as though Dean would have to introduce some new risk (i.e., displeasure) in order to maintain enjoyment suited to the desire position of the gift giver. One possible element in this sense could be the sadistic desire to infect and thus hurt the bug chaser while deriving enjoyment in the process. Placing oneself in this deeply disturbing moral position could indeed be considered a risk. However, this understanding of gift giving is ill suited to his idea of solidarity and of barebacking as ethics.

This would lead us to the following conclusion: The notion of embracing of risk is consistent with the psychoanalytical understanding of the processes of both eroticizing and enjoyment only insofar as enjoyment and desire are not completely detached from the element of the ego, as it is in relation to the loss of this object that enjoyment is experienced as risky, dangerous, painful and so on. Insofar as Dean tries to substitute the positive desire for solidarity with the negative desire that involves the death of the subject, he risks losing touch with the constitutively painful dimension of sexual excitement, and thus of enjoyment in the Lacanian sense. But even the re-introduction of a sacrificial reading of bug chasing would not solve the matter. Because if the bug chaser has sacrificed his life and thus becomes part of bareback culture, it is difficult to see what he hereafter will put at risk. For enjoyment to continue, some pain needs to be repeated. And thus in order to embrace risk in terms of erotization, one needs some*one* who risks some*thing*.

Conclusions: The Ironic Enjoyment of Bug Chasing

The analysis presented in this chapter has argued that Dean's account in *Unlimited Intimacy* produces an idealized image of barebacking desire. The chapter has argued that it is by situating this desire outside the hegemonic sexual economy that Dean is able to construct barebacking as an idealized exception to normative sexual practice, and as an ethical figure. For instance, his understanding of it as a desire for solidarity among barebackers exempts it from the dynamics of power and dominance forming sexual relations. In this way, Dean ignores issues raised by empirical research about how top narratives in barebacking are often marked by ideas of ownership, machismo and aggression in relation to bottoms (Grundy-Bowers et al., 2015: 188), while bottom narratives in contrast tend to draw on romantic notions of intimacy and a desire to please one's partner (Hoppe, 2011: 211–15). Moreover, the chapter has suggested that the notion of bareback desire for solidarity is inconsistent with the psychoanalytical notion of enjoyment that Dean's book rests on. It has more precisely shown that the idea of solidarity does not account for the subjective desire position of the gift giver, and therefore obscures how the gift giver is aroused by seroconversion. Thus, this chapter has claimed that Dean's insistence that barebacking is essentially about ethics, altruism, solidarity and so forth ultimately masks how everyday sexual experience is permeated by risk, danger and death.

This brings us to the question of Dean's hesitance to acknowledge barebacking as a culture of death, and his claim that "[b]areback culture is not all about death" (Dean, 2009: 6). What might this distance to death in Dean's text signal? The heroism of the bug chaser lies in his surrender to the virus that embraces ego death, but also in a form of transcendence insofar as he substitutes bareback solidarity with individual interest, or substitutes unlimited intimacy with individual limited intimacy. In this viral brotherhood, the death of the individual is no longer important. The seroconverted has entered a community of unlimited enjoyment where the only thing at stake is the circulation of the virus. Barebackers are no longer obsessed by death, or haunted by the fears of suffering the displeasures linked to such a death. Yet herein lies the very problem. Because as Dean struggles to avoid reducing bug chasing to death-enjoyment, he ends up with a desire for which death seems redundant. In fact, here bareback desire appears to be not *at all* about death.

In contrast, Lacanian psychoanalysis suggests that enjoyment is originally immersed in the subjective struggle with death, and Stoller's notion of sexual excitement was invoked early on in this chapter as an alternative to Dean's account. In Stoller's work, erotization is structured as an apparatus that translates a sense of threat into something to derive pleasure from (Stoller, 1986: 55). As stated, this relates to the Freudian argument concerning how the subject, on an unconscious level, secretly believes in her/his own immortality. Triumphing over the threat of death by way of enjoyment then allows the subject to maintain a sense of immortality. The downside of Stoller's account is that it runs the risk of reducing enjoyment to a mere defensive mechanism. If we, however, stick to the Lacanian notion of enjoyment as pleasure in displeasure, this reduction seems untenable. In particular, Stoller's position tends to assume a stable point from which the subject appears to be able to master and control trauma. However, excitement also contains an instance the subject is never able to grasp despite all efforts to do so. This excessive instance forces itself upon the subject, and as such disturbs, disgusts, excites and even shatters the ego, precisely as Dean's frequently shows in his analysis. So sexual fantasy and excitement do not only constitute a space in which the subject conquers trauma, threat and danger. It is moreover a privileged site for the emergence in our experience of such threats, not least that of death. Many examples in Dean's book seem to confirm this structure: The intensity of pleasure corresponds to the heightened sense of risk. If "AIDS infects sex with the consciousness of death" (Bersani & Philips, 2008: 28), then this knowledge serves enjoyment.

This also tells us something about the relation between death and barebacking desire. If Dean's reading argues that the incorporation of the virus leads to a form of acceptance of death in life, this suggests that seroconversion establishes an affinity between the barebacker and death. In barebacker solidarity, the individual has transcended fears of death and reached a point of unlimited acknowledgment of otherness. In contrast to this, an analysis that focuses on enjoyment as an apparatus that manages trauma and danger—in the process deriving pleasure from displeasure—would suggest that its affinity with death is only momentary insofar as it oscillates between such an affinity and a certain distance to death. Rather than being either close to or distant from, accepting or denying, death, barebacking desire moves around death. In a process that is tempting to describe as ironic, barebacking moves toward death only to ultimately withdraw from it and establishing a form of distance from it, triumphing over it through enjoyment. And, thus, the fears of the protective doctrine are transcended by turning its object into a means of excitement. Why support a doctrine that can be ridiculed because the object that it fears can be overcome by enjoyment? The barebacker keeps on relentlessly violating/enjoying the symbolic limit that the latex embodies.

In this context, it is interesting to note how Dean fails to relate this discursive irony of bareback discourse to its mode of enjoyment. In fact, the deferral of normative limits in the sexual practice of barebackers is clearly mirrored in its brutally ironic rhetoric. This bareback rhetoric, as it were, often appears to be the perfect embodiment of enjoyment as pleasure in displeasure. Pornographic movie titles like *Need for Seed*, *Breed Me*, *Breeding Season*, *Forced Entry* and *Creampie Milkshakes* or messages posted in online communities like "I had been hearing that (the city) was a good place to chase the bug," "Gono, herpes, syph, sores, hiv, aids, blisters, pus, drip…. Feel the burning in your cock and ass as you cum or get filled. Pleasure spiked with pain!" and "looking for well poz tops who want to impregnate my neg hole" (Graydon, 2007) systematically stage and cancel out the displeasure embodied by vulnerability, disgust and death. Although not triumphed over by sexual excitement, here the threat of death is undone by discursive wit.

Perhaps barebacking desire is not suicidal. Perhaps it is not murderous. However, describing it as "unlimited," "ethical," "altruistic" and as desire for "solidarity" repeats the fundamental gesture inherent in the very reductions and idealizations that Dean challenges. If anything, Dean's text, in its empirical detail and richness, attests to the difficulties of appropriating sexuality for a political or ethical struggle. Such appropriations are as susceptible to generalization and reduction as is the pathologizing gaze of the health discourse. Ironically, they share the underlying ambition to straighten out sexuality, to make some forms of sexuality more natural, proper or true than others. But if sexuality is a performative apparatus that seeks to achieve certain ends while being constitutively split between pleasure and displeasure, it is never a straight matter. It is originally queer and the crown jewel of this queerness is the subject's impossible "relation" to death. Any serious effort to rethink barebacking desire should acknowledge this impossibility, and how it—like sexual practice in general—unfolds as a constant process of ever-new versions of "revival" and "denial" of death. As a result, the analysis must allow for the possibility that different ends are being achieved in and through barebacking. The mere empirical presence of death in barebacking is not in itself proof of a more authentic relation to it.

References

Bersani, L. (2010) *Is the Rectum a Grave? And Other Essays*, Chicago: University of Chicago Press.
Bersani, L. and Philips, A. (2008) *Intimacies*, Chicago: University of Chicago Press.

Cooper, D. (2005) *The Sluts*. New York: Carroll and Graf Publishers.

Crimp, D. (1988) 'How to Have Promiscuity in an Epidemic' in Douglas Crimp (ed.) *AIDS: Cultural Analysis/Cultural Activism*, Cambridge, MA: MIT Press.

Dean, T. (2009) *Unlimited Intimacy: Reflections on the Subculture of Barebacking*, Chicago: University of Chicago Press.

Derrida, J. (1995) *The Gift of Death*, Chicago: University of Chicago Press.

Foucault, M. (1998) *The History of Sexuality: Will to Knowledge*, Penguin books.

Garcia, C. (2013) 'Limited Intimacy: Barebacking and the Imaginary', *Textual Practice*, 27(6), 1031–1051.

Gauthier, D. K. and Forsyth, C. J. (1999) 'Bareback Sex, Bug Chasers, and the Gift of Death', *Deviant Behavior*, 20(1), 85–100.

Girard, G. (2016) 'HIV Risk and Sense of Community: French Gay Male Discourses on Barebacking', *Culture, Health & Sexuality*, 18:1, 15–29.

Gonzalez, O. (2010) 'Tracking the Bugchaser: Giving the Gift of HIV/AIDS', *Cultural Critique*, 75(Spring), 82–113.

Graydon, M. (2007) 'Don't Bother to Wrap It: Online Giftgiver and Bugchaser Newsgroups, the Social Impact of Gift Exchanges and the "Carnivalesque"', *Culture, Health and Sexuality*, 9(3), 277–292.

Grov, C. (2004) '"Make Me Your Death Slave": Men Who Have Sex with Men and Use the Internet to Intentionally Spread HIV', *Deviant Behavior*, 25(4), 329–349.

Grundy-Bowers, M., Hardy, S. and McKeown, E. (2015) 'Barebacking and Sexual Position', *Sexualities*, 18(1/2) 176–194.

Hammond, C., Holmes, D. and Mercier, M. (2016) 'Breeding New Forms of Life: A Critical Reflection on Extreme Variances of Bareback Sex', *Nursing Inquiry*, 23(3), 267–277.

Hoppe, T. (2011) 'Circuits of Power, Circuits of Pleasure: Sexual Scripting in Gay Men's Bottom Narratives', *Sexualities*, 14(2), 193–217.

Kagan, D. (2015) '"Re-Crisis": Barebacking, Sex Panic and the Logic of Epidemic', *Sexualities*, 18(7), 817–837.

Lacan, J. (2002) 'The Mirror Stage as Formative of the *I* Function', in Bruce Fink (ed.) *Écrits: A Selection*, New York: W.W. Norton & Company.

Laplanche, J. (1976) *Life and Death in Psychoanalysis*, Baltimore: John Hopkins University Press.

Mowlabocus, S., Harbottle, J. and Witzel, C. (2014) 'What We Can't See? Understanding the Representations and Meanings of UAI, Barebacking, and Semen Exchange in Gay Male Pornography', *Journal of Homosexuality*, 61(10), 1462–1480.

Palm, F. (2016) 'Sexual Arousal, Danger, and Vulnerability', in L. Folkmarson Käll (ed.) *Bodies, Boundaries and Vulnerabilities: Interrogating Social, Cultural and Political Aspects of Embodiment*, Cham: Springer.

Robinson, A. (2014) 'Barebacking with Weber: Re-Enchanting the Rational Sexual Order', *Social Theory and Health*, 12(3), 235–250.

Stoller, R. (1986) *Observing the Erotic Imagination*. New York: Yale University Press.

8

Me and My Dead Body: Death, Secularism, and Simultaneity

Hedvig Ekerwald

Introduction

A much-discussed subject in thanatology is death anxiety. Numerous scales are invented to measure people's fear of dying and death. In this chapter, another route to knowledge is taken. People are asked for their thoughts about not death abstractly but their own dead body in the unknown future. When trying to imagine one's future dead body, it is undoubtedly hard to find words. Thus, one draws on available discourses and images. The images drawn upon have originated with stories on euthanasia, organ donation, autopsies, and cremation but also more spiritual aspects such as afterlife. Because talking about one's own future death is emotionally, cognitively, and discursively difficult, my thesis was that it might be easier to do so with someone one knows. To this end, I conducted an interview study with 11 peers from my local network in Sweden.

H. Ekerwald (✉)
Department of Sociology, Uppsala University, Uppsala, Sweden
e-mail: hedvig.ekerwald@soc.uu.se

© The Author(s) 2019
T. Holmberg et al. (eds.), *Death Matters*,
https://doi.org/10.1007/978-3-030-11485-5_8

The interviewees strongly identified themselves as secular, with few exceptions. They referred to rationalism, implying that nothing exists other than what the natural sciences can explain. New, more abstract questions were developed based on this finding. How is death subjectively experienced by secular individuals? How do individuals understand the trajectories of their own dying bodies within society's cultural superstructure? How does the supposed secular understanding of death relate to utilitarian ways of thinking, and to humanism and rationality as well as to magical thoughts and feelings? Finally, given that the interviews were performed with Swedes, is there anything in their views on death that could be considered Swedish?

The aim of the analysis is to understand the interviewees' ways of thinking about death by problematizing the notion of secularity. There are three themes in particular that emerge from my analysis, and they will be deepened to illustrate the meaning-making undertaken by the interviewees. These themes are: secular respect for the dead body, cremation as a rational choice, and what is understood as irrational resistance to donating one's organs. But before we begin analyzing the themes, a short theoretical background and description of Swedish society, as well as some notes on the empirical study itself, will be presented.

Background

The present study aims to contribute to two fields of research: cultural death studies and sociology of religion. Even if the field of death studies is relatively young and rapidly growing, with two of its leading journals, *Omega* and *Death Studies*, starting in 1970 and 1985 respectively, the subfield of cultural death studies is even younger. For example, this subfield has investigated phenomena such as the modern belief in angels (Walter, 2016) and ghosts (Davies, 2007), dead celebrities (Albrecht, 2013), unusual epitaphs (Gustavsson, 2015), grieving over pets and memorial websites for deceased pets (Gustavsson, 2015; Redmalm, 2013), and highly individualized funeral rites (Svensson, 2013; Nations et al., 2017). There are also more established topics in cultural death studies such as grief (Walter, 1999) and continuing bonds (Klass et al., 1996; Jonsson, 2015). Cultural death studies have spread widely, even to consumption studies, resulting in a special issue of *Consumption Markets & Culture* on "consumption and death" in 2017. The novelty of the cultural death studies field radiated from the consumption researchers who took part in preparing this special issue:

> In the spirit of the Paris café society, those of us interested in death met in a small, out of the way room at the 2012 Association of Consumer Research (ACR) Conference. The excitement about the possibilities was palpable and I knew we were on to something. (Dobscha & Podoshen, 2017: 383–4)[1]

The questions that research in the area of death studies, especially cultural death studies, pose to my material are whether there are signs of belief in the supernatural, whether the way funerals are arranged today is marked by a strong sense of individualism, and whether the anguish typical of the many death anxiety scales also characterizes my material. The last question can be answered immediately. There is very little death anxiety among the interviewees in my study. Most of them believe they are less afraid of death than the average person.

A much older field than cultural death studies is sociology of religion. It goes back to the seminal work of Émile Durkheim on religion, in French in 1912, and then translated into English in 1915 as *The Elementary Forms of Religious Life*. His radical idea is that religion is the celebratory feelings of a collectivity toward itself. As meaning-making around one's own death often builds on religious discourses, we can assume that secularity might constitute an interesting contrast. This assumption has motivated my analysis.

Secularism has also been part of mainstream sociology, stressed by the binary secular-religious. Traditional societies are said to be religious, while modern, industrial societies are thought to be secular. Modernity is thus linked to secularism (Giddens & Sutton, 2017; Martin, 1978). But when the poor countries of the Global South were industrialized and the rich countries of the Global North transformed into so-called knowledge societies, things changed. Many religious people came to the Northern countries, such as Sweden, through migration, which in turn was caused by decolonization, unjust economic conditions worldwide and the wars in Indochina, Afghanistan, and the Middle East. In the opposite direction, less often observed, I note that European communistic influences in the anticolonial struggle spread secularism in the Global South. Religion and secularism mingled everywhere and the secularism thesis started to be questioned (Moberg et al., 2014). The binary secular-religious began to dissolve.

My study also explores what the context of Sweden could mean for people's way of looking at death and their own dead body. Using secularism as an everyday word, as in Longman Dictionary—"disregard for or rejection of religious beliefs and practices"[2]—Sweden is one of the most secular countries in the world.[3] This is the case even though Sweden had a powerful state church from 1536 up to the year 2000.[4] Building on the many surveys from 1981 and beyond within The World Values Survey network, Ronald Inglehart and Christian Welzel have shown the extreme position of Sweden when it comes to the values of its population (World Values Survey, 2008). Sweden combines being second in the world when it comes to secular-rational values with being first in the world when it comes to self-expression values, or turning this around; Sweden is next to lowest in the world when it comes to traditional values and lowest when it comes to survival values.

Within the World Values Survey (2008), traditional values mean stressing religion, parent-child ties, authority, and nation as well as rejecting abortion, euthanasia, suicide, and divorce. Secular-rational values mean less stress on religion and traditional family values. Authority is less stressed as well, and abortion, euthanasia, suicide, and divorce are more accepted. Survival values mean stressing economic and physical security, values also linked to low levels of tolerance. Self-expression values mean stressing gender equality, environmental protection, citizen participation in the country's decision-making and tolerance of gays and lesbians as well as immigrants.

The work of Ronald Inglehart and Christian Welzel (World Values Survey 2008) and similar research have been criticized by Erika Willander

(2014: 89) for having a restrictive view on what religion is and for claiming global applicability even though this research is marked by "a time-specific American experience of Protestantism." Taking Sweden as the example and basing her reasoning on an investigation of religious affiliation, practice, and beliefs since the 1880s and an analysis of how the concept "sacred" is used on blogs, Willander's surprising conclusion is that religiosity has cultural, collective, and public power in today's Sweden. This is a religiosity without a common belief system; it does not conform to the expectations of churches, but overall, it is not weak. Almost half of the population believes in "some spirit of life force" and has done so for a long time. The Swedish population—portrayed as extreme in Inglehart and Welzel's research, but less extreme in Willander's analysis—has also been said to worship or sanctify nature. For example, among many factors helping Swedish cancer patients feel better, those connected to nature have been shown to be most important (Ahmadi, 2006; Ahmadi & Nader, 2013).

Considering both Denmark and Sweden, Phil Zuckerman (2009: 58) states that one reason for the strong connection between these countries and secularism, so important for this chapter, is the long-standing Lutheran state church[5]:

And since the Lutheranism of Denmark and Sweden is largely state-subsidized through taxes, what that ultimately means is that the churches will all be nicely painted, the gas bills will be paid, the lawns will be mowed, and the salaries of the pastors will be regularly ensured—whether five hundred people come to church every week, or only five.

Another reason Zuckerman gives for the strong connection is the security of the societies—both Sweden and Denmark are highly ranked on different indices of security. Zuckerman (2009: 60) writes: "With such secure lives and healthy societies, the demand for the balm and comfort that religion provides, has waned." The link between insecurity and religion can be called into question, however. In my view, struggling for survival might give less time to worry about one's death and thereby less need for religious comfort than having a secure life. But if we assume that Zuckerman is correct in his idea that more security means less religion, then I would like to add that Sweden has benefitted from 200 years of peace, something unique compared to most countries. The last reason Zuckerman gives is the unusually high proportion of salaried women. According to studies, women are more religious than men, and he proposes that when women entered the paid workforce on a large scale, they stopped teaching their husbands and children religious customs and knowledge.

I would like to add a question of what the recent peak in immigration to Sweden has meant for its secularism. The immigration rate has been much higher in Sweden than in its neighboring Nordic countries, also welfare societies, and almost one-fifth of the population of 10 million in Sweden is now foreign born.[6] Urbanism means a concentration of structural and individual differences, which in turn promotes tolerance and individual freedom. Perhaps differences based on being a migration-linked multicultural society in general, not only in the cities, would have the same consequences—tolerance and individual freedom. If so, the large wave of immigration to Sweden would be one explanation for the country's secularism. Zuckerman does not use migration as a reason to explain "irreligious" Swedes, but regarding a presence of Muslim immigrants, he says that it might not provoke a defensive reaction in the form of strengthening traditional Christian belief among the non-Islamic part of the population. It is more likely that "it will be in the form of an increased embrace and celebration of rational, democratic secularism" (Zuckerman, 2009: 63).

In sum, how research from death studies and sociology of religion can help an analysis of death perspectives among modern Swedes has been presented, and the Swedishness of secularism has been explored, as have explanations for these characteristics. The simultaneous, almost religious emphasis on nature has been mentioned. Based on this background, my study asks how people view death and their own, future dead body. But first, the study itself has to be presented.

The Empirical Study

For this chapter, I have conducted an interview study based on a qualitative sample of 11 persons. The methodologically novel approach is that the sample as a whole consists of people from my own network of close acquaintances. I have known them for decades, with one exception—a woman I have known for only four years. They have all, with the exception of two, met each other on different occasions. For this reason, and in order to maintain confidentiality, little is said about the interviewees apart from in this introduction. It is a predominantly middle-class sample of Swedish people, varying in age from 30 to 95 years, and all interviews were carried out during the spring of 2017. There are six women and five men in the sample, and three of them are foreign born. The present or former occupation of the interviewees are author, cleaner, engineer, medical doctor, nurse, pastor, psychologist, salaried employee, and three academics (from agricultural sciences, natural sciences, and social sciences). The sample is dominated by secular interviewees, but to insure variation, I included some friends who have a more religious worldview—a Christian pastor, a Muslim cleaner and a Jewish academic. None of the participants had recently grieved a close relative or friend who had died, nor had they been diagnosed with a deadly decease themselves. This was seen as important for ethical reasons.

The interview questions cover a large number of aspects of the interviewees' attitudes toward death and their own, future dead body, such as their relation to religion, burial practices, mourning, afterlife, supernatural events, organ donation, autopsy, and euthanasia.[7] The interviews, each around 40 minutes long, have been transcribed in their totality and the material has been coded. Throughout my long history of being a sociologist and with several interview studies behind me, I have only once before interviewed people I know.[8] For a researcher, interviewing people she or he knows gives rise to new knowledge. In my interviews, there was so much that could be assumed and tacitly understood between interviewer and interviewee, and therefore, many elements of the interview were never explicitly stated. A newcomer, reading the transcribed interviews, would find gaps and incomprehensible links, but to me the fabric of the transcribed text is intact. Because I know the interviewees, I could question their answers by, for example, pointing out inconsistencies, and I could dig deeper into sensitive topics than would otherwise have been possible. In this way, I argue that the study challenges assumptions concerning our everyday way of thinking about death. My relationship to the interviewees also had consequences for the point discussed below.

Death, especially one's own death, is a sensitive topic, which makes talking about it difficult and personal. Knowing theoretically that it is a sensitive topic is one thing, perceiving this sensitivity in the actual interview setting is another. Death is like sexuality, heavily exploited in the media, and at the same time very closely tied to our personality and surrounded by privacy, and often also by silence. According to the death denial thesis proposed by Ernest Becker (1973), we all deny that we are going to die and we even build our individuality around this denial process. His thesis could have deterred me from interviewing, but I found that the interviews brought me, the interviewer, and the interviewee closer together. My feeling was one of thankfulness to the interviewees for sharing with me some of their innermost thoughts. For me, conducting these interviews felt good, and there seemed to be a corresponding feeling among the interviewees. They seemed to appreciate us discussing these existential questions.

In the World Values Survey (2008), a secular worldview is analyzed. But is the specific sample of Swedes in my study secular? Subjectively, it is absolutely the case. Among the 11 interviewees, only two claim to have a religious worldview: the Protestant pastor and the Muslim cleaner. The others answer my question on whether they regard themselves as religious, agnostic or secular by indicating that they are "mainly secular," "secular," or "very secular," or similar. The term secular was not defined in my interviews, instead taken as an everyday word. But what do we find if we investigate the content of this secular self-perception? This question can be answered by analyzing three themes from the interviews—secular respect for the dead body, cremation as a choice seen as rational and irrational resistance to donating one's organs. The themes illustrate how the secular Swedish interviewees subjectively perceive death. The first theme provides an answer to a question a religious person might ask concerning whether secular people disrespect the dead human body.

Secular Respect for the Dead Body

One not particularly uncommon representation of secularism in Sweden seems to be the following: secular people are rational and they know how to weigh statistical risks. They know everyone is going to die, a 100 percent risk, but contrary to some religious people, they do not need to fear ghosts at night while alive or punishment in hell after death.[9] Perhaps this way of thinking explains why one interviewee, the nurse, says early on in the interview that the reason she is less afraid of death may be that she is "rather rational." A different representation is expressed by two other interviewees in my study. They think it would in fact be good if they had a religious belief. They have observed how religious friends have accepted disappointments and unhappiness in life more easily. Whatever happens is not their fault, it is their fate and they can surrender to God.

I ask the "rather rational" interviewee about the limits of rationalism. I want to know her views. What causes human beings to want to honor the living person who has died, by taking care of her or his dead body respectfully? She answers: "Yes, you might wonder about that. But it is of course … it has to be connected to religion, an eternal life and…" I interrupt her by saying that, even without religion, mankind would not just throw the dead bodies over the city walls, as Diogenes suggested. Here, Diogenes' view on death is taken from Thomas Laqueur's (2015) major oeuvre *The Work of the Dead: A Cultural History of Mortal Remains*. Laqueur contrasts Diogenes the Cynic with the rest of mankind. Diogenes, Laqueur writes (2015: 1), now quoting Cicero, "ordered himself to be thrown anywhere without being buried. And when his friends replied, 'What! To the birds and beasts?' 'By no means,' saith he; 'place my staff near me, that I may drive them away.' 'How can you do that', they answer, 'for you will not perceive them?' 'How am I then injured by being torn by those animals, if I have no sensation?'" According to Laqueur, human beings have never done with their fellows what Diogenes wanted people to do with his dead body.[10]

My interviewee agrees with Laqueur's notion, which I described for her, and she takes up the Tutankhamun exhibition in Stockholm 2016:

All archeology shows, you know, that we have at all times treated death in a … yes, but not always, actually. But funeral ceremonies, there have really been such ceremonies in all cultures […] There has of course always been a link between treating human beings in a dignified way and treating the dead body in a dignified way.

Treating a person in a dignified way and also treating that person's dead body in a dignified way are two actions that are linked. I interpret this to mean that a secular person who believes that death means the individual ending still wants to treat the body of the dead person with respect and veneration. If you respect people, you respect their dead bodies. This respect for the dead body is not linked to religion. Death invites veneration among us all.

But could disrespect actually have a hidden link to religion? If the soul leaves the body at the moment of death, the body is just like the skin the snake sheds or the cocoon the newborn butterfly leaves behind. The leftovers do not matter. Religious rituals, however, do contradict the notion of a hidden link. In contrast to Diogenes, religions celebrate respect for the dead body. The rite of passage from life to death is often tended to by religious institutions. In some religious thinking, specific rituals are required to allow the soul to leave the body in an orderly manner. If the religious rituals are not performed correctly, there is a risk for an unhappily binding of the soul to the place of the body, transforming the dead person into a restless ghost.

Another interviewee, a doctor, puts forward a materialist explanation of two old burial traditions. She mentions that in Arctic countries where it used to be impossible to bury people during the winter due to the hard, frozen soil, it became natural to develop the custom of keeping dead people in designated cold houses until the warmth came back in spring and allowed digging in the soil. On the other hand, in hot countries where dead people decompose almost immediately it became natural to develop the custom of burying people within a very short time after death: "And then we simply make a story about it, why it should be so."

What would such a materialistically bent interviewee say about Diogenes? To understand the interviewee's meaning-making, we will see below how she shares norms of respecting the body of a dead person at the same time as she above evidenced a materialistic view regarding our representations of dying and human remains.

Do you think that staff shall be taught to handle them [dead human beings] gently? That they should not talk about everything in the same room after they've died?
Yes, somehow I think so…

…that you should try to learn to be disciplined when you are…

Just as I think you should be so in life, I think. And you are not going to sit during a childbirth and watch a soccer match. Then you can go somewhere else to watch that soccer match. Something, I think…

Yes, but then you still think that there is something in a dead body that is so connected to the human being that it once was, although there is nothing superstitious about it, that you still ought to…

From the beginning it is … yes, and that has to do with how we … they are of course not so terribly different from themselves [while alive]. And that has to do, I think, with how my representation of it is. And what I should carry with me from it, and things like that, you know.

Yes, is it a fine childbirth, or a fine funeral? That is, funeral … dying and everything.

Yes, yes, yes.

Then it's easier to be comforted or to…

Yes, and that you remember it as something good in some way. And I think like this, that is, I've reflected on this thing that people absolutely want to show a lot of pictures of dead people who are torn to pieces. I think that it's doubtful from the point of view of respect for both life and death, somehow.

Yes, so then you could say that it exists in a modern, secular human being, if I can call you that…?

Yes.

…a position to continue to say no to Diogenes!

Yes.

The same interviewee brings up the medical expression "sanctity of life" and does so in connection with stem cells. She explains that the most powerful stem cells are taken from fetuses. A mother who has a sick baby can help it by becoming pregnant again and using the unborn fetus in the new pregnancy as a supplier of stem cells to save her born baby. The life of the fetus is then lost: "There is something like the sanctity of life in a way that you want to…" and then she interrupts herself. I ask her if she means that the fetus becomes a producer of utilities and she agrees.

We have now seen two secular persons struggling with putting the notion of respect for a dead person's body into words. Even if the dead body signals the end of the individual, we still want to treat it with respect. Because the interviewees mean that if you honor people, you respect also their dead bodies, and this respect for the dead body is not linked to religion.

Cremation as a Rational Choice

There is a lot of variation among my interviewees when it comes to norms concerning euthanasia, organ donation, and autopsy. But there is one shared norm expressed by the interviewees, and that norm concerns cremation. Most of the interviewees would prefer to be cremated. Cremation is a strong norm in Swedish society in general. In statistics on cremation, Sweden belongs to the top ten countries in the world (Kremationsstatistik, 2017). Japan tops the list, while China, Russia, and the US are in the middle of the statistical distribution. Low percentages of cremation are found in Catholic countries such as Italy and Poland. In Sweden, 81 percent are cremated. Cremation in Sweden is not a sign of atheism, as both religious and non-religious people are cremated. Still, there is a correlation showing that more secular countries have a greater proportion of cremation.

The governmental burial toll guarantees a burial plot, and there is no difference in costs between cremations and interments. However, for the interviewees cremation is also a question of space and costs. The lack of space for burials with coffins in modern cemeteries is stressed by many interviewees.[11] Connected to the space and cost argument, one interviewee states that cremation is rational, reasonable, and modern as well as practical. Several informants stress the aspect of practicality. Dealing with an urn with ashes instead of a big coffin is practical. For instance, ashes can be easily transported in a private car.

It is not only physically easy, but also mentally easy. Cremation ashes are much less frightening than corpses are for ordinary people. One interviewee, the engineer, recalls how he once drove the remains of his dead mother-in-law for many hours in the car, from the crematorium to the churchyard in another city. He was alone in the car with the urn with ashes. As my interviewees are my friends, I remembered the event itself when it occurred, and in my memory he had not found it ghostly or horrible or unpleasant. He responds: "I was younger then, perhaps I didn't think about it so much."

Another argument for cremation is hygiene—burning is connected to cleanliness. For example, hospitals burned the clothes used by tuberculosis patients after they had died. The idea of hygiene has been associated with cremation since it began (Åhrén, 1994, 2002, 2009). This image of cleanliness is brought up by the interviewees when talking about cremation.[12] A concept close to cleanliness is the Swedish word *aptitlig*, meaning savory or appetizing. Cremation makes corpses more "appetizing," a word used by two interviewees. One interviewee talks, using similar food metaphors, about "worms that are going to chow down on your eyes, no, damn it all, that's not funny!" To put it bluntly, one interpretation of what the interviewees express concerning the cremation theme is that a corpse is horrible, not clean, not appetizing—something that rots and spreads germs. Ashes are much less frightening. Eva Åhrén (2002, 2009: 246) contextualizes this longing for purity in industrialism and modernity: "By means of steel, fire and engineering the horrors of putrefaction were overpowered. Purity, enlightenment and activity defeated disintegration, darkness and passivity."

An alternative, perhaps even futuristic image not shared by the interviewees is one based on the organic cycle. This could be an image of the dead body slowly dissolving into the earth thanks to helpful bacteria, insects, and worms, making the soil fertile, and then being slowly sucked up by the roots of flowers and trees and helping them grow. Decomposition processes are beneficial and necessary for the planet. For the individual, they mean that she or he will finally be merged with the earth and united with nature. Alongside the preference for cremation among the interviewees, there is disagreement concerning the question of whether the ritual of the cremation-bound scattering of ashes is a personal or an impersonal act. One interviewee, an academic, says that scattering ashes is "in a way totally impersonal" and with ashes "you cannot place a concrete human being at a concrete place." Another, a young civil servant, says:

> Then there is this scattering-your-ashes business. However, that's a more modern habit. Everyone can understand that. I don't know how common it is, but this … you can think that it fits in … that you should be a unique

individual and do things in your own way, outside institutions. It's like, 'I want my ashes to be scattered on exactly this or that place that fits me!' That's easier if you are cremated than if you're a corpse that's going to be dug down, 'dig me down there and over there!' That would be impractical.

This scattering of ashes disagreement illustrates in an unusually clear way how the symbolic level is projected onto the material level with a certain degree of randomness. The same thing, scattering your ashes, can seem truly individualistic or very impersonal.

The fact that the absolute majority of Swedes have adopted cremation as a norm has removed the former heathen connotations of cremation. Today, as mentioned, both religious and secular Swedes adhere to the cremation norm. The concrete, collective imagination surrounding the heavily energy-demanding and mercury-emitting process of cremation is that it is good, modern, and effective. Subjective rationality signifies the choice of cremation. But rationality is not all-embracing.

The Irrational Resistance to Being Donated

Recently, five major Swedish universities published ads under the heading "Did you know you can donate your body to a scientific institution after death?"[13] The four-column text includes the following criterion for becoming a donor: "You see your own body as an object, which can be handled freely, i.e. without restrictions of a religious or existential nature concerning what we will be allowed to do with the deceased."[14]

Being more or less secular, do my interviewees see their own body "as an object, which can be handled freely"? It does not seem so. One longer excerpt with an interviewee, one of the three academics, illustrates how such an instrumental view of one's body is undermined by other ideas:

> **Have you taken a stand on donating your organs when you die?**
> They're too old. No human being would have any use for them.
> **You don't know that. There may be a retina in your eye that they could use.**
> No, no, no! Nothing like that, thank you.

Why not?
Because I'm selfish.
Why?
Eh, because I think that you should … if you…
Be burnt up as a whole? [Laughter]
What?
Be burnt up as a whole?
I know it sounds insane, because if you're burnt up it doesn't matter. But I'd rather that they don't carve me up before I'm burning.
So, and then you don't want an autopsy on yourself either?
No, I'd rather not have an autopsy. No! But it's totally irrational.
Yes, yes, but there are irrational things connected with this, right?
Yes, absolutely!
But then I wonder, do you have any general stand on organ donation?
I think that if there are young people who you could help, then I think it's completely OK. But I'm 69 years old, so I don't believe there is anything that's good enough in me to be of use to them.
So it's more like they can freely donate their organs, all those who want to? Or perhaps you even encourage your son, or you say "have you entered your organ donation…?"
I would never do that.
No. Why not?
Because I'm superstitious.
Why? What do you mean?
Well, to bring that up at all with those closest to me, then I would go around and think "did I in any way cause them to die untimely?"
Yes, yes, yes, I understand [laughter]
Totally insane, but you asked.

Among the interviewees, responding like this interviewee did, saying that their organs are too old for donation, is common. The older interviewees think their organs are of no worth. The fact is, however, that tissues like the cornea can be used from donators who are over 80 years old.[15] In the interview quoted above, I oppose to her assertion of the worthlessness of her organs. But she holds on to her statement that she does not want to donate her organs. Her reason now is that she is "selfish." I then juxtapose her earlier wish to be cremated with her wish not to donate organs. Should this be interpreted as her wanting to be intact at the moment of cremation? The dialogue goes on and the interviewee agrees with my suggestion that she wants to be cremated intact. She hears what she has said and comments on it: "But it is totally irrational." What does this mean? How can one's feelings around one's future dead body be consoled by the thought that the body will be safely burnt up while intact? This desire is also evident when we are discussing autopsy. She would rather not have an autopsy. My comment on this seemingly irrational assertion is the following, showing a certain bias in my interviewing: "Yes, yes, but there are irrational things connected with this, right?" This is a comment she affirms: "Yes, absolutely!"

I continue testing her meaning-making around organ donation in an attempt to understand the underlying ideas. Regarding her "irrational" wish to be cremated intact, does it influence her stand on organ donation generally and, more specifically, taking her own son as an example? Here another factor comes into her thinking—superstition. She cannot bring up that topic with her son. Misery would be brought on him if she were to encourage him or other family members and friends to think about donating their organs after death. If anyone were to actually die, she would go into magical thinking[16]: "Did I in any way cause them to die an untimely death?" Here too she hears what she just said and comments: "Totally insane, but you asked."

This intellectual person is harboring thoughts, feelings, and values that she herself calls "totally irrational" and "totally insane." She finds herself caught up in contradictions, which the dialogue itself made visible. The feelings are there, but acknowledging any logic in them is impossible.[17] This excerpt provides a clear example from my interviews of how we can have a paradoxical relationship to our own future dead body. This interviewee's paradoxical understanding of her own death is certainly something she shares with many of us. It should be added that unwillingness to donate organs is not typical in my sample. The young civil servant says: "Yes, I think that the world would be a much better place if we donated our organs to each other."

Another possible example of a paradox in the face of one's own death is the following. In everyday life we demand dignity. Death triggers existentialist thoughts about the meaning of life and the grief of having to leave loved ones. It is also connected to a certain everyday fear, visible among my interviewees, concerning dignity. They fear they might die in an undignified, shameful way. One interviewee, the engineer, talks about the death of an acquaintance who fell to the ground during a carnival. The man was fully sober, but people passed him by, only seeing an old, drunk man, not a severely sick person in need of immediate help. The old man died on the street. Even if many secular, modern individuals believe they will be absolutely nothing, non-existent after death, they nonetheless worry about how they will be represented and perceived when they are gone.

Could this worry about dying in an undignified way, in combination with a secular worldview, also be called paradoxical? I would say no. If a secular person's view on death as annihilation can be portrayed using the image of a wall, in comparison to a religious person's view on death as a door (Testoni et al. 2015: 60), it could be considered paradoxical to worry about what happens when the self is annihilated. But many secular people can easily see that the world and life go on after their death. They are not solipsistic, but instead care about what happens to their family and friends when they themselves are dead. Dead or alive, they belong to a group in the form of family, friends and others, and the group lives on. Is the nature of the above examples only paradoxical because the interviewees do not expect an afterlife? In the case of worrying about an undignified representation of one's dead body, this may be the case. The desire to be cremated intact is different. As I see it, this means that, for any living person, it is psychologically difficult to see oneself as dead, and the paradoxes are automatically fed by that difficulty. This reasoning would apply to both religious and secular persons.

Conclusions

The aim of this chapter has been to analyze 11 interviewees' ways of thinking about death by problematizing their notion of secularity. Three themes emerged through my analysis: the secular respect of the dead body, cremation as a rational choice, and an irrational resistance to being donated. When a topic is rarely on the agenda for discussion—such as one's own death—discourses on that topic are probably weaker than discourses on more trivial and frequent topics. This allows a variety of views to become visible, which has been seen in the present study. The common thread in this multitude of views, however, is secularism. Religion in its institutional form is weak in the lives of the interviewees. But there are limits to the rationalism that one might assume based on knowing about their secularism. These limits are exposed in the paradoxes that occur when talking about oneself as dead. In my interviews, there are also accounts of experiences of death and dying, really showing that my interviewees do not feel alienated from death—they have sat by the side of dying persons, and they have transported the ashes of relatives to cemeteries far away. They have stood in awe of a dead human being.

Their irrational thoughts can be discussed. Is it I, the interviewer, who has tried to force the interviewees into two different boxes—one secular and one religious—and who has demanded logic in their statements? Instead of logic, the researcher Ann af Burén (2015) uses the concept coherence, and she proposes a model of how people live with *simultaneity*, which contradicts coherence. This is related to situational religiosity, discussed by sociologists of religion. Situational religiosity can be exemplified by describing how religious interpretations depend on the social context. In Sweden, according to af Burén (2015: 183), it seems to be almost shameful to tell someone that you have had an out-of-the-ordinary experience. In contrast, Yael Keshet and Ido Liberman's (2014) study of secular traditionalist Israelis consulting rabbis shows that their expectations of out-of-the-ordinary events are actually ordinary. These secular, though traditionalist, Israelis who consult rabbis see a halo around the rabbi, they tremble and cry when they are in his company, and miracles are happening. Situational religiosity describes these differences. af Burén instead uses the notion of simultaneity. She emphasizes that her interviewees express religious and non-religious explanations for events at the same time. These explanations co-exist. She quotes the sociologist of religion, Mark Chaves, who states that "people's religious ideas and practices are fragmented, compartmentalized, loosely connected, unexamined, and context dependent. This is not a controversial claim; it's established knowledge" (Chaves, 2010: 2, quoted in af Burén, 2002: 37).

I agree that human beings are so constituted that coherence in think-ing may come only as a result of hard work. Coherence is not typical for human beings when thinking about the world, and perhaps especially, as in the present case, when thinking about their own future dead body. In this respect, secular people are not so rigidly secular, and religious people are not so deeply religious. af Burén calls her interviewees "semi-secu-lar."[18] This is a fitting description of my interviewees as well. Willander (2014) characterizes such semi-secular persons as having a religiosity although they are not active churchgoers. They believe in "some spirit of a life force." The surprising result of Willander's study is that such semi-secularity, as af Burén would call it, has been stable in Sweden for a very long time, "over the last 100 years," despite great changes in the laws and regulations surrounding religion (Willander, 2014: 217).

In sum, my study and similar studies indicate that the Swedishness in talk about death is characterized by the custom of cremation and a mul-tifaceted secularism, far from being the polar opposite of religion. When given the opportunity, a varied cultural repertoire is used to make sense of one's own future death. On the whole, my small qualitative sample of Swedes have illustrated that, in everyday life, many of us do not think much about our own death. We contemplate our own ending and fear illnesses and accidents, but the concrete details of dying do not seem to be on the agenda as long as we are in good health. Also absent from the agenda is the moral dilemma implicated in today's healthcare politics about death, with one exception in my sample—the doctor. Laqueur (2015: 551–3) hypothesizes that we are entering a new age, "not of being dead but of becoming dead [...] For the first time in human history, there is always something that can be done to gain extra hours, days, or even months of life," and "dying has also entered realms of decision-making where it never appeared before." This dilemma, although not elaborated on by my interviewees, is profound and will be with us during the com-ing decades. My study suggests that, even in the context of a technical revolution in healthcare related to death and dying, secularism in Sweden will not reduce us to adopting instrumental and utilitarian views.

Notes

1. Could this interest have links to the fact that the cohorts worrying today about death are bigger than ever before as they are born in the baby boom during the years around 1945? They are now approaching the end of life.
2. Longman dictionary of the English language (1984/1991).
3. For critical discussions on today's secularism in Sweden, see af Burén (2015), Kittelmann Flensner (2015), Berglund (2017), and Zuckerman (2009).
4. https://www.svenskakyrkan.se/statistik: Today as a free church, the Church of Sweden still has 6.1 million members of a population of 10 million people. Accessed 22 October 2017.
5. The state church in Sweden ended in 2000 while *Den Danske folkekirke*, Church of Denmark, is still a state church (Wikipedia https://en.wikipedia.org/wiki/Church_of_Denmark, accessed 1 November 2017).
6. Statistics Sweden, "Summary of Population Statistics 1960–2017": The population is 10,142,686 in March 2018 with 8.9 percent foreign citizens, 18.5 percent foreign born, and 24.1 percent either foreign born or born in Sweden with two foreign born parents.
7. Concerning the quotes, this must be said—in spoken language, the stream of thoughts are meandering, breaking up sentences, starting anew, jumping to something else, and so on, perhaps even more so in conversations among friends as in my interview study. The spoken language is still intelligible when you are there, hearing it. Spoken language is also difficult to transcribe both as the facial expressions are lacking and as it contains so many small words that despite their shortness forward important nuances. In this chapter the Swedish interview quotes have been translated into English, still another obstacle that might obscure clarity. All this makes the transcribed quotes difficult to read but the messages will hopefully transcend the transcription anyway.
8. Together with Monica Blom I conducted interviews with the participants in a birth prophylaxis course in 1980 just after we all had had children. Monica and I were two of the eight mothers and eight fathers participating in the course, led by the famous birth prophylaxis teacher Jeanette Brandt. I wrote an unpublished report based on the interviews.
9. Ghosts are normally not part of protestant religion and those who are atheists can still feel haunted by dead significant others. In incorporated death discourses borders are permeable.
10. Sky burials should probably be regarded as an exception.

11. In Sweden every person registered in the Swedish Population Register pays 0.22 percent of his or her income annually in toll to the government for a place in a cemetery (the burial toll). You then get a grave and you can keep that grave for 25 years without paying more. You can choose between cremation and burial without any extra expenses.

12. On the cleanliness subject it can be said that crematoria in Sweden, despite efforts to clean the flue gases, still leak out 110 kg mercury or quicksilver every year from the burned amalgam in the teeth of the corpses and this is a significant share of the total emissions of mercury in Sweden which in 2001 was 650 kg (Wängberg, 2010). It is contradicted without mentioning Wängberg's study, by SKKF, Sveriges kyrkogårds- och krematorieförbund (2017) with arguments based on methods not accounted for. The journal *NyTeknik* writes that in 2010 according to SKKF 29.4 kg mercury was let out from crematoria while according to the governmental Swedish Environmental Protection Agency the amount let out in 2010 was instead 114 kg (NyTeknik, 2013-02-14).

13. The universities are Karolinska Institutet, Linköping University, Sahlgrenska Academy at Gothenburg University, Umeå University, and Uppsala University. The advertisement was placed on page 3 in a special journal, "Innovativ vård" ("Innovative care"), produced by the company *Mediaplanet*, and it came with the daily *Dagens Nyheter* in September 2017.

14. The Swedish word *man* (in French *on*) is complicated and here translated with both "you" and "we." Here I give the quote in Swedish: "Man ser den egna döda kroppen som ett föremål, som kan hanteras fritt, d.v.s. utan förbehåll av religiös eller existentiell natur om vad man får göra med en avliden."

15. https://www.1177.se/Vasternorrland/Stall-en-anonym-fraga/Fragor/Finns-det-nagon-ovre-aldersgrans-for-att-fa-donera-organ/, accessed 27 June 2018.

16. See, for example, Tykocinski (2008).

17. When she exclaims "Totally insane!" she uses a stronger word than "crazy" (Swedish: *tokigt*), namely the word *vansinnigt*, which is more like the word I chose for the translation, "insane."

18. Despite the differences in situational religiosity, I would like to compare semi-secularity with *Masorti*, a Hebrew word referring to "people who do not necessarily view themselves as being religious, but rather as someone who observes Jewish tradition, including certain religious elements thereof" (Keshet & Liberman, 2014: 109). There are probably many persons with Protestant background in Sweden corresponding to this "Masorti" type in their life style.

References

Ahmadi, F. (2006) *Culture, Religion and Spirituality in Coping: The Example of Cancer Patients in Sweden*, Uppsala: Acta Universitatis Upsaliensis.

Ahmadi, F. and Nader A. (2013) 'Nature as the Most Important Coping Strategy Among Cancer Patients: A Swedish Survey', *Journal of Religion and Health*, 52(4), 1177–1190.

Åhrén, E. (1994) *Renande lågor: Den svenska eldbegängelserörelsens framväxt under 1800-talets sista decennier* (Purifying Flames: The Growth of the Cremation Movement During the Last Decades of the 19th Century), Stockholm: Stockholm University, Department of History, Avdelningen för idéhistoria.

Åhrén, E. (2002) *Döden, kroppen och moderniteten*, Stockholm: Carlssons bokförlag.

Åhrén, E. (2009) *Death, Modernity, and the Body: Sweden 1870–1940*, Rochester, NY: University of Rochester Press.

Albrecht, M. M. (2013) 'Dead Man in the Mirror: The Performative Aspects of Michel Jackson's Posthumous Body', *The Journal of Popular Culture*, 46(4), 705–724.

Becker, E. (1973) *The Denial of Death*, New York: Simon & Schuster.

Berglund, J. (2017) 'Secular Normativity and the Religification of Muslims in Swedish Public Schooling', *Oxford Review of Education*, 43(5), 524–536.

af Burén, A. (2015) *Living Simultaneity: On Religion Among Semi-Secular Swedes*, Södertörn Doctoral Dissertations, Stockholm: Södertörn University.

Chaves, M. (2010) 'SSSR Presidential Address: Rain Dances in the Dry Season: Overcoming the Religious Congruence Fallacy', *Journal for the Scientific Study of Religion*, 49(1), 1–14.

Davies, O. (2007) *The Haunted: A Social History of Ghosts*, Basingstoke: Palgrave Macmillan.

Dobscha S. and Podoshen, J. S. (2017) 'Death Consumes Us: Dispatches from the "Death Professors"', *Consumption Markets & Culture*, 20(5), 383–386.

Durkheim, É. (1915 [1995]) *The Elementary Forms of Religious Life*, New York: Free Press.

Giddens, A. and Sutton, Ph. W. (2017) *Sociology*, Cambridge: Polity Press.

Gustavsson, A. (2015) 'Death, Dying and Bereavement in Norway and Sweden in Recent Times', *Humanities*, 4(2), 224–235.

Jonsson, A. (2015) 'Post-Mortem Social Death: Exploring the Absence of the Deceased,' *Contemporary Social Science*, 10(3), 284–295.

Keshet, Y. and Liberman, I. (2014) 'Seeking Empowerment and Spirituality in the Secular Age: Secular and Traditionalist Israelis Consulting Rabbis', *Sociology*, 48(1), 92–110.

Kittelmann Flensner, K. (2015) *Religious Education in Contemporary Pluralistic Sweden*, Gothenburg: University of Gothenburg, Dept of Literature, History of ideas, and Religion.

Klass, D., Silverman, P. R. and Nickman, S. L. (eds.) (1996) *Continuing Bonds: New Understandings of Grief*, Abingdon: Taylor & Francis.

Kremationsstatistik 2016. (2017) Sveriges kyrkogårds- och krematorieförbund.

Laqueur, T. (2015) *The Work of the Dead: A Cultural History of Mortal Remains*, New Jersey: Princeton University Press.

Longman Dictionary of the English Language. (1984/1991) Essex: Longman Group UK Limited.

Martin, D. (1978) *A General Theory of Secularization*, Oxford: Blackwell.

Moberg, M., Granholm, K. and Nynäs, P. (2014) "Trajectories of Post-Secular Complexity: An Introduction", in P. Nynäs, M. Lassander and T. Utriainen (eds.), *Post-Secular Society*, New Brunswick, NJ: Transaction.

Nations, C., Baker S. M. and Krszjzaniek, E. (2017) 'Trying to Keep You: How Grief, Abjection, and Ritual Transform the Social Meanings of a Human Body', *Consumption Markets & Culture*, 20(5), 403–422.

NyTeknik. (2013-02-14) https://www.nyteknik.se/energi/22-ton-metall-gravs-ner-6404805, accessed 28 June 2018.

Redmalm, D. (2013) *An Animal Without an Animal Within: The Powers of Pet Keeping*, Dissertation, Örebro: Örebro University.

Statistics Sweden. (2018) 'Summary of Population Statistics 1960–2017', www.scb.se, accessed 14 May 2018.

Svenska kyrkan, statistics, https://www.svenskakyrkan.se/statistik, accessed 22 October 2017.

Svensson, I. (2013) *Liket i Garderoben: Bögar, Begravningar och 80-talets Aidsepidemi* (The Corpse in the Closet: Gay Men, Funerals and the Aids Epidemic of the 1980s), Stockholm: Ordfront förlag.

Testoni, I., Ancona, D. and Ronconi, L. (2015) 'The Ontological Representation of Death: A Scale to Measure the Idea of Annihilation Versus Passage', *Omega*, 71(1), 60–81.

Tykocinski, O. E. (2008) 'Insurance, Risk, and Magical Thinking', *Personality and Social Psychology Bulletin*, 34(10), 1346–1356.

Walter, T. (1999) *On Bereavement: The Culture of Grief*, Buckingham: Open University Press.

Walter, T. (2016) 'The Dead Who Become Angels: Bereavement and Vernacular Religion', *Omega: Journal of Death and Dying*, 73(1), 3–28.

Wängberg, I. (2010) *Utredning av Kunskapsläget Angående Rening av Rökgaser vid Krematorier* (Investigation of the state of knowledge regarding the treatment of flue gases at crematories), Stockholm: IVL B 1883.

Wikipedia, https://en.wikipedia.org/wiki/Church_of_Denmark, accessed 1 November 2017.

Willander, E. (2014) *What Counts as Religion in Sociology? The Problem of Religiosity in Sociological Methodology*, diss., Uppsala: Dept. of Sociology, Uppsala University.

World Values Survey. (2008) http://www.worldvaluessurvey.org/WVSContents.jsp, accessed 22 October 2017.

Zuckerman, P. (2009) 'Why Are Danes and Swedes so Irreligious?', *Nordic Journal of Religion and Society*, 22(1), 55–69.

Part III

Persons and Non-Persons

9

Digital Mourning Labor: Corporate Use of Dead Celebrities on Social Media

Magdalena Kania-Lundholm

Introduction

After Prince's sudden death in April 2016, people from around the world gathered to pay tribute to this legendary pop icon and artist. Social media became popular channels for fans, celebrities, political and other public figures to express sorrow and pay homage to the artist. Even brands, organizations and companies—such as Chevrolet, Cheerios, *The New Yorker*, Spotify and Google to name just a few—took to social media to pay their respects with pictures of the star beside purple-themed posts and lyrics.

It seems self-explanatory that using someone's death to one's own commercial advantage may be a problematic or even immoral act, especially using the death of someone who has been admired by fans across the globe. At the same time, only a few brands received harsh criticism from users, causing them to delete their posts. Others continue posting messages referring to passed celebrities on their social media channels. It would seem that paying tribute or homage to a dead celebrity has become

M. Kania-Lundholm (✉)
Department of Sociology, Uppsala University, Uppsala, Sweden
e-mail: magdalena.kania@soc.uu.se

© The Author(s) 2019
T. Holmberg et al. (eds.), *Death Matters*,
https://doi.org/10.1007/978-3-030-11485-5_9

177

a customary way for global brands and organizations to communicate. It is a way to show they stay up to date with media news flows, especially those concerning many people and involving affective relationships, like the ones between pop stars and their fans. In the age of social media, social networking sites and platforms are now part of every major brand's marketing scheme. Thus, reactions to popular news and events are increasingly becoming a key aspect of that scheme. When a celebrity dies, fans take to social media to remember and to mourn. When global brands and companies attempt to do the same, they risk being accused of turning death into an advertising spectacle.

In the age of mediatization, where media are increasingly integrated into all spheres of society and social life, we experience the *mediatic turn* alongside the *affective and emotional turn* (Giaxoglou & Dövelling, 2018; Couldry & Hepp, 2017). Media communication technologies and social media, in particular, have contributed to the expansion of death and mourning from more private and locally defined spaces into public, global events. This is also the case for the anti-police violence online activism described by María Langa and Philip K. Creswell in Chap. 10, this volume.

Information about the death of a celebrity reaches fans across the globe in a matter of minutes or even seconds, as soon as it is publicly shared on social media. At the same time, however, when it comes to commemorative practices, we are moving away from official institutionalized rituals to more personal, vernacular practices and expressions. For instance, social media services such as Instagram facilitate digital practices of mourning and remembrance and offer the *platform vernacular* for individuals to share their memories and feelings (Gibbs et al., 2015). Consequently, we can speak of a double logic of online death that prompts global coverage of the news (typically the death of a celebrity) and personalized, local, informal and often emotional responses to it. These responses are guided by specific norms of mediating emotion in digital mourning which include, for example, what content is appropriate to share and what the appropriate reactions are to information about someone's death (Wagner, 2018).

Like any other type of mediatized practice, mourning on social media is not an isolated event, but rather connected to other social practices.

When it comes to celebrities and pop stars, the proliferation of postselves and commodification of the afterlife are a growing and documented phenomenon. In other words, the symbolic immortality of stars has become an important token in late capitalism, particularly for proliferation of the transcendence markets (Kearl, 2010). This is to say that with regard to pop culture, social media and remembering celebrities who have passed away, death might in fact be a moment of injecting new life. Questions remain, however: Who has the right and authority to take advantage of someone's death? If individual social media users impose implicit norms of conduct on digital mourning practices, do global brands do the same? Is there a contradiction between logics of mourning and online death, on the one hand, and commercialization, on the other? Why do they not necessarily go hand in hand?

While some of these questions will remain purely rhetorical, the goal of this chapter is to understand the process through which social media become venues for self-promotion of global brands to share memories and pay tribute to celebrities who have passed away. More specifically, the goal is to understand how global brands can exploit and capitalize on celebrity death through social media users' work. This is to say that social media users do not necessarily only consume the free services offered by social networking sites. Instead, the practices they perform, such as communicating and socializing, involve the process of generating information that is further commodified and sold to advertisers. Such information becomes central to the process of data accumulation in digital Big Data capitalism (Fisher, 2015). This chapter asks: How can we understand the fact that celebrity death is employed by global brands for self-promotion and profit? What is the role of social media users in this process? The next two sections provide a brief overview of previous studies focusing on the mediation and commercialization of celebrity death. In the subsequent section, I discuss the phenomenon of branding and introduce the concept of digital labor in the context of social media. The final section describes the process through which global brands extract value by engaging users in performing *digital mourning labor*, which is a form of immaterial, affective digital labor purposefully aimed at and performed by social media users. Finally, I provide concluding remarks and a few suggestions for future research.

Public Responses and Mediating Celebrity Death

Celebrity can be defined as a mediated construct and persona that is both shaped and consumed by audiences (Evans & Hesmondhalgh, 2005). This construct is the result of an interplay between the mediated public image and the private person presented to the world (Van den Bulck & Claessens, 2013). Celebrity death has become one of the driving forces behind television and newspaper coverage. Among the most prominent examples are the media coverage and public displays of grief following the death of Natalie Wood and John Belushi in the 1980s (Magee, 2014) and Princess Diana's death in 1997 (Walter, 1999). Scholars have examined the impact of celebrity death on, for instance, children and adolescents, as well as on anxiety and cancer awareness among the public (Keays & Pless, 2010). Moreover, the impact of celebrity suicide and death on public mourning has previously been the topic of scholarly scrutiny (Gibson, 2007). Celebrity death has also been made visible in the media through, for example, the embalming process. When a celebrity dies, it is their living incarnation—the famous visage—that takes center stage in media coverage (Davies, 2010). Media also use different frames in order to convey reactions to deceased celebrities. For example, they may focus on exceptional qualities, such as the talent and fame of the celebrity, or frame the story around ethical issues, thus provoking debates about sexuality, domestic violence, divorce and suicide. As the study of the suicide of Flemish celebrity singer Yasmine illustrates, these media frames are not necessarily simply mimicked by audiences, but rather negotiated and even opposed in a variety of ways (Van den Bulck & Claessens, 2013).

Responses to celebrity deaths have also been connected to consumer practices (Radford & Bloch, 2012; Van den Bulck & Claessens, 2013). Because celebrities are often perceived as distant, fans turn to products they can purchase and, in this way, remain closer to their idols. Consuming goods associated with dead celebrities is one of the coping strategies used when dealing with a profound sense of loss and grief. As Radford and Bloch (2012) suggest, there is a possibility that, in death, celebrity can achieve a mythological status that transcends both class and culture. For instance, James Dean, Marilyn Monroe and several other dead celebrities have become something of a "human brand" that can potentially generate revenues for media and corporations. By manipulating the celebrity image and brand, media have the capacity to tone down the more mundane and "earthly" aspects of celebrity and focus on endorsing the mythic ideal.

Branding Celebrity Death: From Persons to Delebs

As mediated constructs, celebrities are also commodities created by media industries that are targeting audiences. Thus, celebrity has also been defined as a commodity and a vehicle of consumption created within the capitalist order, where its presence both encourages and legitimates consumption (Rojek, 2007). In such a context, celebrities are synonymous with capital, although the connection is perhaps not so obvious if we think of famous and widely mediated figures such as the Pope or Princess Diana. Mediated celebrity images become a brand that operates even outside of the primary context in which they have appeared. In other words, celebrities may be famous for film-making or their music, but they are also the subject of gossip columns and occur across a wide spectrum of other media contexts.

Branding can be defined as a technique used to enhance the exchange value of commodities. One of the main goals of branding is to make commodities attractive, unique and appealing, so that they can be traded in the competitive context of global markets and eventually purchased by consumers. The market value is often produced in an affective relationship between brands and consumers. In many cases, consumers are entangled through partnership with brands, a process through which they can closely identify with a product, for example, an Apple computer or Nike shoes. In the context where market value is produced in an affective relationship with brands, we can also speak of the emergence of affective and immaterial labor, which will be discussed later in this chapter. Consumers not only benefit from purchased goods, but through the act of identifying with a particular brand, they also "work" for it. Value is thus produced through the fetishizing of social action as a marketed commodity, the invisible social relations of production as well as the emergence of new modes of objectification and exploitation (Rojek, 2007; Banet-Weiser & Mukherjee, 2012).

In a society that values mediated fame, celebrity culture flourishes. The reception, success or failure of a celebrity is closely related to an understanding of their constructed and mediated image/brand and audience responses to it. Consequently, celebrities are considered "texts and signs" rather than real persons (Long & Wall, 2009). If we consider celebrities to be socially constructed and widely mediated brands, then we need to acknowledge the "polysemy, or multiplicity of meanings that celebrities evoke" (Long & Wall, 2009: 97). As Gamson suggests, name recognition is critical to commerce and "celebrities are most useful if they can draw attention regardless of the particular context in which they appear [...] the less attached a name is to a context, the more easily it transfers to new markets" (Gamson, 2001: 271). When a celebrity dies, the status of that person is often elevated to an iconic image and maintained further by media and audiences. Fans maintain this image by, for example, purchasing celebrity-related commodities, maintaining websites and posting information on networking sites. The market of dead celebrities, also known as *delebs*, is large and growing (D'Rozario, 2016). Likewise, the *digital afterlife industry* and commercial interests that are shaping it have recently received some critical scholarly attention (Öhman & Floridi, 2017).

Today, celebrities are not only constructed media subjects, but rather brands themselves. A UK-based company, Starcount, tracks activity on profiles of at least 11 different social networking sites including Facebook, YouTube, Twitter, Weibo and Orkut. Each dead celebrity receives a number of stars reflecting followers and activity. The top of the list includes Michael Jackson with over 200 million stars, Bob Marley and Tupac Shakur with about 40 million stars.[1] What scoring services like this one offer is the idea of the total social media impact of a given celebrity, including their reputation. The problem with global corporations tweeting about dead celebrities can be related to the current status of celebrities and the fact that, as brands, they are also sites of production of value and an industry in their own right (Hearn & Schoenhoff, 2016). In 2001, *Forbes magazine* began its annual ranking of postmortem top-earning dead celebrities. A popular measurement tool developed to assess the familiarity and appeal of celebrities and brands known as "the Q Score" has a separate "Dead Q" tool to measure the consumer appeal of dead celebrities. This is a growing global industry that capitalizes on delebs, with an estimated annual revenue exceeding two billion dollars in the U.S. alone.[2]

In a global culture, celebrity deaths can be transnationally mediated and reach global markets. In late modern societies, death becomes a mediated phenomenon and people often experience it for the first time via media technologies. In a study of the public mourning of Australian TV star Steve Irwin, Gibson argues that there are "celebrities or major national or international public figures whose deaths are the first to make their mark on the biography and psyche of individuals" (Gibson, 2007: 415). She suggests that there is a strong link between mourning of celebrities and the commercial interests that turn these deaths into public, media events. Celebrity deaths are commercially exploited by media, and their media presence continues long after death. In some cases, famous persons such as Michael Jackson, Bruce Lee, Marilyn Monroe or Fred Astaire have appeared on everything from soft drinks to clothing, chocolate and perfume (Penfold-Mounce, 2015). The phenomenon of *digital necromancy* describes a process in which dead celebrities are brought to life not only by featuring in advertisements, but also by, for example, creating holograms that present their own concerts (Davidson, 2013). This was the case for the hologram that appeared in 2012 at the Coachella music festival featuring the late rapper Tupak Shakur. In this way, from rather volatile and demanding "real" persons, delebs become brands that are easier to both manage and exploit (Penfold-Mounce, 2015).

In recent years, social media have become increasingly mobilized for and intertwined with the rituals of celebrity death and mourning (Courbet & Fourquet-Courbet, 2014). Celebrity death in relation to social media user's practices includes, for example, the process of introjection by fans who focus on selective and positive recollection of the celebrity's image and further mythologizing of it (Radford & Bloch, 2012). Studies on death and mourning in technology-mediated culture emphasize, among other things, how new technologies have changed the field of death studies. This includes, for instance, addressing issues such as mechanisms of loss and commemoration, mourning and suicide communities, online sites for support and counseling and various commercial grief sites (Sofka et al., 2012). More recently, specific platforms, such as Twitter, have been examined as online spaces of mediated relationships between celebrities, fans and the pop culture industry. For instance, Van den Bulck and Larsson (2017) analyze Twitter responses to the death of David Bowie. They argue that online mourning is led by the Twitter "elite," which consists of celebrities, artists, media and music industry figures rather than "regular" fans. With regard to content, analyzed tweets focus mostly on expressions of grief, information exchange and tribute to Bowie's work (Van den Bulck & Larsson, 2017). However, even if the relationships between a celebrity and fans are *parasocial* (in the sense of being one-sided and "virtual"), the feelings of mourning and grief are "real" as expression and emotional labor (Van den Bulck & Larsson, 2017; cf. Hochschild, 1983). In other words, regarding the role of social media in public mourning of celebrities, Twitter is a space for *both* expression of emotions and exchange of information (Hoe-Lian Goh & Lee, 2011; Holiman, 2013; Lansdall-Welfare et al., 2012; Mallow, 2015; Van den Bulck & Larsson, 2017).

Thus far, a number of studies on dead celebrities and social media have focused primarily on the nature of social media responses. As illustrated above, scholars were interested in, for example, knowing who dominated the discussions and whether social media, Twitter in particular, can potentially serve as open and democratic spaces for "ordinary citizens" to shape the public debate. In this chapter, however, I specifically address the social media use of global brands that share information about and references to dead celebrities as well as the role social media users (elites and "ordinary" users alike) can potentially (and often involuntarily) play in this process. In an attempt to understand this relationship between corporate owners and social media users, the next section looks at a specific form of immaterial labor, namely digital labor, which generates new forms of human sociality and productivity.

Digital Labor in the Age of Social Media

One of the characteristics of the postindustrial economy is the emergence of new forms of value generation, new relations between production and consumption, and new types of work, including industries such as advertising, management and finance. Immaterial labor is defined as labor that produces the informational and cultural content of the commodity and is at the crossroads of the relationship between production and consumption (Lazzarato, 2001). What is specific to the results of immaterial labor is that commodities are not necessarily destroyed in the process of consumption, but rather transform and create the cultural environment of the consumer (Lazzarato, 2001). This means that immaterial labor produces not only the commodity itself, but also a *social relationship* that emerges as a result of it. With the decline of production-based industries and the rise of a new information-based economy and new kinds of knowledge workers, the boundaries between labor and leisure, work time and free time, work and play are continuously being blurred. In the context of the media, critical scholars such as Smythe (1981) have pointed to the active role of audiences in the creation of media value that revolves around immaterial, cognitive and emotional types of labor. He suggested that media sell audiences to advertisers and that, in return, audiences do work by learning to desire and purchase particular products (cf. Fisher, 2015).

Social media offer a particular space in which cognitive, emotional and communicative aspects of human sociality can be subsumed by capital. Digital labor, which is a type of immaterial labor executed in the context of social media, refers to activities that require cognitive and emotional investment, such as memorializing and grieving for the dead. In the past decade or so, social media have become venues of exploited user participation. As Fuchs argues: "Digital labour on social media means that yet more time that is spent *outside of the paid work* conducted in factories and offices is becoming exploited" (Fuchs, 2015: 116, my italics). Because social media are associated with free time, leisure and communication, social media users do not receive compensation for their online participation, which takes the form of liking, sharing, uploading, posting and other digital practices. At the same time, companies generate profit from user activities, they take advantage of the information that is generated by users, for example, in the case of targeted advertising (Allmer et al., 2015; Fuchs, 2015; Scholz, 2011). Social media users, like consumers, might consider themselves empowered and creative, but are nonetheless serving networking sites' platforms and their owners by providing both intentional (such as posting, sharing, tweeting) and unintentional information (data that users produce while doing something else) (Fisher, 2015).

Digital labor emerges in the context of transformation of leisure time into labor time, paid labor into unpaid labor and consumption time into production time. It is in the context of cognitive capitalism and the knowledge economy that changes in the quality of work require a broader understanding of labor. Concepts that capture this process include, among others, *digital prosumption* (Ritzer & Jurgenson, 2010), *playbour* (Scholz, 2011) and *crowdsourcing* (cf. Allmer et al., 2015). They all belong in the culture of speed, acceleration and pressure for constant change that defines the current status quo of modern societies (Rosa, 2005). In other words, in order to stay creative, innovative and active, one has to be "on the run." Some argue that this need for immediate gratification and constant change is driven by the human fear of death, which results in "panic flight reactions," often in the form of conspicuous consumption (Rosa, 2005, in Fuchs, 2015: 101). In words of the critical scholar Hartmut Rosa: "We are not running towards the bright horizon but rather running away from the dark abyss behind our backs" (Rosa, 2015, n.p.). In the era of social media marketing, the boundaries between original, independent editorial posts and posts that have been sponsored and paid for are becoming increasingly blurred. For instance, global brands often make use of corporate social media by investing heavily in collaborations with so-called influencers, namely bloggers and vloggers (video bloggers), each with between 30,000 and two million followers (Kay, 2017). Additionally, to remain in the market, stay competitive and generate value, global brands not only need to seek out new opportunities and collaborations, they are also expected to act as individuals and take stances on breaking news, including the death and mourning of celebrities (Kerns, 2016).

What counts as digital labor? Perpetual blogging, commenting, liking, sharing, posting and tweeting reflects not only some aspects of human sociality, but also the new forms of productive activity that can be transformed into commodity in the form of data and metadata. For instance, Mosco (2017) mentions up to 75 different types of data Facebook and its advertisers can gather about users. These data include basic information, from the user's name, age, ethnicity to his/her grocery store, restaurant and vacation preferences. All of these data can be bought, mined and used for the purpose of targeted advertising and value generation. In this way, social media users are involuntarily inserted into global data flows and subjected to controlled algorithmic identities (Mosco, 2017). In other words, old forms of structural dominance, such as capitalist exploitation of the value created by people's work, take on new forms online (Lindgren, 2017). In the following section, I introduce the concept of mourning labor in an attempt to understand what happens when emotions and information concerning dead celebrities are shared by global brands on social media.

Digital Mourning Labor: Celebrity Death and Global Brands on Social Media

Using dead celebrities to sell commodities is not necessarily a new phenomenon. One of the first practices of this sort is a Coca-Cola commercial from 1991 where Elton John sings with reanimated celebrities such as Humphrey Bogart, Louis Armstrong, Cary Grant and Groucho Marx (Davidson, 2013). Cost is one of the factors that encourage brands to go with delebs, who are considerably cheaper than the living stars. At the same time, using dead celebrities sparks controversies, mostly ethical in nature. Brands may be subject to accusations of "grave robbing" (Davidson, 2013), as in the case of the shoe company Dr. Martens, which in 2007 commissioned an advertising campaign from the UK-based advertising agency Saatchi & Saatchi. The advertisement featured the late leader of Nirvana, Kurt Cobain, sitting on a heavenly cloud, wearing an angelic robe and a pair of black Dr. Martens boots. The ad read: "Dr.

Martens. Forever." The advertisement was one of several featuring dead rock stars such as Sid Vicious from The Sex Pistols and Joey Ramone from The Ramones. Later that year, the company was forced to apologize and remove all advertisements. They acknowledged that featuring dead rock stars in their ads was a mistake. They had to apologize in particular to Cobain's ex-wife, Courtney Love, who found it "outrageous" that a company was allowed to gain commercially from using her husband's image (Fleeman, 2007).

One of the reasons some find using delebs in commerce to be disrespectful is that death and mourning are perceived as belonging to private, intimate and "authentic spaces" not previously touched by market forces (Banet-Weiser, 2012). At the same time, as suggested by Foucault, the spread of market principles to previously non-marketized areas or "the application of the economic grid to a field [...] defined in opposition to the economy" (Foucault, 2008: 240) constitutes the governing principle of neoliberalism. With the rise of the mass consumer society and mass media, the promotional power of the celebrity persona grew to the point of becoming an economic condition, and "a metaphor for value in modern society" (Marshall, 1997: 7). Moreover, during the 1970s and 1980s, the focus of media has moved from mass to niche audiences and increasingly personalized target marketing. In other words, marketing strategies are being adapted to existing technology affordances.

I define *digital mourning labor* as a kind of immaterial, affective digital labor purposefully aimed at and performed by social media users. It is initiated by commercial actors, such as global corporate brands, that employ their social media platforms to share emotions of grief, nostalgia, mourning and information about dead celebrities. Mourning labor, like any other form of immaterial labor, benefits from different forms of human sociality that are turned into productive activity and further transformed into commodity, most likely in terms of data flows. Hence, social media users' work can be exploited *both* by global brands that make users purchase advertised commodities and by corporate social media owners who can gather users' data.

In relation to this, it has to be noted that global brands and celebrities (living or dead) are the predominant and most common actors on social media. Despite the notion that social media are democratic spaces of participation and creativity for all citizens, social media are largely dominated by multimedia companies. This means that, in practice, global companies, celebrities and advertising dominate, and that the tendency is for corporations and capitalist logic to colonize social media (Fuchs, 2017).

In the context of social media marketing, mixing the seemingly mutually exclusive logics of death and commerce has yet another angle. Namely, directly after death, control over the celebrity brand, its metrics and value can be temporarily limited and thus potentially "highjacked" and monetized by others. By sharing information and grief with social media users, global brands seem to take for granted that the practice of "prosumption," in terms of social media users sharing, liking, commenting and retweeting, will be business as usual. For example, after Prince's death in 2016, several companies and media outlets took to social media to pay tribute and express feelings of grief. The music streaming service Spotify tweeted: "We join the world in mourning the loss of a genius, a legend, and an inspiration to generations of artists and fans." *The New Yorker* posted a picture of an upcoming cover with the motif of *Purple Rain*—a direct reference to one of Prince's famous songs. Moreover, tech giants like Google and Snapchat temporarily switched to the color purple for their logos. Similarly, after the death of David Bowie that same year, several global and popular brands from the music and fashion industry shared their grief. The jeans brand Diesel tweeted: "RIP #DavidBowie the man. The myth and the legend will live on forever." The fashion designer Marc Jacobs wrote Bowie's own lyrics from *Quicksand*: "I'm not a prophet or a stone aged man, just a mortal with potential of a superman. I'm living on." The tweet also pictured a thunderbolt, signature sign of Bowie and a hashtag RIP DavidBowie.

However, the affective, grieving aspect at the intersection of the global, corporate brand, on the one hand, and the celebrity brand, on the other, may sometimes cause disruption and voice social media users' criticism. This is when "unfortunate corporate social media reactions"[3] take place. For instance, the plastic shoe manufacturer Crocs posted an image of a white pair of their shoes with a tagline: "Your magic will be missed but your inspiration lives on forever. #DavidBowie," a tweet that after harsh criticism for brand promotion was deleted.

Similarly, the tech giant Microsoft was forced to apologize after tweeting an invitation for people to remember the late Amy Winehouse by purchasing one of her albums on a platform owned by the company.[4] Also, after Prince's death, the cereal manufacturer Cheerios posted a picture saying "Rest in Peace" with a purple background and a single Cheerio above the "I." The tweet was shortly removed by the company, which issued an apologetic statement saying they wanted to acknowledge the loss of Prince—who was also from Minnesota, but it was removed out of respect for Prince and those who mourned his death.[5] Other brands that received criticism from social media users for problematic reference to dead celebrities include the companies Maker's Mark (bourbon whisky brand), Hamburger Helper and Pringles. In all of these cases, social media users' criticism occurred when the connection between mourning a dead star and advertising a product became so obvious that expressions of grief and mourning could be interpreted as yet another means to promote the brand. This is the case particularly when mourning on the part of companies is a strategy to encourage customers to purchase their products (like Microsoft) or when the product itself is too distant from celebrity's own brand that it becomes obvious they would not endorse it if they were still living (like in the case of Crocs). These examples are of course anecdotal in nature, and my goal is not to prove any general trend. However, it is important to emphasize that, regardless of whether companies receive users' criticism when sharing information about dead celebrities and "paying tribute" to them, the users perform mourning labor when they decide to comment on, share or like the post. In other words, it could be argued that the contemporary logic of promotion, which requires that global brands act as "friends" with their customers, also triggers the affective labor of mourning and grief.

Social media have not only tipped the balance between the private and the public, but also opened up new venues and opportunities for promotion and public mourning. The affective and critical responses of social media users do interfere with the process of exploiting a celebrity image for profit after the celebrity's death. Thus, brands know they have to respect social media, and they handle their accounts accordingly. In the reputation economy, brands are particularly concerned with their images and scores (cf. Hearn & Schoenhoff, 2016). One tweet can make a difference, as in the case of United Airlines, which received harsh criticism on Twitter for forcibly removing one of its passengers from a plane.[6] Unsurprisingly, marketers produce manuals offering advice for brands on how to "responsibly" approach their followers. For instance, the suggestion "don't sell, just share" can be particularly useful when sharing expressions of mourning and grief, which are not necessarily opportunities for commerce. In the process of sharing, however, the immaterial, affective labor of users is obscured. Thus, in a way, global brands can exploit both the images of dead celebrities and social media users at the same time.

The process of digital mourning labor is marked by the affective relationship between social media users/fans and global brands. In this unequal relationship, global brands not only want to take advantage of the affect generated by the celebrity, but in the process of acknowledging the celebrity's death, they also turn attention away from the persona of celebrity toward the brand and the product itself. Digital mourning labor relies on social media users' work and on the affective relationship fans have with their idols. By associating dead celebrity with their own product, global brands are attempting, albeit often implicitly, to turn fans into consumers and, furthermore, into producers of free content. In other words, global brands exploit the possibility of conflating the roles of fans, potential promoters and marketers (cf. Hearn & Schoenhoff, 2016).

Generally speaking, making a profit from the affective relationship between the brand and the consumer, namely turning consumers into fans and later into producers, can be a successful strategy. In other words, taking advantage of the affective relationship developed between consumers and brands has proven to be a central marketing model in late capitalism. It can sometimes fail, however, because by engaging with affective labor, here mourning a dead celebrity, it uncovers the problematic, invisible relations of production in the late capitalist economy. This may explain why some users reacted so critically when certain global brands posted tributes to dead pop icons on their social media channels. It may be that, for some fans, consumption of products they associate with their idols is the only way to approach these idols and deal with their grief. Consequently, there is also strong resentment exhibited toward those who try to take advantage of their relationship with the celebrity and their grief.

Conclusions

This chapter aimed to understand how global brands can exploit and capitalize on celebrity death through social media users' work. Neither mediation nor commercialization of celebrity death is a new phenomenon. However, with the rise of new technologies and social media in particular, the marketing and branding strategies of companies often need to adapt to new technological affordances. At the same time, old forms of structural dominance, including capitalist exploitation of the value created by social media users' work, also take place in these new online contexts. I suggest that, along with changes accompanied by a shift in the quality of work in cognitive capitalism, the meaning of labor became broader and came to include immaterial aspects that have previously been associated with leisure and play (cf. Terranova, 2000). Answering the two questions posed at the beginning of this chapter—namely how we can understand global brands making use of dead celebrities for self-promotion and profit as well as the role of social media users in this process—requires understanding the new conditions of cognitive capitalism and the role of social media in the digital economy.

When global brands express grief in relation to a recent celebrity death, they do attract attention, especially when they use a hashtag with a given celebrity's name or initials. Social media users perform digital mourning labor that is immaterial, but that can materialize in the form of profit generated by global brands. This includes short-term profits, such as when customers purchase certain products, but also long-term profits, when customers continue to do so because they identify with the brand. At the same time, social media users' work can be exploited by corporate media platform owners through data mining. These practices rely heavily on affective, immaterial labor, which includes users' relationship with the dead celebrity. In other words, global brands capitalize on the meaning and attachment individuals feel in relation to their dead idols. However, when the commercial interests of global brands become too obvious, users protest and criticize, and brands have to apologize, but the prosumer work typically goes unnoticed. The concept of *digital mourning labor* introduced in this chapter pertains particularly to the celebrity image or brand, which, after death, continues a mediatized and commercial life of its own. If we agree with the idea that celebrities become brands on their own while alive, then these brands often continue living even after the celebrities' physical death. The phenomenon of global brands employing references to dead celebrities illustrates that, at the crossroads between public mourning of a celebrity and commercialization of his/her image/brand, there is very little space left for feelings of grief and loss.

By mixing the mutually exclusive logics of death and mourning, on the one hand, and the logics of commerce and profit, on the other, global brands extract value by engaging users in performing digital mourning labor, which is immaterial but materializes in the form of profit generated by the online networking sites and platforms. Consequently, it can be argued that value is not only extracted from users' immaterial labor, but also from the symbolic meaning and value of celebrity death that global brands capitalize on.

Future research could explore this process further, particularly by empirically focusing on cases of mourning labor in larger samples of material from, for example, Twitter or Facebook. Also, we need to better understand what types of responses are most common, which kinds of cases of mourning celebrities online trigger social media users' criticism and which do not, and what norms are regulating this process, if any. Last but not least, it would be interesting to explore the concept of symbolic immortality in relation to dead celebrities' social media presence. For instance, *N.E.R.D.* is the 2017 title of the album by Pharell Williams and stands for *No One Ever Really Dies*. Such statements go a long way in the digital political economy of social media and dead celebrities' place in it.

Notes

1. https://www.forbes.com/pictures/mfl45mffd/social-networking-lives-of-the-dead-celebrities/#a39fcdb13f8c, accessed: Dec. 2017.
2. http://www.cbc.ca/radio/undertheinfluence/nobody-s-dead-anymore-br-marketing-deceased-celebrities-1.2801803, accessed: Dec. 2017.

3. http://www.somethingawful.com/news/corporate-twitter-prince/, accessed: Dec. 2017.
4. http://www.news.com.au/entertainment/music/microsoft-blasted-for-amy-winehouse-death-tweet/news-story/80ff41320c9be7814b2a22a364 7f3da9, accessed: Dec. 2017.
5. https://www.cnbc.com/2016/04/22/global-brands-join-tributes-to-musi-cian-prince.html, accessed: Dec. 2017.
6. http://nordic.businessinsider.com/twitter-responds-to-man-being-dragged-off-united-airlines-flight-2017-4?r=UK&IR=T, accessed: Dec. 2017.

References

Allmer, T., Sevignani, S. and Prodnik, J. A. (2015) 'Mapping Approaches to User Participation and Digital Labour: A Critical Perspective', in E. Fisher and C. Fuchs (eds.) *Reconsidering Value and Labour in the Digital Age*, London: Palgrave Macmillan.

Banet-Weiser, S. (2012) *Authentic. The Politics of Ambivalence in a Brand Culture*, New York: NYU Press.

Banet-Weiser, S. and Mukherjee, R. (eds.) (2012) *Commodity Activism: Cultural Resistance in Neoliberal Times*, New York: New York University Press.

Couldry, N. and Hepp, A. (2017) *The Mediated Construction of Reality*, Polity Press.

Courbet, D. and Fourquet-Courbet, M. (2014) 'When a Celebrity Dies … Social Identity, Uses of Social Media and the Mourning Process Among Fans: The Case of Michael Jackson', *Celebrity Studies*, 5(3), 275–290.

Davidson, J. (2013, August 2) 'Digital Necromancy: Advertising with Reanimated Celebrities', *Time*, http://business.time.com/2013/08/02/digital-necromancy-advertising-with-reanimated-celebrities/, accessed 30 May 2017.

Davies, C. (2010) 'Technological Taxidermy: Recognizable Faces in Celebrity Deaths, *Mortality*, 15(2), 138–153.

D'Rozario, D. (2016). 'Dead Celebrity (Deleb) Use in Marketing: An Initial Theoretical Exposition', *Psychology & Marketing*, 33(7), 486–504.

Evans, J. and Hesmondhalgh, D. (2005) *Understanding Media: Inside Celebrity*, Maidenhead: Open University Press.

Fleeman, M. (2007, May 24) 'Dr. Martens Shoes Apologizes for Kurt Cobain Ad', *People*, http://people.com/celebrity/dr-martens-shoes-apologizes-for-kurt-cobain-ad/, accessed 29 May 2017.

Fisher, E. (2015) 'Class Struggles in the Digital Frontier: Audience Labour Theory and Social Media Users', *Information, Communication & Society*, 18(9), 1108–1122.

Foucault, M. (2008) *The Birth of Biopolitics: Lectures at the Collège de France, 1978–1979*, Basingstoke: Palgrave Macmillan.

Fuchs, C. (2015) *Culture and Economy in the Age of Social Media*, New York: Routledge.

Fuchs, C. (2017) *Social Media: A Critical Introduction*, London: Sage.

Gamson, J. (2001) 'The Assembly Line of Greatness: Celebrity in Twentieth-Century America', in C. L. Harrington and D. D. Bielby (eds.) *Popular Culture. Production and Consumption*, Oxford: Blackwell.

Giaxoglou, K. and Dövelling, K. (2018) 'Mediatization of Emotion on Social Media: Forms and Norms in Digital Mourning Practices', *Social Media + Society*, Special Issue: Mediatization of Emotion on Social Media: Forms and Norms in Digital Mourning Practices, 4(1), 1–4.

Gibbs, M., Meese, J., Arnold, M., Nansen, B. and Carter, M. (2015) '#Funeral and Instagram: Death, Social Media, and Platform Vernacular', *Information, Communication & Society*, 18(3), 255–268.

Gibson, M. (2007) "Death and Mourning in Technologically Mediated Culture", *Health Sociology Review*, 16(5), 415–424.

Hearn, A. and Schoenhoff, S. (2016) 'From Celebrity to Influencer. Tracing the Diffusion of Celebrity Value Across the Data Stream', in D. Marshall and S. Redmond (eds.) *A Companion to Celebrity*, Chichester: Wiley & Sons Inc.

Hochschild, A. R. (1983) *The Managed Heart: Commercialization of Human Feeling*, Berkeley: University of California Press.

Hoe-Lian Goh, D. and Lee, C. S. (2011) 'An Analysis of Tweets in Response to the Death of Michael Jackson', *Aslib Proceedings*, 63(5), 432–444.

Holiman, J. M. (2013) *iGrieve: Social Media, Parasocial Mourning and the Death of Steve Jobs*, MA Dissertation, Southern Utah University, USA.

Kay, K. (2017, May 28) 'Millennial "Influencers" Who Are the New Stars of Web Advertising', *The Guardian*, https://www.theguardian.com/fashion/2017/may/27/millenial-influencers-new-stars-web-advertising-marketing-luxury-brands, accessed 29 May 2017.

Kearl, M. C. (2010) 'The Proliferation of Postselves in American Civic and Popular Cultures', *Mortality*, 15(1), 47–63.

Keays, G. and Pless, I. B. (2010) 'Impact of a Celebrity Death on Children's Injury-Related Emergency Room Visits', *Canadian Journal of Public Health*, 101(2), 115–118.

Kerns, C. (2016, December 19) 'On Brands, Death and Social Media', *Marketing Land*, http://marketingland.com/brands-death-social-media-200622, accessed 25 April 2017.

Lansdall-Welfare, T., Lampos, V. and Cristianini, N. (2012) 'Nowcasting the Mood of the Nation', *Significance*, 9(4), 26–28.

Lazzarato, M. (2001) 'Immaterial Labor', trans. Coilli, P., Emory, E., http:// frontdeskapparatus.com/wp/wp-content/uploads/2012/10/Immaterial-Labor-Maurizio-Lazzarato.pdf, accessed December 2017.

Lindgren, S. (2017) *Digital Media & Society*, London: Sage.

Long, P. and Wall, T. (2009) *Media Studies. Texts, Production and Context*, Essex: Pearson Education.

Magee, S. (2014) 'Rest in Mediated Peace: How *Entertainment Tonight's* Coverage of Nathalie Wood's and John Belushi's Deaths Helped Shape Celebrity Death Coverage Today', *Celebrity Studies*, 5(3), 291–304.

Mallow, S. (2015) *Losing Robin Williams: An Analysis of User-Generated Twitter Content Following the Sudden Death of a Celebrity*, University of Northern Iowa, Honors Program Theses, Paper 191, http://scholarworks.uni.edu/cgi/ viewcontent.cgi?artic-le=1182&con-text=hpt, accessed 4 December 2017.

Marshall, D. (1997) *Celebrity and Power: Fame in Contemporary Culture*. Minneapolis: University of Minnesota Press.

Mosco, V. (2017) *Becoming Digital. Towards a Post-Internet Society*. Emerald Publishing.

Penfold-Mounce, R. (2015) 'Not Just for Halloween: Dead Celebrities Comes Back to Haunt Us All Year Round', *The Conversation*, http://theconversation. com/not-just-for-halloween-dead-celebrities-come-back-to-haunt-us-all-year-round-41733, accessed 29 April 2017.

Radford, S. K. and Bloch, P. H. (2012) 'Grief, Commiseration and Consumption Following the Death of Celebrity', *Journal of Consumer Culture*, 12(2), 137–155.

Ritzer, G. and Jurgenson, N. (2010) 'Production, Consumption, Presumption: The Nature of Capitalism in the Age of the Digital Prosumer', *Journal of Consumer Culture*, 10(13), 13–36.

Rojek, C. (2007) *Cultural Studies*, Cambridge: Polity.

Rosa, H. (2005) *Social Acceleration. A New Theory of Modernity*, New York: Columbia University Press.

Rosa, H. (2015) 'Social Acceleration and the Need for Speed. An Interview with Hartmut Rosa', https://www.versobooks.com/blogs/2158-social-accelera-tion-and-the-need-for-speed, accessed December 2017.

Scholz, T. (ed.) (2011) *Digital Labour. Internet as Playground and Factory*, New York: Routledge.

Sofka, C. J., Gilbert, K. R. and Cupit, I. N. (eds.) (2012) *Dying, Death and Grief in an Online Universe*, New York: Springer.

Smythe, D. (1981) *Dependency Road: Communication, Capitalism, Consciousness and Canada*, Norwood: Ablex.

Terranova, T. (2000) 'Free Labour: Producing Culture for the Digital Economy', *Social Texts*, 18(2), 33–58.

Van den Bulck, H. and Claessens, N. (2013) 'Celebrity Suicide and the Search for the Moral High Ground: Comparing Frames in Media and Audience Discussions of the Death of a Flemish Celebrity', *Critical Studies in Media Communication*, 30(1), 69–84.

Van den Bulck, H. and Larsson, A. O. (2017) 'There's a Starman Waiting in the Sky' Mourning David #Bowie on Twitter', *Convergence: The International Journal of Research into New Technologies*, online first: https://doi.org/10.1177/1354856517709670.

Wagner, A. J. M. (2018) 'Don't Click "Like" When Somebody Has Died: The Role of Norms for Mourning Practices in Social Media', *Social Media + Society*, Special Issue: Mediatization of Emotion on Social Media: Forms and Norms in Digital Mourning Practices, 4(1), 1–11.

Walter T. (ed.) (1999) The *Mourning of Diana*, Oxford: Berg Press.

Öhman, C. and Floridi, L. (2017) 'The Political Economy of Death in the Age of Information: A Critical Approach to the Digital Afterlife Industry', *Minds & Machines*, 27, 639–662.

10

Aligned with the Dead: Representations of Victimhood and the Dead in Anti-Police Violence Activism Online

María Langa and Philip K. Creswell

Introduction

#Blacklivesmatter began with death. In February 2012 Trayvon Martin, an African American teenager, was shot and killed by George Zimmerman. Martin was walking home from a 7-Eleven with Skittles and an iced tea when he was killed. In July 2013, Zimmerman was acquitted of murder charges and three activists began writing on Twitter, Facebook and Tumblr with a simple message: #BlackLivesMatter. It was in 2014, however, that #BlackLivesMatter took to the streets en masse, protesting the deaths of Michael Brown in Ferguson, Missouri and Eric Garner in New York City. Both Brown and Garner were killed by police officers and became iconic cases that fueled growing awareness of a problem in the United States—the killing of African Americans by police. The movement propounds mourning as an open dynamic which "bears both the vulnerability inherent in black lives and the instability regarding a future for those lives... Black Lives Matter aligns with the dead, continues the

M. Langa (✉) • P. K. Creswell
Department of Sociology, Uppsala University, Uppsala, Sweden
e-mail: maria.langa@soc.uu.se; philip.creswell@soc.uu.se

© The Author(s) 2019
T. Holmberg et al. (eds.), *Death Matters*,
https://doi.org/10.1007/978-3-030-11485-5_10

199

mourning, and refuses the forgetting in front of all of us" (Rankine, 2017: Kindle loc. 326–32).

In this chapter, we analyze the ways activists represent the dead online through the affordances of digital technologies in a cultural context in which African Americans are criminalized both in life and after death. We utilize Charles S. Peirce's (1992 [1894]) semiotic triad of *index*, *icon* and *symbol* to analyze the way that activist groups represent victims of police shootings on their websites and social media accounts. We find that activists reconstruct the deceased's personhood by identifying them with a larger victimized collective and with the protestors themselves as potential victims of racialized police violence. In this process, the dead not only become full persons again but also postmortem political actors. The dead join the fight against police killings of African Americans.

Over 1000 American citizens are estimated to die at the hands of police every year (Amnesty International, 2015).[1] Of those who are killed, African Americans—particularly men—are overrepresented among the victims, with one study placing the likelihood of African Americans being shot by police 3.49 times higher than the general population (Ross & Hills, 2015). The criminalization of African Americans—which is both a historical legacy (Tolliver et al., 2016) and evident in modern media (Smiley & Fakunle, 2016)—affects how both police and the public imagine the killings of African Americans (Tolliver et al., 2016). As a result, African Americans live in fear of the police (Brunson & Miller, 2006; Desmond et al., 2016), experiencing existence as fragile and grief as inevitable. Parenthood is treated with the fear of the unthinkable—but eminently all-too-thinkable for African Americans—that one's child or oneself will be killed by the police (Coates, 2015; Rankine, 2017).

In the wake of killings, the same well-trodden debates begin. The lives of victims are discussed at length, their victimhood resting on their perceived moral character. Fake pictures of Trayvon Martin posing as a "thug," were broadcast on Fox News as though his teenage posing justified his murder (Smiley & Fakunle, 2016). The death of Michael Brown in Ferguson became a debate about whether he had stolen cigarillos from a convenience store minutes before he was "shot six times, twice in his head and left facedown [*sic*] in the street [...] for four hours after his shooting" (Rankine, 2017, Kindle loc. 305–07). These debates underline that the defining element of victimhood is innocence; victim and perpetrator are polarized, demanding absolute innocence from the former (McEvoy & McConnachie, 2012). Alleged crimes deprive victims of personhood just as they were deprived of due process. Victims are deemed culpable for their own deaths. Like Giorgio Agamben's (1998) *Homo Sacer*, they are judged by society and sent back to a community that has permission to kill them. Said differently, their alleged criminality renders them socially dead (Králová, 2015). Black Lives Matter is an ongoing memorialization of those who have died—or were denied justice—at the hands of the state. As Rankine (2017) writes, the movement aligns with the dead and continues mourning.

The case of Black Lives Matter and anti-police violence activism affords us with an opportunity to study the modes of representation of the dead in both online memorialization and political claims-making. We ask, therefore, two questions in this chapter. First, how are the dead represented visually by Black Lives Matter and associated websites? And second, how do activists deal with the criminalized status of the victims of police violence in this representation? In short, we ask, how do activists represent those who are doubly dead, both biologically and socially; those who were deprived of their personhood status through criminalization both pre- and postmortem? We approach this by analyzing the Black Lives Matter Internet presence, their website, as well as their Twitter, and the associated Mapping Police Violence, We the Protesters and Campaign Zero websites. Using Peirce's semiotic triad to analyze visual and textual materials, we find that activists represent the dead *indexically* through statistical aggregation, *iconically* through individual cases and *symbolically* through the identification with the protestors. These different modes of representation help to reconstitute the dead's personhood through a threefold victimhood: *objective victimhood*, *exemplary victimhood* and *collective victimhood*. This approach challenges a unidimensional understanding of victimhood and is accomplished by connecting the dead to the living, who become possible victims, and by sidestepping the individualized narrative of culpability through aggregation. These findings show that technology affords activists with the ability to argue for the personhood of the victims of police violence.

Studying Online Activism, Death and Representation

The role that grief plays in the mobilization of social movements has been highlighted by researchers and activists (Milstein, 2017). Protestors publicly mourn the wrongfully deceased in what Michael Humphrey and Estela Valverde call "political mourning" (Humphrey & Valverde, 2007: 181), making their private grief a public display with demands of justice. Mourning, memorialization and grief are at the core of groups such as anti-femicide protestors (Mendoza, 2017), anti-war movements (Jones, 2009) or anti-AIDS protestors (Gould, 2001). In this context, the dead can appear as martyrs of the cause, sanctified through the details of lives lived in innocence (Olesen, 2013) or be used to galvanize support (McLaren, 2013; Mendoza, 2017) through acts of political mourning. Some movements portray the dead with grotesque images, like in the anti-abortion, environmental and anti-war movements (Haffman & Young, 2010). Representing the dead, then, becomes of relevance for activists seeking justice. However, representing genocides, large-scale killings of minority groups or massacres is a difficult task. The horror of death has led witnesses to highlight the uniqueness of events and find abstract modes of visual representation, which often dehumanized the victims, the perpetrators, or both (Burucúa & Kwiatkowski, 2015).

Digital media's affordances provide both activists (Earl & Kimport, 2011), and private grievers (Meese et al., 2015), with new tools for representing the dead. Memorialization and grieving practices have changed with the introduction of the Internet (Walter et al., 2012), with an increased personalization of grieving practices and the individuation of the deceased (Krysinska & Andriessen, 2015). Mourners continue their bonds with the deceased through different practices (Klass et al., 1996), and today the bereaved turn to the Internet to extend and continue their relationships with the dead (Irwin, 2015). This extension can be characterized as an afterlife (Meese et al., 2015), and it allows the deceased's unique identity to continue existing in perpetuity (Walter, 2018). Furthermore, mourning and memorialization online shifts mourning from a private experience to a public one, associated with a community of mourners (Clancey, 2015). Online mourning practices do not only connect communities of mourners who may not previously had access to them (Nguyen, 2015), but can also offer a way for unrecognized groups to have a grievable presence online (Devgan, 2013). The Internet is also a strongly visual medium where activists frequently make claims online through pictures, memes and videos (Askanius, 2013).

However, qualitative researchers in the social sciences predominantly study texts. The study of social movements from a visual or aesthetic perspective has been less common, though it has ticked up in recent years (cf. Doerr et al., 2013). Attention to visual data for the study of social movements has been highlighted as a way making qualitative data more robust (Philipps, 2012). Many researchers extend the notion of discourse to visual analyses (Doerr & Milman, 2014), by, for example, attempting to understand a "visual rhetoric" (Jones, 2009, para. 9). Others have worked directly with Goffman's concept of *keying* in visual analysis (Luhtakallio, 2013). Many of these studies analyze online cases, such as the audio-visual expressions of movement claims in YouTube videos, using the tools of social semiotics (Askanius, 2013).

Representing the Dead: Anti-Police Violence Activism and Visual Representation Online

Inspired by these approaches, we collected materials that were shared and/or created by the following activist groups: Black Lives Matter, Mapping Police Violence, Campaign Zero and We the Protesters, focusing on images but accounting for their context. The three latter movements emerged from Black Lives Matter. Mapping Police Violence was created with the purpose of "collecting comprehensive data on police killings nationwide to quantify the impact of police violence in communities" (Mapping Police Violence, 2017: n.p.). Campaign Zero shares a planning team with Mapping Police Violence and emerged from Black Lives Matter members in 2015, when the latter group was criticized for "demonizing" police and not proposing a plan with solutions to police brutality (Friedersdorf, 2015). The initiative was launched by four activists who met during the Black Lives Matter protests surrounding the shooting of Michael Brown in Ferguson, Missouri, in 2014 and is referred to as a Black Lives Matter initiative in media reports (Varagur, 2017, first published in 2015). We the Protestors also shares a planning team with Mapping Police Violence and Campaign Zero and links directly to both websites.

In this chapter, we do not analyze the entire corpus of the contents of these platforms. We have chosen, instead, to focus on the representation of the victims of police violence directly through images and graphics. However, this necessitated a careful exploration of the platforms, which provided information from negative results: the non-representation of victims. Screen captures were taken systematically during the collection of online content and accompanied with notes throughout the process (Boellstorff et al., 2012). Screenshots have a double benefit of capturing visual aspects of the platforms we analyzed. First, they allowed us to capture the context of graphics, images and text and, second, they retain important information such as the captured section's URL and the precise date and time of the shot. This allowed for the notations to focus on impressions and the interactive elements of the websites (such as animations, links, expansions). In total, we analyzed a corpus of 130 screen captures with notes taken during the exploration of these online contents. The screenshots were first analyzed vis-à-vis the notes taken during the process. Then we coded them according to our semiotics-inspired theoretical framework. Finally, we connected the categories with Black Lives Matter's goals of framing police violence as a social problem and the dead as victims of it. This uncovered a logic in the representation of the dead and Black Lives Matter's fight against police violence through the construction of victimhood.

Peirce's Semiotics as a Framework for Analysis

The choice of Peirce's semiotic triad—index, icon and symbol—allows us to address the visual representation of victims of police violence analytically in connection with the issue of the personhood and criminalization of the dead, as well as the resulting issue of victimhood. Our analytical framework rests on the premise that there are different levels of abstraction that relate signs to any given object of representation. By *sign* we mean anything that signifies a relationship between itself and an *object*, which can be material things or abstract concepts. For example, little gray figures (sign) signify dead bodies (object), or a skull-and-crossbones signifies poison. This is the most basic depiction of semiosis or signification—the process through which a sign signifies a meaning.

The nature of the relation between the two basic elements of this process (sign and object) is the *ground* of signification. According to Peirce, the ground of a sign can be indexical, iconic or symbolic. Thus, the ground determines whether the sign can be categorized as an index, an icon or a symbol. An index is related to its object through a sensorial or material connection between the sign and the object; smoke means fire, blood on the sidewalk or a chalk outline of a body means a murder. An icon is a sign which represents a larger group, class or kind of objects. An icon resembles the object being represented, but the object is broader than itself; the use of Mike Brown to represent all victims of police violence is iconic. A symbol is a sign that is abstracted from the material or sensorial nature of the object; the white dove symbolizing peace or a staff with a serpent wrapped around it symbolizing medical treatment. Symbolic representation is established by convention, not because of a resemblance or a material connection to the object. Symbols are usually the best resource to represent abstract ideas. Mike Brown, for example, could become a symbol of the fight for justice.

The interpretation of a sign involves other signs that can modify or qualify its meaning. The interpretant is a sign that interprets another sign, this is why the process of semiosis could be infinite (Monelle, 1991). Any given sign connects to a network of interrelated interpretants that "should presumably help to connect signs, and thereby their users and interpreters, to their objects" (Hilpinen, 2007: 612). The network of interpretants, then, can modify any sign into an infinite expansion of meanings that could classify it as an index, icon or symbol—or all of them at once—by changing the focus of analysis. To stabilize this in our analysis, we establish two interpretants of interest—activism and criminalization, which function as the context or lens of the interpretation. Taking activism and criminalization as the interpretant, we postulate that activists created the materials we analyzed with the objective of advancing their cause against police violence. Moreover, we postulate that activists are representing the victims of police violence in a context of the racialized criminalization of the victims.

This way, we simplified the model to understand index, icon and symbol as forms of representation that progressively incorporate more conventionally established meanings and levels of abstraction into the communication of an object (Table 10.1). Therefore, the representation is more subjective, value-oriented or ethical, including more conventionalized meanings regarding an object that has been constructed as an objective social issue (Berger & Luckmann, 1989 [1966]). Furthermore, we highlight that this communication is taking place in the context of activism against police violence and the criminalization of victims, by establishing them as the interpretants. In the analysis that follows, we describe three modes of representation: indexical, iconic and symbolic in connection to the construction of the deceased as victims of police violence as a social problem.

Table 10.1 Analytical framework

	Interpretant: Anti-Police Violence Activism and Criminalization		
	Indexical Representation	*Iconic Representation*	*Symbolic Representation*
	Mark left by the object	Sign represents a larger group; a class or kind of object	Sign and object are related purely by convention
Object: Fatal Victims of Police Violence	Non-resemblance	Resemblance	Non-resemblance
	Low level of abstraction; sensorial connection between sign and object	Middle level of abstraction; one sign represents a class of objects	High level of abstraction; usually the sign expresses abstract ideas
	e.g., smoke means fire; statistics of police violence	e.g., use of the image or story of high-profile case of police shooting to represent all	e.g., use of American flag colors to incorporate abstract idea of the nation

Indexical Representation: On Objective Victimhood

The most prominent form of indexical representation in the analyzed material is the use of statistics and graphics. Similar to Beauchamp's (2007) findings about the use of statistics in anti-trans violence, statistics became a primary form to represent victims, rather than focusing on iconic deaths. However, as we will see, the mechanisms at play in this process are not so straightforward as they are exposed more systematically through the three forms of representation in our model. That is, the move toward "symbolic deaths" in our case does not emerge directly from statistics, but from a whole array of representations on different levels of abstraction.

Mapping Police Violence, part of the Campaign Zero network, presents updated statistics as well as monthly and annual reports with access to raw data. The landing page on Mapping Police Violence is an interactive map of the United States that highlights with red marks the occurrence of police killings. This map also provides a timeline animation. As the timeline moves, shootings are marked with an orange flare—resembling a gunshot. One can click on the marks, causing a pop-up window with a picture of the victim to appear. This window features a short reference to their person, the incident that ended their life, and a link to the news source on the killing. The description of the incidents is concise, which contrasts the dramatic use of colors, especially the bright red and the use of deep black for the map of the United States. Moreover, the information provided about the victims is a bare minimum—categorical identifiers like age, race and place of residence. Only the pop-up frame provides users with a window into the victim's identity. Here, victims are represented as a data point in the statistics of police killings. Furthermore, the website's start page is dedicated to highlighting aspects of police violence in the United States using graphics—not text.

In this graph, there are no attempts to hide cases that may suggest criminal behavior, despite that the suggestion of criminality is a sensitive matter due to a context of the criminalization of victims, where the smallest suspicion of even minor crimes can be a justification for the use of deadly force. In this sense, the provision of a picture, name and description of the incident appears as literally emerging from the statistical and geo-graphical data. The degree of victimhood of the person is irrelevant in this indexical form of representation, because the personal information emerges directly from the statistical data which presents police violence as an objective, measurable social problem. Each person who was and is killed by the police is a flare on the map of the United States.

Similarly, a year calendar on Mapping Police Violence shows the vic-tims as a number on each date, highlighting the number of deaths like a heat map in yellow, orange and red. With this representation, whether the victim committed a crime or not recedes into the background. Every death is a consequence of the use of force by police. The aggregation of the representation of these deaths in the statistics presents this force as excessive and stemming from something bigger than any individual number. Cases are displayed by integrating visual and textual informa-tion, while using animation, time-lapses and the interactive emergence of elements from professional graphics. There is minimal reading required and the websites focus on the perception of visual elements, movement, time and interaction. While AIDS quilts may have simultaneously humanized victims and demonstrated the spread of the disease (Gould, 2001; Jones, 2009), they were limited spatially and temporally. Interactivity affords movements a unique opportunity to represent the dead in multiplex ways simultaneously. These representations deftly side-step individualization and, as we will see later, offer users the ability to select their own iconic victims.

Conversely, in a separate section, the activists behind Mapping Police Violence have created a gallery that commemorates only the unarmed victims of police violence. Under the heading *Here are the names and stories of unarmed black people killed by police*, one finds larger images of the victims and a longer account of the encounters with police officers who ended their lives. The fact that these people were unarmed and, therefore, more "innocent" promotes the creation of a separate memori-alized space for those whose victimhood status is what we call "exem-plary." *Exemplary victims* are a step further from being only a data point. They are ascribed personhood—humanized—with a biography.

Nonetheless, this section is headed with graphics on the statistics of unarmed black people killed by police. The accounts of the shootings in the gallery have a journalistic style; they are short, with limited, less affective descriptions. No personal information is provided other than the basics. There are no deeper narratives about victims' lives outside this event, contrary to what the title suggests. It is only the use of candid or personal photos which offers a window into the victim's life. These pictures could be part of an *iconic* representation, as an example which stands in for all African American victims of police violence. However, there are still elements of indexical representation, as the activists are not offering up an iconic case to stand for all others. The strength is not on the profound innocence of one—who is to represent all—but rather the stories, if short and concise, of all victims. It is the difference of the individuality of nails in a box and that of the idiosyncratic details of someone's life. In this gallery, the short stories highlight the former, while the pictures are a snapshot of the latter. Together they bring forth what these people share—personhood and victimhood.

Mapping Police Violence frames the representation of victims in a similar manner to journalistic databases like "The Counted" by *The Guardian*. This website provides statistical and geographical data on police killings in the United States, making use of a strict, journalistic style to account for each case. Cases are placed in a yearly timeline and users can scroll through them, filter them by category and click for more information. The *Washington Post* databases are the most judicious of the three regarding design and the use of photographs; but it still makes use of pictures for the illustration of the cases in the database. The *Washington Post*'s databases generate the feeling of aggregation in different ways, like an animation which shows the total deaths rising from zero each time someone enters a page.

In sum, the three websites use statistical data and graphics in similar ways, representing the dead indexically but with the possibility of user selection. The activist group, however, frames police violence in the United States not only as an objective social problem but also as an issue of racism against African Americans. The statistics highlight black persons killed by police. Therefore, this extension of victimhood created by the indexical representation of police violence would, ultimately, seem to extend only to African American victims.

Mapping Police Violence featured no personal narrative or exemplary tales of victimhood in their gallery of unarmed victims. The decision to assign all victims of a category with equal space and information in each website's database is closer to an indexical form of representation than an iconic one, since it is presented as emerging directly from the data rather than a selection by a victimhood criterion. Some cases, like those of children, could be expected to generate stronger emotional reactions, but responses to the material are left to users of the websites, not the creator of the content. The gallery, along with the individual pictures and descriptions in general, can be seen as functionally iconic in the sense that the user can navigate through cases that may come to represent the rest of the victims. However, given the way the information is presented, activists need not make that decision. Users are offered a choice, which we interpret as implying that the decision does not matter regarding the victims of police violence as a social problem.

During the time when we were collecting our material, from February of 2017 to March of 2018, Mapping Police Violence changed the layout of their gallery of unarmed victims. Rather than increasing the amount of information, they made it more uniform with the rest of their database. A similar move to represent victims more equally can be seen on the journalistic websites, as well. *The Washington Post* chose a panel of gray, standard human figures to represent victims. Hovering one's cursor over a victim provides information about that individual victim. This form of representation, which is also used by Campaign Zero, is the one described by José Emilio Burucúa and Nicolás Kwiatkowski (2015) as the silhouettes, ghosts and multiplication formula that emerged following World War II. Such a formula focuses on the accumulation of victims and their absence. *The Guardian* has aesthetically equated the victims' pictures through the editing of colors and contrast, making all the different pictures look similar in their database.

Iconic Representation: On Exemplary Victimhood

One consequence of Mapping Police Violence's style is that the iconic representation of the victims is left to the user. Each individual user can select cases and assess their victimhood. This stands in contrast to the three heavily edited pictures of the victims of police violence on the Black Lives Matter website. Each victim, with their names and hashtags, adorns the banner: #philandocastile, #delwarnsmall and #altonsterling. In this context, these images are an example of *iconic* representation since these three high-profile cases stand for all victims on this website, which does not feature a gallery or memorial section. Black Lives Matter makes use of iconic and other forms of visual representation, not related directly to the victims, but to black culture more broadly and other causes for which the group advocates.

On their Twitter page, there are more cases of iconic representation. First, the central heading on Twitter is a digital painting of Trayvon Martin whose death inspired the hashtag, and which led to the formation of the movement. When assessed as a whole, the victims represented are no more than 10 out of the totals of roughly 1000 deaths per year. These victims, then, represent a much larger whole.

The victims represented iconically are generally high-profile cases which have sparked protests around the country. They tend to coincide with cases that exemplify police wrong-doing and for which there is evidence of the victim's innocence or immediate surrender to the police. The cases that become high profile, however, seem to be those in which footage or pictures of the killing are available. However, other victims are also represented iconically, if less frequently, even when their cases are not well-known. For example, in Black Lives Matter's Twitter we found an image commemorating the death of a young woman. Her personhood is highlighted through the statement that she "is not another hashtag." Instead, she is a child and someone who was loved by family and friends and who "deserved more" than dying in police custody. Her story here represents thousands more cases of children, or innocents, who were loved by their families, who deserved more than execution. Dead victims who were, in short, *persons*.

Several memorial images such as this can be found in Black Lives Matter's Twitter and Instagram. Such images are closer to the way other movements represent their dead as martyrs, highlighting their exemplary innocence. However, the predominant way in which victims are represented iconically is in large pictures carried by protestors on the street.

The practice is reminiscent of the way the protesters in Argentina raise signs with the faces of those killed by the last dictatorship. Drawn on blank pages, on printed pictures stuck on cardboard or painted on large waving flags, the faces of the dead are brought into the fight, raised as banners to the sky. It is this way of representing the dead that connects the iconic and symbolic representations of the dead in the Black Lives Matter movement.

Symbolic Representation: On Collective Victimhood

A step further in the direction of broadening the spectrum of the victims' meaning for activist groups is the symbolic form of representation. Victims come to express not just police brutality but also the movement of protestors themselves. In this way, activists bridge both the movement's past and future and its online and offline presence (Askanius, 2013). The majority of the images where victims are present, even if indirectly, are protest pictures. In the case of Black Lives Matter, Trayvon Martin has become a symbol used by the movement—especially on Twitter. The image of the three victims on Black Lives Matter's start page is accompanied by a phrase about the movement: "The Black Lives Matter network advocates for dignity, justice, and respect" (Black Lives Matter, 2017: n.p.). Similarly, images of protesters holding pictures and signs of victims claim them for the movement. At the same time, by identifying the victims with the protestors and the public, victims are given their personhood back. They come to represent the movement, turning them into more than victims; they are symbols of the change that is needed.

A further step in the direction of relating the victims to the movement against police violence is the predominance of images which also turn protestors into victims. Using pictures of the victims and protest pictures, Black Lives Matter includes protestors, and the public, as potential victims of police violence and relates to the group's collective identity. On Black Lives Matter's Twitter account, for example, a boy wearing a Trayvon Martin T-shirt raises a sign that reads "Don't shoot! I'm just young, black and walking." Such representation is consistent with slogans like "hands up, don't shoot" and "we can't breathe," which reference the deaths of Mike Brown and Eric Garner, respectively. The individual's victimhood is emphasized since s/he becomes associated with a larger collective. An example of this is the performance of protestors lying on the streets as though they are dead—so-called die-ins—directly embodying the victims through this performance. The Campaign Zero website, which contains many images of this kind, uses one of these pictures to illustrate their vision or cause. We the Protesters provides an "activist toolkit" in which they include a compilation of protest signs pictures. Many of them feature names and pictures of victims. Other signs turn the protestors even more directly into victims with texts such as "You are killing us," "We all are Michael Brown," or "Our daughters will be next."

Another form of symbolic representation is the use of colors for the design of the websites. The selection of design elements such as color is contextual and conventional and almost impossible to assess with certainty in terms of its meaning. However, there are two interesting aspects of color use in the analyzed material. First, Black Lives Matter's black and bright yellow colors are currently being used by groups against police violence in Canada and the United Kingdom, among other places. The globalization of the movement can expand their political mourning to other places and then victims of police violence in the United States could be identified with victims of police violence around the world. Second, Mapping Police Violence's use of color for graphics on its start page is centered on red and blue on a white canvas, evoking the American flag. Moreover, red is used to represent negatives and blues positive aspects of statistics. For example, states with high rates of police killings are shown in red, while the ones with low rates are blue or light blue. The figures representing the killings where officers have not been tried are in red, while the ones who have are in blue. Regardless of the possible connections to red or blue—red representing blood or blue the abolitionists during the Civil War—victims are represented through references to the American flag. These victims, like Philando Castile (Fig. 10.1), are inscribed with the nation as a distinctly American problem—with seven stars for the number of times he was shot—and thus with citizenship and personhood.

He Lived
by THE LAW
& DiED By
The Law

Philando
Castile
32 years.
No CRIMINAL
RECORD.
KiLLED in FRONT
OF This Daughter

Fig. 10.1 A tribute to Philando Castile shared on Twitter by Gianluca Constantini after Castile's killing in 2016

Constantini's memorial to Philando Castile, however, was not found on the Black Lives Matter or Campaign Zero website or Twitter. In fact, similar images vindicating the innocence of victims of police shootings directly with references to the persons' past life were less common than we expected. When the dead become symbolic, they symbolize the movement for change, the protestors and all possible future victims. They are given a kind of retrospective political agency—whether they were involved in the movement or not—and they come to represent a larger collective who struggles to end police violence. This way, the criminalized victims become full persons again.

Conclusions: On Victimhood, Death and Activism

> You must always remember that the sociology, the history, the economics, the graphs, the charts, the regressions all land, with great violence, upon the body. *Between the World and Me*, Ta-Nehisi. Coates (2015: 10)

The violence that falls on the bodies of African Americans killed by police officers continues after death. The Black Lives Matter movement fights against this violence both pre- and postmortem. Our analysis shows how activists carry on part of this struggle. The recognition of the dead as victims of structural and state violence is a central aspect of counteracting the effects of the postmortem violence that robs the dead of their personhood—criminalization. As our analysis shows, the content of these websites and social media pages constructs a threefold victimhood for those killed by police which may be an attempt to counter criminalization discourses through visual choices, rather than explicit argumentation. First, *objective victimhood* is constructed through indexical representation of the dead. Police violence emerges as an objective social problem that ended the lives of those represented in graphics and statistics. Second, *exemplary victimhood* emerges when some victims become icons that represent the whole number of the dead. In the Black Lives Matter movement, however, this representation falls short of representing the dead as martyrs and focuses on the dead *as persons* who had friends and family and lived as people do. Finally, most iconic representations are a link toward the construction of what we have called *collective victimhood* using symbolic representation. Black Lives Matter and its associated websites symbolically relate the dead to activists, protestors and the movement through images of protest or pictures of victims associated to the values and goals of the movement.

In a situation where killings are legitimized by delegitimizing the persons being shot, constructing the dead as victims is a key issue (see Fürst & Idevall Hagren, Chap. 11, this volume, for a similar argument). Black Lives Matter does not focus on a binary and absolute understanding of victimhood and therefore builds up from more than just exemplary cases of victimhood. Rather, they emphasize the humanity of each person—victim or potential victim, criminal or not—derived from discourses of human rights and the sacredness of every person (Joas, 2013). However, by representing victims indexically, Mapping Police Violence also sidesteps individualizing discourses of culpability and offers a different argument. Furthermore, the move to symbolic representation extends police violence and the rest of the victims to the struggle against police violence and racial discrimination more generally. Such an extension also means that protestors—and even the public—become potential victims, contributing with their own personhood to undermine the alleged criminal status of the fatalities.

The representation of the dead in Black Lives Matter and associated groups online makes a double move that places the focus on the social and not the individual—one toward aggregation and the other toward collective action. The representation of victims embedded in statistical aggregates and collective protests shifts the focus from debates about individual innocence to collective victimhood and collective action against structural violence inflicted upon African Americans, while some iconic cases serve as a highlight of the lives lost. The dead, then, recover their value as citizens and persons by being turned into postmortem political actors. Their deaths are the dire consequence of a social problem. The victims become protestors, protestors become victims, and together they struggle to end police violence in the United States.

Note

1. The United States federal government does not keep official statistics, and it is difficult to quantify the issue with precision (Klinger, 2011). Amnesty International (2015) estimates that between 400 and 1000 persons are killed by police every year. These estimates coincide with the statistics gathered by activist groups and journalists (see, e.g., Mapping Police Violence and The Counted by *The Guardian*).

References

Agamben, G. (1998) *Homo Sacer: Sovereign Power and Bare Life*, Stanford, CA: Stanford University Press.

Amnesty International. (2015) 'Deadly Force: Use of Lethal Force in the United States', http://www.amnestyusa.org/research/reports/deadly-force-police-use-of-lethal-force-in-the-united-states, accessed 13 February 2018.

Askanius, T. (2013) 'Protest Movements and Spectacles of Death: From Urban Places to Video Spaces' in N. Doerr, A. Mattoni, and S. Teune (ed.), *Research in Social Movements, Conflicts and Change: Vol. 35. Advances in the Visual Analysis of Social Movements*, Bingley: Emerald Insight.

Beauchamp, T. (2007) 'The Limits of Virtual Memory: Nationalisms, State Violence, and the Transgender Day of Remembrance', *InterAlia: Pismo poświecone studiom queer*, 2, 1–16.

Berger, P. L. and Luckmann, T. (1989 [1966]) *The Social Construction of Reality: A Treatise in the Sociology of Knowledge*, New York: Anchor Books.

Black Lives Matter. (2017) 'Black Lives Matter | About', http://www.blacklives-matter.com/about, accessed 28 March 2017.

Boellstorff, T., Nardi, B., Pearce, C. and Taylor, T. L. (2012) *Ethnography and Virtual Worlds: A Handbook of Method*, Princeton, Oxford: Princeton University Press.

Brunson, R. K. and Miller, J. (2006) 'Gender, Race, and Urban Policing: The Experience of African American Youths', *Gender and Society*, 20(4), 531–552.

Burucúa, J. E. and Kwiatkowski, N. (2015) *Cómo Sucedieron Estas Cosas: Representar Masacres y Genocidios*, Buenos Aires: Katz.

Clancey, G. (2015) 'The Diaspora of the Dead: Civic Memorialization in the Age of Online Databases', *Mortality*, 20(4), 390–407.

Coates, T.-N. (2015) *Between the World and Me*, New York: Spiegel & Grau.

Desmond, M., Papachristos, A. V. and Kirk, D. S. (2016) 'Police Violence and Citizen Crime Reporting in the Black Community', *American Sociological Review*, 81(5), 857–876.

Devgan, S. (2013) 'From the "Crevices in Dominant Memories": Virtual Commemoration and the 1984 Anti-Sikh Violence', *Identities*, 20(2), 207–233.

Doerr, N., Mattoni, A. and Teune, S. (2013) 'Toward a Visual Analysis of Social Movements, Conflicts and Political Mobilization', in N. Doerr, A. Mattoni, and S. Teune (eds.), *Research in Social Movements, Conflicts and Change: Vol. 35. Advances in the Visual Analysis of Social Movements*, Bingley: Emerald Insight.

Doerr, N. and Milman, N. (2014) 'Working with Images' in D. Della Porta (ed.), *Methodological Practices in Social Movement Research*, Oxford: Oxford University Press.

Earl, J. and Kimport, K. (2011) *Digitally Enabled Social Change: Activism in the Internet Age*, Cambridge: MIT Press.

Friedersdorf, C. (2015, September 24) 'Will Black Lives Matter Be a Movement That Persuades?' *The Atlantic*, https://www.theatlantic.com/politics/archive/2015/09/will-black-lives-matter-be-a-movement-that-per-suades/407017/, accessed 13 February 2018.

Gould, D. (2001) 'Rock the Boat, Don't Rock the Boat, Baby: Ambivalence and the Emergence of Militant AIDS Activism', in J. Goodwin, J. M. Jasper, and F. Polletta (eds.), *Passionate Politics: Emotions and Social Movements*, Chicago: The University of Chicago Press.

Haffman, D. and Young, M. P. (2010) 'War Pictures: The Grotesque as a Mobilizing Tactic', *Mobilization: An International Quarterly*, 1(15), 1–24.

Hilpinen, R. (2007) 'On the Objects and Interpretants of Signs: Comments on T. L. Short's Peirce's Theory of Signs', *Transactions of the Charles S. Peirce Society*, 43(4), 610–618.

Humphrey, M. and Valverde, E. (2007) 'Human Rights, Victimhood, and Impunity: An Anthropology of Democracy in Argentina', *Social Analysis: The International Journal of Social and Cultural Practice*, 51(1), 179–197.

Irwin, M. D. (2015) 'Mourning 2.0: Continuing Bonds Between the Living and the Dead on Facebook', *OMEGA – Journal of Death and Dying*, 72(2), 119–150.

Joas, H. (2013) *The Sacredness of the Person: A New Genealogy of Human Rights*, Washington, DC: Georgetown University Press.

Jones, R. (2009) 'The Aesthetics of Protest', *Enculturation*, 6(2), http://www.enculturation.net/6.2/jones, accessed 07 February 2017.

Klass, D., Silverman, P. R. and Nickman, S. L. (ed.) (1996) *Continuing Bonds: New Understandings of Grief*, Washington, DC: Taylor & Francis.

Klinger, D. A. (2011) 'On the Problems and Promise of Research on Lethal Police Violence', *Homicide Studies*, 16(1), 78–96.

Králová, J. (2015) 'What Is Social Death?' *Contemporary Social Science*, 10(3), 235–248.

Krysinska, K. and Andriessen, K. (2015) 'Online Memorialization and Grief After Suicide: An Analysis of Suicide Memorials on the Internet', *OMEGA – Journal of Death and Dying*, 71(1), 19–47.

Luhtakallio, E. (2013) 'Bodies Keying Politics: A Visual Frame Analysis of Gendered Local Activism in France and Finland', in N. Doerr, A. Mattoni, and S. Teune (eds.), *Research in Social Movements, Conflicts and Change: Vol. 35. Advances in the Visual Analysis of Social Movements*, Bingley: Emerald Insight.

Mapping Police Violence. (2017) 'Planning Team', https://mappingpoliceviolence.org/planning-team/, accessed 13 February 2018.

McEvoy, K. and McConnachie, K. (2012) 'Victimology in Transitional Justice: Victimhood, Innocence and Hierarchy', *European Journal of Criminology*, 9(5), 527–538.

McLaren, K. (2013). 'The Emotional Imperative of the Visual: Images of the Fetus in Contemporary Australian Pro-Life Politics', in N. Doerr, A. Mattoni, and S. Teune (eds.), *Research in Social Movements, Conflicts and Change: Vol. 35. Advances in the Visual Analysis of Social Movements*, Bingley: Emerald Insight.

Meese, J., Nansen, B., Kohn, T., Arnold, M. and Gibbs, M. (2015) 'Posthumous Personhood and the Affordances of Digital Media', *Mortality*, 20(4), 408–420.

Mendoza, E. F. O. (2017) 'Feminicide and the Funeralization of the City: On Thing Agency and Protest Politics in Ciudad Juárez', *Theory & Event*, 20(2), 351–380.

Milstein, C. (ed.) (2017) *Rebellious Mourning: The Collective Work of Grief*, Kindle edn, Chico: AK Press.

Monelle, R. (1991) 'Music and the Peircean Trichotomies', *International Review of the Aesthetics and Sociology of Music*, 22(1), 99–108.

Nguyen, H. T. (2015) 'Wiring Death: Remembering on the Internet', *КУЛТУРА/Culture*, 11, 65–76.

Olesen, T. (2013) '"We Are All Khaled Said": Visual Injustice Symbols in the Egyptian Revolution, 2010–2011', in N. Doerr, A. Mattoni, and S. Teune (eds.), *Research in Social Movements, Conflicts and Change: Vol. 35. Advances in the Visual Analysis of Social Movements*, Bingley: Emerald Insight.

Peirce, C. S. (1992). 'What Is a Sign?', in N. Houser & C. Kloesel (eds.), *The Essential Peirce: Vol. 1 (1867–1893)*, Bloomington, IN: Indiana University Press. (Original work published 1894).

Philipps, A. (2012) 'Visual Protest Material as Empirical Aid', *Visual Communication*, 11(1), 3–21.

Rankine, C. (2017) 'The Condition of Black Life Is One of Mourning', in C. Milstein (ed.), *Rebellious Mourning: The Collective Work of Grief*, Chico: AK Press.

Ross, C. T. and Hills, P. J. (2015) 'A Multi-Level Bayesian Analysis of Racial Bias in Police Shootings at the County-Level in the United States, 2011–2014', *PLOS ONE*, 10(11), e0141854.

Smiley, C. J. and Fakunle, D. (2016) 'From "Brute" to "Thug": The Demonization and Criminalization of Unarmed Black Male Victims in America', *Journal of Human Behavior in the Social Environment*, 26(3–4), 350–366.

Tolliver, W. F., Hadden, B. R., Snowden, F. and Brown-Manning, R. (2016) 'Police Killings of Unarmed Black People: Center Race and Racism in Human Behavior and the Social Environment Content', *Journal of Human Behavior in the Social Environment*, 26(3–4), 279–286.

Varagur, K. (2017, January 15) 'How Black Lives Matter Activists Plan to "Check the Police"', *The Huffington Post*, https://www.huffingtonpost.com/entry/police-union-contract-project_us_565f4193e4b08e945fedb444, accessed 13 February 2018.

Walter, T. (2018) 'The Pervasive Dead', *Mortality*, *16*, 1–16.

Walter, T., Hourizi, R., Moncur, W. and Pitsillides, S. (2012) 'Does the Internet Change How We Die and Mourn? Overview and Analysis', *OMEGA – Journal of Death and Dying*, 64(4), 275–302.

11

Frames of Death: Media Audience Framing of a Lethal Drone Strike

Henrik Fürst and Karin Idevall Hagren

Introduction

A silent shaky black and white YouTube video shows a number of dark silhouettes moving on the ground.[1] The perspective is that of a drone plane, crossing the skies of Iraq, controlled from a military compound in the US. The drone pilot engages fire, and from the ground an explosion emerges. The silhouettes disappear. While we do not know much about the context or the people killed, the title of the video clip, uploaded on 11 April 2008 by an organization associated with the US Armed Forces, frames it as "UAV Kills 6 Heavily Armed Criminals," which tells us that six suspected enemies of the US Armed Forces were killed in a drone strike.[2]

H. Fürst (✉)
Department of Sociology, Uppsala University, Uppsala, Sweden
e-mail: henrik.furst@soc.uu.se

K. Idevall Hagren
Department of Scandinavian Languages, Uppsala University, Uppsala, Sweden
e-mail: karin.hagren.idevall@nordiska.uu.se

© The Author(s) 2019   **221**
T. Holmberg et al. (eds.), *Death Matters*,
https://doi.org/10.1007/978-3-030-11485-5_11

However, this title is only one possible framing of the message from the video clip. The audience commenting on the video clip is also framing the meaning of the deaths the video clip allows us to witness. In a media landscape increasingly dominated by participatory media and semi-anonymous audiences, such as YouTube commentators, this construction of death has clear political stakes (e.g. Langa & Creswell, Chap. 10 in this volume). Nonetheless, this chapter is one of the very few studies paying attention to *how* audiences are framing the media message in the context of war propaganda in participatory media. Understanding this framing process sheds light on the construction of killing and death, and its legitimacy in the dissemination of war propaganda, in the age of drone warfare and participatory media.

The rise of drone warfare[3] intersects with the rise of YouTube. YouTube has become a common place for distributing videos of war and death. The Iraq War is the first example, where both soldiers and the army publish videos on YouTube from an ongoing war (Andén-Papadopoulos, 2009).[4] What is perhaps different from other previously studied types of media outlets, such as war propaganda in news reporting (Boltanski, 1999; Chouliaraki, 2006; Hiebert, 2003; Sontag, 2003), is that YouTube allows people to interact and comment in the comment field adjacent to the video clip (see also Heemsbergen & Lindgren, 2014). Seemingly anonymous participants express themselves in relation to their own localized media consumption, which becomes part of a potentially global communication about the content of video clips. Acting as Internet "prosumers" (Ritzer & Jurgenson, 2010), commentators on YouTube not only act as an audience and consume the media content, but also produce media content using the affordances offered by the technology. Hence, they are part of a participatory culture (Jenkins, 2006). Their utterances, interaction, and media production contribute to the framing of contemporary media events, including that of death and war propaganda, as exemplified in the YouTube video clip under study. Like social media in general, YouTube offers extensive possibilities for users to control framing and take a stance on political controversies. The analyzed video clip thus explicitly calls for opinions *for* the war, and is not meant to encourage pity for the Iraqi victims of the drone killing. And while war images always require and are embedded in some context that gives them meaning (Sontag, 2003), the antagonistic and aggressive use of visual images of war that we see in this case is markedly different from the conventional use of similar material in established media (Chouliaraki, 2006).

Interrogating the processes through which commentators frame killing and death, this chapter is informed by a cultural sociology perspective that conceives of symbolic boundaries as "conceptual distinctions made by social actors to categorize objects, people, practices, and even time and space" (Lamont & Molnár, 2002: 168). The boundaries help people define and categorize how to perceive reality, such as drawing the boundary for what lives should or should not be considered livable. Definitions and categorizations are made through language, and therefore we analyze how the audience uses cultural modes discursively to frame the moral status of victims of drone strikes and to draw symbolic boundaries between legitimate and non-legitimate death and killing. These boundaries are drawn between persons (livable lives) and non-persons (non-livable lives) through different frames that either oppose or justify the depicted killings. In consequence, the boundaries tell us about the moral status of the lives being killed. Hence, we understand the framing of these events as a highly moral process, which allows the commentators to position themselves in different ways in relation to the drone strike, and we raise questions such as: What lives are considered valuable and treated as objects of care and grief? What lives are of no worth and thus killable? What lives do people enjoy seeing destroyed? Analyzing how discourses about death and dying intersect with life and living in a domain where death simultaneously triggers disgust and enjoyment, this chapter explores the ways in which death is both produced and consumed in contemporary social media discourse.

Frames of Drone Warfare

In *Frames of War*, Judith Butler (2009: 1) analyzes the "cultural modes of regulating affective and ethical dispositions through a selective and differential framing of violence." We follow this lead by studying how the value of life and death is constructed and justified affectively through cultural frames. More precisely, the selective and differential framing of violence and death can, according to Butler, be understood through Erving Goffman's frame analysis. Hence, meanings are constructed through layers of frames (Goffman, 1974). In order to analyze how actors ascribe meaning to the clip, we explore the cultural framing of death and killing through the ethical and affective dispositions expressed in the comments.

Butler (2009) argues that if lives are seen as livable (ethical disposition), they are also grievable (affective disposition) (see Redmalm, Chap. 12 in this volume). Non-grievable lives (affective disposition) are simply not lives in the first place (ethical disposition). For normative reasons, Butler talks about grievable and non-grievable lives, which indicates that all lives should be considered precarious, livable, and thereby grievable. However, people's actual ethical and affectual dispositions are not in focus in this conceptual model. In contrast, we argue that Butler overlooks the idea that killing can also be a source of excitement and pleasure (see e.g. Palm, Chap. 7 in this volume). Death is not only grievable or non-grievable, but also, as our case will show, enjoyable or non-enjoyable. Hence our suggestion is that what we are confronted with here can be described as "drone porn." While the word porn has sexual connotations, it should be read here as spectatorial involvement in and arousal or enjoyment of something that may be seductive, although at times morally prohibited. The concept of drone porn highlights responses to distant deaths. Drone porn is the arousal from breaking down the frame that defines a person's life as livable. The moral status of a person is destroyed. The breakdown of the frame and the destruction of moral status are enjoyed as distant domination of the powerless victim through the perceived omnipotent control over life and death.

For some people, viewing the video clip seems to involve feelings of arousal and enjoyment. This excitement also emerges at a distance from the event, that is, from a position of safety. The arousal is therefore produced by combining the obviously violent and dangerous character of the event with the relative safety of consuming such an act through YouTube. Following Palm's (2016) perspective on the dynamics of excitement, drone porn arguably takes place through an oscillation between safety and danger that produces excitement. In this perspective, such oscillation would be at the heart of the dynamic of arousal. The excitement comes from the safety of viewing and experiencing the death and killing at a distance, overcoming one's own vulnerability through the perceived control over this very danger and vulnerability (Palm, 2016). Hence, drone porn could be seen as spectatorial involvement and arousal based on viewing and experiencing the dangers of death at a safe distance. The link between death and pornography has previously been suggested, such as the idea that viewing death in media representations distances the viewer emotionally from acts of death, which parallels the emotional distancing to sex caused by viewing sexual pornography (Gorer, 1984). To sum up, drone porn is expressed as an aesthetic and affectual response to the killing and becomes possible when the life destroyed is seen as not having moral status and, thus, as non-grievable.

While Butler (2009) writes about mourning and grief as a response to the destruction of livable lives, we also introduce the idea of "drone horror." As shall be seen in our analysis, this response is rare but present in our material. Instead of the images evoking pity and compassion for the suffering (cf. Chouliaraki, 2006; Sontag, 2003), drone horror shows that the spectator's enjoyment is in focus, but in its inverse form: disgust. While the moral response concerns the value of a life, the drone porn and drone horror responses are spectatorial, involving the aesthetic side of death and the affectual response triggered by this aesthetics.

Studying the Framings of Livable and Non-livable Lives

Comment sections on the Internet constitute a particular genre of communication, with its own history of politics and policing (Hagren Idevall, 2016; Reagle, 2015). This so-called bottom half of the Internet has been an integral part of YouTube since its inception in 2004. We argue that these comment sections signify the phenomenon of participatory cultures on the Internet. Certain uploaders, some known as "YouTubers," and certain types of video clips gain a following. While we have selected only one case, the results may be transferred to similar types of video clips on YouTube. The comment section arguably signifies a highly current intersection of drone warfare, participatory media, and constructions of actual deaths.

The YouTube video clip selected for analysis had 1297 comments and 2,782,851 views in May 2016, meaning that for every 10,000 viewings, there were four comments.[5] The video clip is bound to gender, age, geographical place, and history, which is shown by the statistics linked to the clip. The number of comments takes the form of an asymmetrical arch spanning from 2008 to 2016, with the highest frequency during the period 2009–12.[6] Most viewers were located in the US, second most in the UK, and third most in Australia and Canada. In addition, the typical viewers are males, most commonly in the age 45–54 years, second 35–44 years, and third 55–64 years.

Participatory culture does not mean that everybody will, or can, participate. Just like any culture, online communities develop their own norms and boundaries, which include certain people and exclude others (Dean, 2001). As the statistics above indicate, this particular comment section is dominated by middle-aged men from the US. From a geopolitical perspective, we can assume that the fact that the majority of commentators are Americans has an impact on the framing of the clip. For example, a distinct "we" is articulated in the comments, referring to "us Americans," most often with Iraqis or Muslims as a contrasting "them." Thus, the discourses of life and death created by this comment section are not universal, but stem from the gaze of those actively participating in the discussions.

In the comment sections, meaning-making is accomplished through language, in text, and therefore we use linguistic methods of text analysis to explore how comments are positioned within the frames presented in Table 11.1 below, constructing certain discourses on life and death. We

Table 11.1 Two frames in the construction of killing by drone strike (response to original framing)

Frame 1. Legitimate kill and moral status of victims as non-livable life	
Moral response	Aesthetic-affectual response
Justified kill	Enjoyed kill (drone porn)
Frame 2. Non-legitimate kill and moral status of victims as livable life	
Moral response	Aesthetic-affectual response
Contested kill	Mourned kill (drone horror)

Source: Authors' own illustration

use methods that explore how commentators use text to take stances on the phenomena they present in their comments and how they communicate with the video clip to which they are responding (cf. Martin & White, 2005). This elaborate analysis shows not only the existence of the different kinds of framings, but also how these framings are made on the linguistic level of meaning-making. The frames draw symbolic boundaries between legitimate and non-legitimate death and killing.

On the YouTube webpage for the video clip, the key frame is the uploader's framing of the event through the title, editing, and description. The construction of death in the comments occurs in response to the video clip and the key frame. In their comments, commentators accept the uploader's framing to different degrees and react to it by either enforcing or resisting it, by expanding or repeating it (Goffman, 1974). We identify two cultural frames that are used by audiences to construct the meaning of killing and death in the video clip. One cultural frame legitimates the killing and the breach of a person's moral status either by justifying the kill or not only justifying, but also enjoying the killing as drone porn. Another cultural frame contests the notion that the kill is justified or not only contests the kill, but also mourns it as drone horror. This description is summarized in Table 11.1.

In an analysis of how responses are articulated, we explore how the victims of the drone attack and the US military, respectively, are being spoken about as well as spoken to. Further on, we analyze to what extent different voices and stances are represented in the comments, for example, by articulating the victim's voice through citation and animation, and how the perspectives of others are being confined, for instance, by disclaimers such as negations (cf. Martin & White, 2005). In addition, positive and negative judgments and appreciations are analyzed to explore the commentators' moral and aesthetic stance on the key frame. Finally, we show how the frames are articulated by illustrating the ways in which attitudes are emphasized, through lexical choices as well as interpunction, such as the use of exclamation marks, smileys, and capital letters. In the following, the results are presented in relation to the two frames according to which commentators respond to the video clip and thus construct life and death in a drone strike killing.

Legitimate Kills and Enjoyable Deaths

In this section, the legitimation of the killing and the construction of the victims as non-livable lives, as non-persons, are discussed as two kinds of responses: *justified kill* and *drone porn*. In the moral response of perceiving the death as a *justified kill*, the killing is legitimized in the comments through moral justifications, claiming that the US had the right to engage fire and that the individuals killed deserved it. These comments respond to the key frame by repeating its understanding of the video clip and adding information to it in order to legitimate the content. Justifications are articulated through propositions that take a stance on the act of killing by using positive judgments. Judgments are made on mainly two themes: the killing was morally right because the individuals hit had weapons and therefore were criminals, and because of the value at risk. The last argument claims that the killing is worth the price in the long run, with respect to both the economic costs of weapons and the costs in human lives.

In one example, we see how a positive judgment is made without any further justifications, but emphasized with three exclamation marks: "Good work!!!" In another comment, a positive judgment of the American army is made with a justification claiming that the victims deserved it, that they were guilty, implicitly saying they had to pay with their lives: "Yeah payback is a bytch huh? … haha … american army is the best … we won so many wars … think about it dumbazz haters." In this example, we also see how the victims are addressed in the question at the beginning of the excerpt. Addressing the victims, who cannot answer, is a way to take a dominant position, ascribing the victims no power at all. This is also common in imperative clauses like the following: "Yaa yaa burn bitches burn thats what u get for threatening our freedom."

Legitimating killing by claiming guilt is often articulated by adding information to the key frame and thus consolidating its meaning. This is the case in the following quote: "If you look closely, the guy in the front has an RGP over his shoulder and an AK, one of the middle guys appears to have a PK M and on [sic] has an Al-Quds/RPK." Evidence showing that the victims have weapons proves they are guilty and justifies the killing as morally right in this situation. Human actors' decisions are not articulated. Yet the quality of the video clip is too low to see whether or not the victims had weapons.

In two of the quotes above, "bitch" is used to refer to the victims. The most common words for the victims in these justifying comments are "terrorists," "insurgents," "ragheads," "enemies" and "bitches." These referential words articulate a negative judgment of the individuals. Moreover, the victims are always referred to as "they," creating a distance between "us Americans" (to which the commentators count themselves) and "the other." The individuals in the clip are Iraqis and Muslims in general.

Justifications including the discourse of costs and value claim that, even though weapons are expensive, it is worth the cost. Making economic calculations concerning the worth of a valuable life has been exemplified by the development of life insurances, where a valuable life is priced (Zelizer, 1979, 1985). However, our findings suggest that the opposite is also possible. People become involved in *economic calculations* to assess the economic costs of *destroying* what is perceived as a *worthless life*, or rather, a negatively valued life. An example of this is shown in the comment below:

> It really is a pain how expensive it is to kill the enemy who are using just a couple hundred dollars worth of weaponry. Then again, considering the lives that can be saved by killing these fanatics it is worth it. It has been the local population that has suffered the most at the hands of these extremists as it is easier to blow up a marketplace than attack a coalition.

The positive judgment of the killing ("it is worth it") draws on the discourse of cost. The justifications construe the act of killing as legitimate and the victims as either guilty or not worthy of living, compared to other values. The lives of the individuals are made non-grievable.

There is, however, one type of comment that justifies the killing, but at the same time seems to make the lives of the victims grievable. As previously stated, justification is sometimes made by letting the weapons determine the guilt. This is also the case in the following comment, but here, the victims are not referred to using negative judgments, but are made into human beings who are loved and thus grievable:

> I admit they were armed and dangerous and they had to be stopped but they were loved by someone and now you think about it for a while and tell me the truth is it nice to make fun of someones [sic] death?

In this example, it is not the frame of justified kill that is contested, but the scorning comments on the clip and the framing of the clip as enjoyment. In the last sentence, this kind of comment is questioned in an interrogative clause, addressing the other commentators.

The audience framing discussed constructs a moral response in which death by drone strike is justified, and the uploader's framing is considered legitimate, constructing the destroyed lives as unlivable. Legitimating the death through this cultural frame constructs the symbolic boundary between the livable and non-livable life. The justifications for the killing are based on moral stances. However, all comments do not deal solely with the moral aspects, but the justification may also be joined by an aesthetic and affectional stance, what here is called *drone porn*. Those who write such comments are primarily spectators. They watch the video clip and then they react to it in an emotional way, expressing feelings and ascribing the clip aesthetic value and thereby adding to the key frame. In the analysis, these expressions are articulated as positive and negative appreciations and positive and negative kinds of affect. In these comments, the stance is more often emphasized through interpunction than it is in comments debating the content.

Drone porn is our term for this spectatorial enjoyment of killing and death by drones. This parallels the human fascination with and desire for repulsive images, such as images of violence and suffering (Goldstein, 1998). Such fascination has at times been associated with the fact that death is a largely hidden facet of life (Gorer, 1984). Drone porn is also similar to war porn. War porn involves the spectacle of creating images that depict the humiliation of people who are being dominated and forced to enact forbidden sexual desires (Baudrillard, 2006). But drone porn is not the same as war porn. In drone porn, the creation of images is not in focus. Rather, drone porn is about the distant yet active consumption of media images of death by drone strike as well as the expressed spectatorial enjoyment and arousal associated with such images. Comments that express drone porn repeat the key frame and legitimate the killing by articulating positive appreciation and affect. In a comment like "its AWESOME cool," positive appreciation is expressed concerning the aesthetics of the clip, emphasized with capital letters. In another comment—"nothing gets our dicks harder than dropping an AGM 114 on some sweaty arab ass!!!"—excitement is articulated with reference to sexual arousal, and it is emphasized, this time using three exclamation marks.

Excitement is articulated in the comments by expressions for laughing and by joking. The short form for laugh out loud (LOL) is commonly used, as well as laughing expressions such as "haha." The emotional response of mockery, irony, and contempt often appears in comments positioning the victims as Muslims, as in the following example: "We sent them to their virgins, admittedly in pieces and rather well done, but Allah can work miracles it is said." Jokes about the victims meeting 72 virgins in heaven draw on Islamophobic discourses, where the joke depicts exclusion through images of Muslims dying (cf. Weaver, 2013). In addition, the jokes become a metaphorical expression for the killing, rendering it something to laugh about.

The emotional reaction transforms the video clip into entertainment, a product to enjoy. Moreover, laughter and jokes are a means to position the victims as "the others" within a racist discourse (cf. Billig, 2001; Malmqvist, 2015). In this process, death is trivialized and the lives of the victims are made not merely into non-grievable lives, but also into enjoyable deaths. The spectatorial gaze turns the scene into fiction, and lives that are fictionalized are not considered livable in the first place (cf. Butler, 2009). However, the process might be reversed: the simulated is extended to the real world (Dorrian, 2014: 52).

Fictionalization is mainly accomplished in two types of comments: comments that use video game metaphors in the response to the video clip and comments that animate the voices of the actors involved, as if they were characters in a film. The war game metaphors are recurrent in the comments. For example, in the comment "just like call of duty 4," an explicit reference to the war game Call of duty is made. In another comment—"enemy AC130 ABOVE!!!!!!!"—the reference is more implicit, in that it uses phrases from the game. Such words ("headshot," "score," "pwned," "killstreak," "points" and "multikill") invoke the voice of the game and make it an actor with the agency to interfere in the meaning-making surrounding the video clip. Therefore, these types of comments also add information to the key frame by putting forward a new perspective.

In the fictionalization, the drone is also made an actor with a voice of its own. The animation of the weapon is common and is often stressed using semiotic resources. In the following quote, "*KABOOM!!!!*," we find an attribution of the weapon/the drone. Here, the victims are also fictionalized by the animation of their voices and a conversion that is made up:

> TERRORIST#1: We will strike down all those who will not bow down to islam, the infidels will perish!! TERRORIST#2: Yes, a great victory will be ours!! We shall … Mustafa, what is that noise? TERRORIST#3: I do not know, it sounds like a missile or … *KABOOM!!!!!*

In the comment, the attribution of the victims is a distancing response to the video. The individuals, positioned as Muslims, are mocked and their dying is trivialized. The discourse of drone porn makes the lives that are destroyed non-grievable because they were never considered livable. The video clip is framed as fiction to be enjoyed and commented on an aesthetic and affective level. The cultural frame of the comments constructs the killing as legitimate and the moral status of victims as non-livable lives. In this frame, drone porn appears as a spectatorial gaze, or an aesthetic and affectual response to the justified killing, where death-by-drone-strike killing is enjoyed.

Contested Kills and Drone Horror

While the comments above repeat and expand the key frame, there are also comments that contest the frame and content of the video clip. This framing thus involves *contesting* the kill and also expanding the contestation by expressing *horror* and disgust for the killing. These comments construct the moral status of the victims as persons, as livable lives. In comments that *contest* the video clip, the killing is not legitimized, and the arguments are based on moral judgments. The contesting is articulated through disclaimers, questioning responses to, and negative judgments about the key frame, as well as propositions expanding it. The most common comment is a questioning response to the title of the clip ("UAV Kills 6 Heavily Armed Criminals"). The proposition that the victims were armed is questioned in interrogative clauses asking for evidence, as in the following comment: "'Heavily armed criminals?' They were walking on the road, in a town, with other civilians nearby, and you fire a Hellfire at them. Awesome job…"

In contrast to the comments that justify the killing, these comments use the positive judgment "civilians" to refer to the victims. By construing them as persons, they are said to be innocent, and the killing was wrong. These individuals are made grievable. This is particularly clear in the quote above, where the victims are said to presumably be someone's father or son. What these comments also indicate, though, is that it might be morally right to kill someone who actually is a criminal, or who is actually carrying weapons. But these particular individuals are not legitimate to kill, because they could just as well have been civilians. The difference between guilt and innocence is thus present here as well. In some comments, this difference is clear, where only the individuals understood as civilians are made grievable through the negative judgments of the drone strike. The judgment is shown in the comment "what about those people walking by just before the explosion? I mean, was one of those guys going to visit his girlfriend? A mailman?" Also in the comment: "You can see 2 people passing before the rocket hits the ground so they died 4 nothing great."

In the first example, an interrogative clause questions the justification of the drone attack by claiming the two by-walkers were civilians. They could have been a mailman or a boyfriend going to visit his girlfriend. In the latter example, a proposition adds information to the key frame; not only the six "terrorists" were killed, but also the two civilians. The contesting constitutes the civilians as grievable. The analysis in this section shows how the audience uses cultural modes discursively to frame the moral status of the victims as livable and the kill as non-legitimate. The audience's attempt to construct the symbolic boundary to include the victims as livable is accomplished by contesting the original framing.

A few comments react to the video clip aesthetically and affectively by expressing horror and disgust for the killing shown, in what is here called *drone horror*. This affective reaction is common in war reporting in the media—reporting that also evokes pity and compassion through images of suffering (Chouliaraki, 2006). The affective response is expressed through comments that take a stance and state an opinion by referring to emotions. The comment "I hate this fucked up world," makes a negative evaluation of the world, it is fucked up, and takes a subjective stance on the world; the commentator hates it. The comment expresses not only hate, but also hopelessness. Another commentator states that the war is "pointless." The killing in the video clip could be understood as an illustration of the war, and the drone horror as a response to this specific case of violence as well as to the situation in "the world."

Drone horror is also expressed in comments that negatively evaluate the content of the video clip. One commentator calls the bombing "inhumane"; another addresses soldiers as a group, writing "what you're doing is evil." Yet another one writes "killing is wrong, isn't it?" In the example below, emotions of reluctance are expressed, "Its creepy," together with a negative appreciation of the posting of video clips like the current one:

> Its creepy watching these video's—They take away the whole essence of human life and the guilt of conscience for taking away another life. It's literally like a Call of Duty game to control one of these things—Not a good thing.

In this comment, a different kind of fictionalization is made than in the drone porn discourse. Instead of associating the content of the video with a war game, the commentator associates the person controlling the drone with someone playing a war game and makes a negative judgment of this type of warfare. The horror is thus a reaction to the violent content of the clip as well as to the act of making the clip public, as a product to consume.

In the few comments expressing drone horror, the lives of the victims are made grievable. The spectatorial and critical gaze adds to the key frame by reacting to it as a product that is not to be enjoyed because of the non-legitimate killing it shows. The aesthetic-affectual response is part of a cultural reframing that constructs a symbolic boundary that portrays the lives destroyed as livable in the first place.

Conclusions: Enjoyment, Superiority, and Inferiority

The drone strike presented in the video clip, the uploader's framing, and the audience response on a social media channel are part of a new amalgam of war propaganda and participatory cultures online. The comments section is not merely a mishmash of individuals' private opinions, but a site for joint meaning-making, where contemporary norms and discourses of morality are constituted. As part of a participatory culture, the video clip triggers not only opinion for or against the war, but also moral and affective stances, expressed by the audience responding to the content. In this context, meaning appears in the reactions. In accordance with Butler's (2009) theories of grievable and non-grievable lives, the comments express stances on what lives are considered valuable and treated as objects of care and grief, as *persons*, and what lives are of no worth and thus killable, as *non-persons*. However, our analysis adds to this dimension an aesthetic-affectual response, where spectatorial enjoyment of death and killing is identified as *drone porn*. We argue that this shift from grieving a life to enjoying the taking of a life correlates with the blurred line between fiction and reality that is jointly created in the participatory culture. The reaction to the video clip as an aesthetic product to consume justifies the moral framing of the killing as righteous.

The concept of drone porn highlights the responses to distant deaths in the form of arousal based on breaking down the frame of a person's life as livable and destroying the moral status of persons. The breakdown of the frame and the destruction of moral status are enjoyed as distant domination of the powerless victim through perceived omnipotent control over life and death. Thus, enjoyment of death creates a distancing division between the superior and the inferior. Comparing the video clip to a war game is one way to create a distance to the killing and the persons being killed. But the distance is also a physical fact in reality, as drone operators are controlling the weapons from a great geographical distance, never having to meet or see the victims other than on a screen. The lack of a physical appearance reinforces the distance and is, perhaps, a prerequisite for the enjoyment of death.

The symbolic distance created through discourse is shown in the perceived anonymous comments that set up symbolic boundaries between "us" and "them." This particular participatory culture also needs to be studied through a geopolitical lens, because most of the people participating in the comment section live in the US or other Western countries, while the victims in the video clip are defined as Muslims and Iraqis. The superior position the commentators take over the victims in the video clip is a situated version of the superior position the US takes in its propaganda for the war in Iraq. The symbolic distancing and physical distancing both create distant enjoyment in the form of drone porn. The combined effect is not only that lives are being destroyed, but also that they are not even seen as livable and precarious in the first place (cf. Butler, 2009).

The phenomena of drone warfare and participatory cultures in social media suggest that we live in an age of technologized anonymity that creates a physical distance to death, but also a discursive and *symbolic distance* to others. Due to this development, high-tech weaponry and distance warfare create a situation in which the armed forces' own troops are not risking their own lives in combat situations (Shaw, 2013). While the causalities and bad memories of previous wars may have stopped militaries from initiating military engagements, these new kinds of highly technologized distance wars may circumvent this hesitation, making it possible for future wars to more easily be initiated (Mann, 2012). Joined by the powerful force of global interconnectedness, online mobilization, and the discursive universes created online, it is possible that findings on the cultural framing of death and killing in participatory media may have further implications in such a future.

Notes

1. An earlier draft of this chapter was presented at the European Sociological Association conference, 7–10 of September 2011 in Geneva, Switzerland. We thank the editors and the Cultural Matters Group at Uppsala University for their comments on earlier versions of the text. We also wish to thank Franz Kernic for suggesting that we study lethal drone strikes.
2. The uploader of the video clip is Defense Video & Imagery Distribution System (DVIDS). DVIDS is owned by Defense Media Activity, which is

a United States Department of Defense (DoD) field activity. DVIDS describes itself as providing "a timely, accurate and reliable connection between the media around the world and the military serving at home and abroad" (https://www.dvidshub.net/about, 29 November 2016).

3. The phenomenon of drone strikes has been around for decades. However, between 2009 and 2016, the Obama administration intensified their drone warfare. Statistics on these drone strikes are both unreliable and hard to come by. Nonetheless, the Obama administration estimated that during this time period 473 drone strikes killed between 2372 and 2581 persons outside the US conventional wars in Iraq, Afghanistan, and Syria (Shane, 2016). Figures and numbers for the drone strikes in Iraq, Afghanistan, and Syria have not been released. But these conventional wars have regularly been reported to involve covert drone operations. The increased use of armed drones can partly be explained by technological developments, but also as a military and political strategy to minimize US military casualties in war and to more effectively kill insurgents through targeted killings. The use of drones for sky-led covert operations and killings has led to ethical conundrums (see Calhoun, 2015). In contrast to being seen as effective for targeted killings, drone operations have been claimed to kill civilians (Shane, 2016). These claims not only lead the Obama administration to reveal statistics about the number of drone strikes outside the conventional wars, but also the number of civilians killed in these drone strikes. The debate about drone warfare has also concerned the stress and trauma experienced by the drone operators effectuating the distant killing (Calhoun, 2015).

4. Officially, the Iraq War was a military engagement authorized by the US Congress, as the US has not declared any wars since the Second World War.

5. The number of times the comments have been read is unknown. Moreover, some comments have disappeared because someone has removed the comment or the account associated with the comment has been deleted. Even though it has been regularly reported that robots make comments (Reagle, 2015), we argue that these comments also become part of the framing process and the construction of death.

6. The cessation of US involvement in the Iraq War in 2011 may explain the decline in the number of comments during the last four years. Moreover, the high numbers of comments from 2009–10 to 2012–13 may also be explained by the highly debated WikiLeaks release of the leaked video clip "Collateral Murder" in April 2010. The video clip shows a helicopter air

strike and includes radio chatter about the attack. It was later reported that two civilian journalists were killed in this attack. The large media coverage following this release and viewings of this video clip may not only have generated an increase in viewings and comments, but may also have set the tone for some of the comments during this period.

References

Andén-Papadopoulos, K. (2009) 'US Soldiers Imaging the Iraq War on YouTube', *Popular Communication*, 7(1), 17–27.

Baudrillard, J. (2006) 'War Porn', *Journal of Visual Culture*, 5(1), 86–88.

Billig, M. (2001) 'Humour and Hatred: The Racist Jokes of the Ku Klux Klan', *Discourse & Society*, 12(3), 267–289.

Boltanski, L. (1999) *Distant Suffering: Morality, Media, and Politics*, Cambridge: Cambridge University Press.

Butler, J. (2009) *Frames of War: When Is Life Grievable?* London: Verso.

Calhoun, L. (2015) *We Kill Because We Can: From Soldiering to Assassination in the Drone Age*, London: Zed Books.

Chouliaraki, L. (2006) *The Spectatorship of Suffering*, London: Sage Publications.

Dean, J. (2001) 'Cybersalons and Civil Society: Rethinking the Public Sphere in Transnational Technoculture', *Public Culture*, 13(2), 243–265.

Dorrian, M. (2014) 'Drone Semiosis', *Cabinet: A Quarterly Journal of Art and Culture*, 54, 48–55.

Goffman, E. (1974) *Frame Analysis: An Essay on the Organization of Experience*, Cambridge: Harvard University Press.

Goldstein, J. (1998) *Why We Watch: The Attractions of Violent Entertainment*, New York: Oxford University Press.

Gorer, G. (1984) 'The Pornography of Death' in E. S. Shneidman (ed.) *Death: Current Perspectives*, Palo Alto: Mayfield Publishing.

Hagren Idevall, K. (2016) *Språk och Rasism: Privilegiering och Diskriminering i Offentlig, Medierad Interaktion*, Uppsala: Uppsala University.

Heemsbergen, L. J. and Lindgren, S. (2014) 'The Power of Precision Air Strikes and Social Media Feeds in the 2012 Israel–Hamas Conflict: 'Targeting Transparency'', *Australian Journal of International Affairs*, 68(5), 569–591.

Hiebert, R. E. (2003) 'Public Relations and Propaganda in Framing the Iraq War: A Preliminary Review', *Public Relations Review*, 29(3), 243–255.

Jenkins, H. (2006) *Convergence Culture: Where Old and New Media Collide*, New York: New York University Press.

Lamont, M. and Molnár, V. (2002) 'The Study of Boundaries in the Social Sciences', *Annual Review of Sociology*, 28(1), 167–195.

Malmqvist, K. (2015) 'Satire, Racist Humour and the Power of (Un)laughter: On the Restrained Nature of Swedish Online Racist Discourse Targeting EU-migrants Begging for Money', *Discourse & Society*, 26(6), 733–753.

Mann, M. (2012) *The Sources of Social Power. Vol. 4, Globalizations, 1945–2011*, Cambridge: Cambridge University Press.

Martin, J. and White, P. (2005) *The Language of Evaluation. Appraisal in English*, Basingstoke: Palgrave Macmillan.

Palm, F. (2016) 'Sexual Arousal, Danger, and Vulnerability' in L. Folkmarson Käll (ed.) *Bodies, Boundaries and Vulnerabilities: Interrogating Social, Cultural and Political Aspects of Embodiment*, Cham: Springer.

Reagle, J. M. (2015) *Reading the Comments: Likers, Haters, and Manipulators at the Bottom of the Web*, Cambridge: MIT Press.

Ritzer, G. and Jurgenson, N. (2010) 'Production, Consumption, Prosumption', *Journal of Consumer Culture*, 10(1), 13–36.

Shane, S. (2016, July 3) 'Drone Strike Statistics Answer Few Questions and Raise Many', *New York Times*, http://www.nytimes.com/2016/07/04/world/middleeast/drone-strike-statistics-answer-few-questions-and-raise-many.html?_r=0.

Shaw, I. G. R. (2013) 'Predator Empire: The Geopolitics of US Drone Warfare', *Geopolitics*, 18(3), 536–559.

Sontag, S. (2003) *Regarding the Pain of Others*, London: Penguin.

Weaver, S. (2013) 'A Rhetorical Discourse Analysis of Online Anti-Muslim and Anti-Semitic Jokes', *Ethnic and Racial Studies*, 36(3), 483–499.

Zelizer, V. (1979) *Morals and Markets: The Development of Life Insurance in the United States*, New York: Columbia University Press.

Zelizer, V. (1985) *Pricing the Priceless Child: The Changing Social Value of Children*, New York: Basic Books.

12

To Make Pets Live, and To Let Them Die: The Biopolitics of Pet Keeping

David Redmalm

Introduction

In Mary Shannon Johnstone's (2016, n.d.) photography art project *Breeding Ignorance*, she visits animal shelters to document the incarceration and mass killing of dogs and cats (Fig. 12.1). She points out that in North Carolina alone, more than 250,000 abandoned dogs and cats are euthanized every year. Seeing puppies gathered in a corner awaiting euthanasia, a pile of cats in a freezer, and dogs put in black trash bags is a forceful reminder that the global kennel complex kills pets on an industrial scale. "We are simply breeding more animals than we have homes for," Johnstone concludes (n.d.: n.p.). This chapter focuses on humans' tension-filled relationship to companion animals. Pets—the animals under humans' care living within or in proximity of the home—are often considered to be friends or part of the nuclear family, and many pets are grieved when they die. Therefore, the very term "pet" is derogatory, as it

D. Redmalm (✉)
Mälardalen University, Västerås, Sweden
e-mail: david.redmalm@mdh.se

© The Author(s) 2019
T. Holmberg et al. (eds.), *Death Matters*,
https://doi.org/10.1007/978-3-030-11485-5_12

241

Fig. 12.1 Mary Shannon Johnstone, a photo of euthanized dogs in plastic bags, from Breeding Ignorance

reduces these nonhuman animal companions to one-dimensional objects of caress—to mere belongings (Redmalm, 2013: 17). But pets are also routinely bred in abundance and are sold, given away, abandoned and quickly forgotten, or euthanized because they are unwanted. Therefore, the word "pet" comprises companion animals' ambivalent position as being *subject to* and the *object of* human care, in between dominance and affection (Tuan, 1984).

The aim of this chapter is to suggest a way of understanding pet keeping in the light of this paradox. This chapter accomplishes this using Michel Foucault's notion of *biopolitics*, a kind of decentralized governing based on the idea that each member of society can be regarded at once as an irreplaceable individual and as a consumable resource. Rather than traditional dominant, totalitarian, or sovereign power that relies on violence and corporeal punishment, the biopolitical state is ruled according to the logic of biopower, a power that has the right "to make live and to let die" (Foucault, 2003: 241). To make pets live and to let them die, to breed, and to euthanize, are equally central to the pet keeping industry. The study of animals and biopolitics is growing, although pets have been underexplored, most efforts focusing on animals in the food industry and in laboratories (see Asdal et al. 2016; Chrulew & Wadiwel, 2017). However, pets are particularly interesting because they are affected by human treatment and change their behavior accordingly, while they to some extent have the freedom to move around in contexts dominated by humans and affect their owners and others. Thinking through pet love and pet death, this chapter argues, also sheds light on the dynamics that make some lives grievable while others are rendered ungrievable (see also Fürst and Idevall Hagren, Chap. 11 this volume for a discussion of Butler's notion of grievability). To make live and to let die are thus also central to the experience of the individual pet keeper—as Carmen Dell'Aversano (2010: 104) puts it, "to love an animal means to allow death into one's life." Most pets have a shorter life span than humans, so choosing to enrich one's life with a nonhuman companion introduces this biopolitical dilemma into one's daily life.

In the first section, titled "To make pets live," I use Foucauldian theory to discuss humans' preoccupation with pets and the social institutions and normative frameworks that make pets live and thrive in human societies. The section follows Heidi J. Nast's (2006) call for a "critical pet studies," a research field that draws on a Foucauldian notion of power to identify the social structures that have made pet love possible and increasingly popular during the twentieth and twenty-first centuries. In the second section, "Threshold," I turn to the work of Giorgio Agamben, who relies on Foucault's work on biopolitics to examine the peculiar analogy between the status of pets and human citizens of contemporary democratic states. Pets exist at the intersection of the line between invaluable and disposable life, and the line between human and animal. Agamben argues that these two distinctions were integral to the formation of larger societies, which is why I suggest that pets help humans take a biopolitical approach to human life. This analogy between human and nonhuman animals—their shared biopolitical condition—will be further explored in the subsequent section: "To let pets die." When pets die the tragedy of an individual fate and biopolitical norms and calculations converge. Drawing on the work of Judith Butler, and my previous studies of expressions of grief for pets (e.g., Redmalm, 2015, 2018), I show how pets' ambivalent status is accentuated, and their biopolitical condition is laid bare, when pet owners face their pets' transience and death. I argue that pet keeping can be regarded as a demarcated zone where norms surrounding life and death can be played with, managed, and reproduced. In the relationship between pet and owner, humans are allowed to address pets' biopolitical subjectivity in a relatively secure and delimited manner, which helps reinforce the wider biopolitical condition in contemporary societies. With the section "The ever after" I ask: Is there life after the politics of life and death? I suggest that by taking into consideration the shared precariousness between humans and animals, and the exchanges of wordless gestures fundamental to the relationship, the relationship between humans and other animals could open up an alternative "ever after" from within a biopolitical playground.

To Make Pets Live

Foucault's (1978, 2003) concept of biopolitics refers to the way society is governed through the statistical monitoring and measurement of bodies, sexuality, migration, and ways of life; disciplinary institutional machineries; and a set of knowledge and norms redistributed to the wider population. This is a decentralized form of power, or *biopower*—a power that has the right "to make live and to let die" (Foucault, 2003: 241). Biopower is employed through a number of biopolitical technologies, among others a "natalist policy" (Foucault, 2003: 243). The state needs to secure a certain birth rate and a certain level of health among its citizens to continue to exist, and thus ideas regarding reproduction and norms of the nuclear family, as well as health ideals, are distributed throughout society. "Letting die," or what Agamben (1998) calls *thanatopolitics*, is an extension of biopolitics. Thanatos was a god of death in Ancient Greek mythology, and the term designates the technologies used for disposing of superfluous or unwanted life. The uneven distribution of wealth and the prioritization of economic gain over environmental concerns, which considerably decrease the lifespan of a large number of people worldwide, are examples of contemporary forms of thanatopolitics deployed in post-world war democratic states.

With a nod to Foucault's *Birth of the Clinic*, Donna Haraway (2008: 139) argues that "the birth of the kennel had all the constitutive discourses in place from the first appearance of the formation." Rather than an actual geographical place or a specific organization, Haraway regards the kennel as a material-semiotic node at which technology, knowledge, power relationships, and norms converge. The kennel is a set of technologies for breeding nonhuman animals according to humans' expectations. The kennel is also a set of normative ideas about maintaining a healthy nonhuman gene pool through breeding and selection in order to maximize the quality of human life. Thus, the kennel is indeed characterized by a "natalist policy," just like the modern democratic welfare state. The "letting die" aspect of biopolitics is also clearly visible in the kennel: surplus dogs are routinely killed in an anonymizing machinery that makes it possible to let them die. Nonhuman animals with unwanted physical and behavioral traits are sterilized or prevented from procreating. Pet owners also sometimes let beloved pets die—pets are regularly euthanized when their owners do not feel they are living life to the fullest due to illness or old age.

The fact that pets are bought and sold on a market is one reason why they so conveniently fit into the biopolitical scheme. Pet keeping takes place within a juridical and ideological framework—termed *animal welfarism* by Francione (2000)—that presupposes that humans own animals, and that animals are resources for human pleasure. Pets are mass produced and constantly available, but nonetheless imbued with uniqueness and authenticity, turning them into irreplaceable and invaluable individuals. Pets make perfect commodities, because they can be mass produced, yet remain unique (Boggs, 2013: 186; Redmalm, 2014; for a similar argument, see Kania-Lundholm Chap. 9 this volume on the commodification of dead celebrities). This enables humans to regard pets as things while at the same time benefiting emotionally from the relationship. It also allows them to treat one or a few nonhuman animals as pets, while excluding other animals from ethical concern. Thus, pets without a human caretaker are categorized as strays, as feral, or perhaps as pests, and are rendered "killable" within the animal welfarism paradigm (see Holmberg, 2017). The thin line between pet and pest is just as thin as that between biopolitics and thanatopolitics.

According to Foucault, power is enacted through a bipolar technology: It is both normative and disciplinary in an embodied manner—"it can also be direct, physical, pitting force against force, bearing on material elements" (Foucault, 1977: 26; see also Foucault, 1978: 139). Society engages the citizen in disciplinary processes in schools, hospitals, and prisons, whereby a "soul" is produced "around, on, [and] within the body" (Foucault, 1977: 29) of the citizen. In this way, docile souls and docile bodies are created that fit neatly into the larger normative biopolitical scheme. These docile subjects do not necessarily have to be human, although Foucault focused on matters of human subjectivity. Several scholars have suggested that the subject of such a power can be both human and nonhuman (see Kirk, 2017: 201; Palmer, 2001; Wolfe, 2013: 37). The kind of decentralized and relational power Foucault conceptualized is rarely transparent to the beings subjected to it, these scholars argue. Subjects regularly reproduce power relationships without being conscious of doing so, which means that a nonhuman being acting within a certain social structure can actively reproduce that structure. Whether that nonhuman being is aware of what is going on is a non-issue, just as human cognition was largely a non-issue for Foucault.

Following this line of argument, it is possible to say that pets have subjectivity and are imbued with a "soul" in Foucault's sense (Palmer, 2001, 2003: 52; Chrulew, 2017). As long as pets are framed as relatively free within an anthropocentric context, this opens the door to governing nonhuman "free" subjects within disciplinary and biopolitical frameworks. Palmer (2001) argues that fences, doors, leashes, neutering, and spaying, as well as instrumental training methods are all disciplinary technologies that have dominant features, but they also presuppose that pets have some kind of scope for agency and "freedom" (see also Rose, 1999). A fence may seem inhibiting, but within the fencing, pets are allowed to act on at least some impulses and interests. Likewise, neutering and spaying eliminate some behaviors and drives in the pet, but will also make the pet more widely accepted in a human-centered community and thus freer, albeit in a narrow sense. Neutering and spaying are also biopolitical technologies, in that they are used to control reproduction. Another disciplinary-biopolitical technology is pet pharmacology. Wolfe (2013: 54) notes that Reconcile, a drug identical with Prozac, is given to dogs to treat separation anxiety. People who live with pets on Prozac may experience them to be slightly duller, but also more predictable and reliable from a human perspective, and the pets can thus be allowed some leeway in the lives of humans. Seen in this light, pet pharmacology can be regarded as a dominant, disciplinary, and biopolitical technology—all at once.

Even the mere act of touching is a disciplinary technology: pet owners are generally advised to touch and handle their pets from early age to create docile bodies—to make them insensitive and compliant to human treatment (Palmer, 2001; Wadiwel, 2017). However, it is interesting to note that bestiality is always associated with stigma and social prohibition, unlike the act of killing an animal (Wadiwel, 2017). Passing the threshold between petting and a sexual act would threaten the distinction between humans and other animals, while killing does not. While the idea of bestiality threatens the boundary between humans and other animals, both "disciplinary" caressing and killing appear to fit into the biopolitical scheme that modern societies assume.

Pets must be framed as "free" if they are to be governed, which also means that pets can actively participate in the reproduction of disciplinary power relations and the proliferation of biopolitical normativity. One example of this is the Obama Family's dog Bo Obama (Skoglund & Redmalm, 2017). By framing Bo Obama as a free and slightly unruly individual, the imagery around Bo and Barack Obama gains normative efficiency. Whether it is Barack Obama playing football or running through the White House corridors together with Bo, or his children playing with the dog against the backdrop of the White House—such press photos give the powerful leader a human face. Bo Obama thus assists in the proliferation of family norms and reproduces normative aspects of "doggy-biopolitics" (Skoglund & Redmalm, 2017).

Some scholars have suggested that, at least to some extent, the very fabric of the family is changing into a "furry family" (Power, 2008) or a "posthuman family" (Charles, 2016; see also Fox, 2006; Smith, 2003), which blurs the boundary between human and animal and decenters the human subject. Yet, after having taken a closer look at Haraway's kennel, inclusion of pets in the family can be regarded as a way of maximizing both human and nonhuman life, in alignment with a biopolitical logic. Thus, although pet keeping includes boundary-transgressing features, these practices, as Charles (2016: 10) puts it, "exist alongside others which reinforce it." Individual pets are appreciated as friends and family members, but the elevation of an individual pet presupposes a system in which humans have the power to decide whether their pets should live or die as well as the ultimate power over all other animals.

Threshold

A biopolitical analysis of pet keeping shows that pets exist on the threshold between invaluable and disposable life. Agamben has theorized this threshold, as well as the threshold between humanity and animality, which makes his theoretical work imperative to the understanding of pet keeping. In this section, I discuss how Agamben can shed light on the fundamental biopolitical function of pets. Human biopolitical subjects can mirror themselves in pets: Pets and humans are subjected to a similar set of biopolitical technologies, yet pets exist on the opposite side of the human-animal divide, which gives humans power over pets through these technologies. I argue that the idea of the pet helps humans think about life in terms of biopolitics.

Agamben adopts Foucault's notion of biopolitics, but while Foucault associates the birth of biopolitics with Enlightenment ideas and ideals, Agamben (1998) argues that because the birth of the state far precedes modernity, so does biopolitics. The administration of all larger societies—societies where all members do not act in direct relation to each other, and where the community is secured by symbolic means—relies on society members' ability to think of the other members both as kin and as an abstract number, as both fellow humans and as resources in food production and warfare. Agamben thus argues that every state formation is founded on the distinction between political life, *bios*, and non-human life belonging to the domain of nature, *zoē*, which lacks the rights of the citizen and is excluded from the state. The idea of political life thus presupposes a notion of something outside the reach of state power, which means that the formation of the state builds on an "inclusion of what is simultaneously pushed outside" (Agamben, 1998: 18).

For Agamben, *bios* is reserved for humans, although not all humans qualify as *bios*. Agamben argues consequently that political life is fundamentally precarious. *Bios* can at any moment be reduced to a state close to *zoē*, which Agamben (1998: 13) calls "bare life": a state where one adheres to normative expectations in constant fear of being bereaved of the fundamental rights associated with *bios* (see also Butler, 2009: 16; Stanescu, 2012). The liminal creatures roaming the boundaries between *bios* and *zoē* are no longer fully human, but not quite animal either. He refers to these beings as *homines sacri* (sacred humans), a concept borrowed from the juridical term for the lawless in ancient Roman law. Agamben suggests that in contemporary liberal democracies "the realm of bare life [...] gradually begins to coincide with the political realm" (Agamben, 1998: 9) and that bare life "now dwells in the biological body of every living being" (Agamben, 1998: 140). This means that the marginal *homines sacri* are becoming the norm through the expansion of the state apparatus, and the increasingly flexible juridical framework fueled by the neoliberal deconstruction of the state and the "war on terrorism." Thus, the making of bare life is a constant threat against humans in contemporary nation states. But do not many nonhuman animals face the same conditions, given that animals are both widely anthropomorphized and objectified and used as resources in modern societies?

Agamben does not discuss the biopolitical status of nonhuman animals, instead he is first and foremost interested in the notion of "the animal" in the sense of animality. In other words, Agamben is interested in "the animal" as an idea because, as he argues, the reproduction and constant negotiation of the boundary between humans and animals are crucial to the making of *homines sacri*. In relation to ideas about "the animal," humans define themselves as humans, although there is no singular way of actually separating humans from all other animals. Humans can separate themselves from others by ascribing them animal characteristics. Psychoanalysis and modern biology have also identified an "inner animal" within the human—humans can define themselves as human by claiming to isolate and control their animal within. Agamben (2004: 26–7) calls this constant negotiation of an inner and outer human-animal boundary *the anthropological machine*, "an optical machine constructed of a series of mirrors in which man, looking at himself, sees his own image always already deformed in the features of an ape." The anthropological machine ensures that humans are distinguished from other animals, but also that there is a constant conceptual dependency between the two poles. Thus, human society partly relies on an impending threat of becoming animal, which makes humans adhere to a specific normative idea of being human, while those who refuse or do not fit into this conception are excluded (Alt, 2011: 148).

This threat is most prominent in what Agamben (1998) refers to as *zones of indistinction*—places such as refugee camps, concentration camps, and prisons. These places are organized to create bare life—to produce a context where the boundary between valuable and disposable life is dissolved so that life can be seen as *bios*, yet treated as *zoē*. This presence of bare life reminds the wider population of their precarious biopolitical condition. Kirk (2017) suggests that there are zones of indistinction designed to turn nonhuman animals into a similar liminal state—into *animalia sacri*. Laboratory animals, he suggests, enter into a zone of indistinction where the line between *bios* and *zoē* has ceased to exist, because they are both reared and cared for, but most often killed after the experiment. The kennel, in Haraway's sense of the word, can also be seen as a zone of indistinction, and pets as *animalia sacri*. While pets are in a vulnerable position in anthropocentric societies, many pets are privileged compared to millions of humans, especially in the face of the humanitarian crises of the twentieth and twenty-first centuries. Wolfe (2013: 54) concludes that "many animals flourish not in spite of the fact that they are 'animals' but *because* they are 'animals.'" Pets thus exist in an ambivalent zone of indistinction—a sort of *benevolent camp* (Diken, 2004)—that comes not only with hazards but also with privileges.

Within this zone, humans' relationship with pets forces humans to face the close connection between *bios* and *zoē*, and to negotiate their relationship both to their animal pet and to their own inner animal. Through interviews with pet owners, I have previously shown how they put the anthropological machine to work and draw on quasi-scientific explanations to conceptualize their pets' behavior as animal behavior (Redmalm, 2013). This allows the owners to distance themselves from their animals. But these biological explanations can also be applied to the humans themselves: Owners of, for example, dogs, cats, and rats can recognize their own mammal selves in their pets' characteristics, behaviors, and needs. A clear indication of this ambiguous stance is that dog owners, as well as some cat owners, often use the words "pack" and "family" interchangeably. Pets are often referred to by humans as family members, but pet owners also refer to themselves as their pets' pack members. In this way, both humans and nonhumans achieve the status of biological as well as political life within the frames of the relationship. Another indication is that cat and dog owners sometimes joke about their animals being true carnivores. Dogs will take the alpha position the first chance they get. Cats are referred to as "killing machines" and would bite their owners' head off if only the cats were big enough.

Some of the features of pets associated with *zoē* are deeply valued by pet owners. They often emphasize that their pets teach them an "animal" way of living. Such a way of life emphasizes the importance of play and of living for the moment rather than accumulating belongings or climbing the career ladder (Redmalm, 2013). Yet all these traits are focused around the individual, and the sphere of the home and the closest community. In other words, the traits gained from pet ownership can be seen as ways of maximizing the human individual's life, turning that individual into someone with a docile mind in tune with the biopolitical machinery. Thus, through pet keeping, the close connection between *bios* and *zoē*, and between bio- and thanatopolitics, is reflected, managed, and reproduced. Pet ownership is not only a mere symptom of biopolitics, it is also an arena where humans can learn to conceive of life according to the biopolitical scheme by engaging with pets—creatures who incorporate *bios* and *zoē* at the same time. Carnivorous companion animals bring violence and death into the everyday and turn it into something natural. Consequently, pet keeping prepares pet owners to accept their own biopolitical condition.

Although contemporary forms of pet keeping are associated with the affluence of the post-war Western world, this ambiguous approach to nonhuman animals far precedes modernity. In fact, both biopolitics and the idea of a nonhuman animal companion seem to date back to the first sedentary societies and the early states. There is archeological evidence that early states made proto-biopolitical calculations of both human laborers and herds of domestic animals, and slaves as well as livestock were managed through controlled reproduction and continuous surveying in these societies (Scott, 2017). In the biopolitical state, the majority benefits from the disadvantaged minorities, soldiers are sacrificed to protect the rest of the population, and both human workers and nonhuman animals suffer to secure the life quality of the privileged. Citizens will thus have to accept that life can essentially be separated into two categories, invaluable and disposable, and that any given life must be able to pass between these categories for the survival of the state. But this also means that when humans pass into *zoē*, it enables a movement in the opposite direction: A low threshold between *bios* and *zoē* also allows nonhuman animals to achieve the status of *bios*. Archeologists have found remains of dogs in graves many thousand years old at various locations, some as old as from the first sedentary societies in the Eastern Mediterranean from the pre-Nauftian (23,000–11,500 BCE) and Nauftian (13,000–9800 BCE) eras (Collier, 2016). The character and context of the findings suggest that the buried animals were considered to be persons, or unique individuals, possibly with a "soul." I therefore wish to suggest, somewhat speculatively, that the formation of early larger sedentary societies made it possible for humans to conceive of the idea of a nonhuman companion—the idea of the pet. In turn, pets' presence in larger societies has facilitated the reproduction of the biopolitical condition. In the next section, I will further explore the connection between biopolitics and the mourning of individual animals.

To Let Pets Die

Butler (2004, 2009) has explored how normative frameworks structure the experience of loss so that some lives are grieved, while other lives can come to an end without a single tear being shed. While Butler argues that grief is central to human communities—we grieve those we think of as included in a "we"—Butler's perspective on grief does not presuppose that a grieved life is necessarily a human life. Indeed, she has described her approach as "a non-anthropocentric framework for considering what makes life valuable" (Antonello & Farneti, 2009: n.p.; see also Stanescu, 2012). Her approach thus allows us to study to what extent animals are made grievable. Butler connects her theorizing of grief to the work of Agamben, and points out that, because human lives are not always grieved, we cannot rely on the human/animal distinction alone to understand how life becomes grievable. Rather, it is a matter of which lives are regarded as livable, meaningful, and intelligible—a line of thought close to Agamben's distinction between *bios* and *zoë*.

Relying on Butler's conceptualization of grief, and my own work on pet grief in various contexts, I will now discuss how the tension between *bios* and *zoë* is handled in expressions and representations of grief for pets. Pet owners often compare losing a pet to losing a friend or a family member (Redmalm, 2015). Furthermore, there are a number of services available to pet owners who have lost a nonhuman animal companion, such as condolence cards for bereaved pet owners, mortuaries specializing in pets, and therapy and self-help books on how to deal with the loss of a pet (Redmalm, 2018; Witt, 2003). However, pet owners also risk meeting social sanctions as a consequence of the norms surrounding human-animal relationships (Morley & Fook, 2005). Therefore, humans grieving the loss of a pet are referred to delineated social and geographical spheres, like pet cemeteries (Witt, 2003: 765) or friendship networks (Redmalm, 2015).

Butler's perspective can be summarized in three points. First, for a life to be grieved, it must be regarded as irreplaceable. According to Butler (Butler, 2004: 20f; 2009: 14, 98), we become who we are through our relations to others, so when someone important to us passes away, we cannot remain the same. Second, there is an unpredictable force in the loss of a grievable life—the existential uncertainty that a grievable loss brings with it makes it transformative (Butler, 2004: 46). Third, there must be a shared embodied relationship between the grieving person and the grieved (Butler, 2004: 26–7; 2009: 29–31). We are born dependent on others, and intimate relationships are often physical, Butler explains

(Butler, 2004: 31; 2009: 14). Therefore, loss is always a bodily experience.

Pets are generally described as *irreplaceable* beings who will be remembered forever when they die. In interviews with pet owners (Redmalm, 2015), in condolence cards (Redmalm, 2016, 2018) and in dog handbooks (Redmalm, 2014), the loss of a pet is repeatedly compared to that of a human friend or family member. Many tombstones at pet cemeteries also describe the deceased pet as an irreplaceable family member, and the owners as "moms" and "dads" (Redmalm & Schuurman, 2017). But pets are also to some extent made exchangeable in the way they are talked about as biological beings, as members of a breed or species with certain characteristics that are appreciated independently of the individual expressing them (Redmalm, 2015). For example, while human condolence cards basically never depict humans, most pet condolence cards have photographs, paintings, drawings or silhouettes of nonhuman animals (Redmalm, 2018). Rather than paying respect to the individual that has been lost, the cards instead focus on the fact that the recipient has lost a member of a species—a dog, a cat, a rat.

When turning to the second aspect of grief, the *unpredictable* force of loss, the same ambivalence can be found. Unpredictability is both visible and downplayed in various ways in expressions of grief for nonhuman animals. Dedicated pet owners can talk extensively about how deeply affected they were by the loss of a beloved pet. At the same time, a pet's death can be planned: death seldom arrives suddenly, but is often the result of a decision that has been carefully thought trough and discussed with a veterinarian. Accordingly, handbooks for dog owners urge readers to plan for the coming and going of pets in their lives. For example, Coile (2003: 89) writes that the bereaved pet owner should start looking for a "second once-in-a-lifetime dog" because "another Chihuahua is a welcome diversion and will help keep you from dwelling on the loss of your first love." It is common among pet owners to plan loss and pet adoption in this way, which can be seen as a way to curb the unpredictability of loss. The unpredictability of loss can also be handled by framing the pet's death as something natural. Pet cemeteries are often planned and managed in harmony with the surrounding green area and the shifting seasons.

The emphasis on the connection between pets and nature as part of the same circle of life frames pet loss as predictable and "natural."

Finally, in relation to the third aspect of grief—the *embodied* character of grievable loss—pet owners regularly talk about their own bodily experience of loss, as well as the bodies of dying pets. Many pet owners describe how animals who have died leave an almost palpable absence behind, and how the loss can be felt as physical pain (see also Chap. 2). But many pet owners attest that they also actively scan their elderly pets for bodily signals of pain, signals that can be used as grounds for a euthanasia decision. Pet owners thus take the role of the empathic friend, sharing the pet's suffering, on the one hand, and the owner proper, trying to decide whether the living commodity is still operative or needs to be terminated, on the other. Agamben (1998: 142) argues that "[e]uthanasia signals the point at which biopolitics necessarily turns into thanatopolitics." From a biopolitical perspective, pets' lives need to be maximized to benefit the lives of humans. But from a thanatopolitical perspective, lives that are not lived to the fullest, and are not considered to be fully human, are rendered disposable. One dog handbook urges the reader to "[l]et him [the dog] die while he's living" (O'Neil, 2008: 231). This formulation truly comprises Agamben's point about euthanasia.

Mourning pets is a balancing act between proximity and distance, between making pets grievable and ungrievable, between embracing life and letting die. Mourned pets move back and forth between *bios* and *zoē*, and the close paradoxical connection between these kinds of lives is accentuated. This way of approaching the lives of animals is fortified by many animals' short lifespan: Many pet owners will experience several unique nonhuman lives come and go during their own lifespan. In consequence, pets' death can be experienced as extremely painful and as manageable—both reactions to loss are present at the same time and equally real. By extension, this stance on pet loss and grief mirrors the biopolitical mechanisms ensuring that humans can be at once persons and resources. When the ambivalence becomes acute in the moment of loss and in times of grief, this also means that humans' ambivalent relationship to other animals in general is reinforced. Through pet grief, pet owners learn to think of *bios* and *zoē* in tandem.

The Ever After

In his analysis of the present state of Western liberal democracies, Agamben suggested that bare life "now dwells in the biological body of every living being" (1998: 140). As I have argued, "every living being" should be understood in a wide sense, including nonhuman animals, which means that humans and other animals share the same biopolitical condition. This does not only have fatal, thanatopolitical consequences for nonhuman animals. The inclusion of pets in the biopolitical scheme also means that pets proliferate and flourish in human societies. In turn, humans' lives are enhanced—humans benefit emotionally and physically from living with pets.

Scholars studying multispecies biopolitics have suggested that the inclusion of pets in the biopolitical scheme can turn biopolitics against itself. McHugh (2011: 20) suggests that the parallel biopoliticization of human and nonhuman lives enables "biopolitical potentials of love." Boggs (2013) follows a similar line of reasoning and posits that when humans make nonhuman animals into commodities, the fact that pets can respond to this commodification debunks capitalism's commodity fetishist fantasy and makes possible economies of desire and reciprocity as alternatives to capitalist logic. Stanescu (2012) in turn suggests that loss highlights the fundamental condition of precariousness, or the condition of bare life, that humans share with other animals. If humans took into consideration their shared status of bare life that contemporary society imposes on humans and other animals alike, it could work as a starting point for ethical responsibility for other animals. Indeed, Butler (2004, 2009) argues that we challenge the very frameworks of grievability when we make someone grievable in conflict with prevalent norms, that is, when we recognize as grievable life that is generally regarded as bare life or *zoē*.

However, as I have suggested, there is also a risk that negotiation of pet grief will reinforce the anthropological machine that makes *bios* and *zoē* coincide. Elevating animal life to a human-like status is itself a kind of politicization of life, and such elevation of some nonhuman lives does not counteract future distinctions between *bios* and *zoē*—between invaluable and disposable life. As a closed realm, pet keeping, including the rituals and practices around pet loss, becomes a way to momentarily play with the boundaries between *bios* and *zoē*. Life in the kennel becomes a reminder that within biopower, there is never a clear demarcation between *bios* and *zoē*, and between human and animal, to begin with.

Agamben also theorizes a way to exist beyond biopolitics, and similar to Stanescu's suggestion, he turns to a form of existence rooted in the body. In a society where life itself was not politicized, inhabitants would find common ground through nothing but the lack of a common ground, a belonging, or a shared identity—a society "without presuppositions and without subjects," as Agamben (1993: 70) writes. Agamben (1999; ten Bos, 2005) argues that the "gesture" could be key to thinking about such a society. The gesture is a wordless act that, in sharp contrast to the biopolitical rationale, lacks linguistic categorizations and teleology, and does not belong to an organizational structure. Here, it is possible to make an anti-anthropocentric reading of Agamben: The emphasis on the gesture is a way to challenge the politicization of life without reproducing human life as the norm. Above I discussed petting as a disciplinary technology, but petting can also serve as a gesture in Agamben's sense in some situations. Wadiwel (2017: 311) suggests that petting can be a way of creating local forms of resistance against biopolitical normalization, through the creation of an "exceptional friendship" in contrast to "the large scale war against animals." I will end this chapter by giving an example of such a context.

Conclusions

This chapter set out to explore the paradox that pets are both subject to and the object of human care—that pets are both treated as autonomous subjects with their own interests and unique traits, and objects that can be purchased, sold, and disposed of depending on their owners' needs and wishes. I have suggested that pet keeping can be regarded as a demarcated zone where norms surrounding life and death can be played with. In this way, pets help humans conceive of and also accept the biopolitical predicament that humans and many other animals share. Sometimes, this playfulness leaks out from the delimited sphere of the kennel, away from categorizations of life and identity negotiations to an uncharted and rougher territory. This happens when exchanges of gestures and "exceptional friendships" across species boundaries (Wadiwel, 2017) force humans to reconsider the commodification of life, animal welfarism, or other biopolitical technologies and rationales. In these cases, the human-pet relationship, which is usually confined to the home and the private sphere, is made political. Let me end this chapter by discussing an example of a gesticulation that highlights the biopolitical framework that simultaneously differs between and shapes human and nonhuman lives—a gesticulation that potentially points ahead toward a life in the ever after that follows biopolitics and anthropocentrism.

A photograph from Mary Shannon Johstone's project *Breeding Ignorance* opened this chapter. In a later project called *Landfill Dogs*, Johnstone decided to take dogs facing euthanasia out on a trip to a landfill where the dogs will be buried when euthanized, together with household trash. Every dog in the project is photographed behind bars, and then during the trip. In the latter photographs, the dogs move around freely. In a few images, a human is also visible, touching, playing with, or jumping around together with the dogs. Although Johnstone hopes that the photos will attract possible adopters, she knows that most of the dogs will not be saved. The immediate purpose of the trip is simpler: "Each dog receives a car ride, a walk, treats, and about 2 hours of much-needed individual attention," she explains (landfilldogs.com/about). For two hours, the exchange of wordless gestures, rather than disciplining and normative expectations, is in the center of the interaction—an exchange that does not immediately generate economic gain, or rely on stereotypical ideas about what a human and what an animal are. For a moment, the dogs transcend their precarious position in the bio- and thanatopolitical scheme.

Gestures and bodily expressions can always be categorized as symbols or reduced to behaviorist reactions. But Johnstone has found a way of bringing out Agamben's gesture without at the same time reproducing a biopolitical constellation of *bios* and *zoē*. And she does so without resorting to the conceptually well-ordered sphere of the interpersonal human-pet relationship, where boundaries between invaluable and disposable life, and between life and death, can be transgressed relatively safely.

Instead, she chooses a highly thanatopoliticized place as playground. By the landfill, the dogs' liminality is not used to normalize the fundamental, biopolitical condition that humans and other animals share. Instead, this liminality is made into the topic of an intervention against biopolitics itself. Here, the exchanges of gestures between Johnstone and the "landfill dogs" bring the relationship between politics, life, death, and play into broad daylight. Through the exchange of gestures, and the display of these gestures through her art, Johnstone recognizes that the dogs are grievable, not as humans or as animals, but as *animalia sacri*—as beings existing on the threshold between *bios* and *zoē*, both conceptually and very literally, given their impending fate (Fig. 12.2).

Fig. 12.2 Mary Shannon Johnstone, "Akimbo" from Landfill Dogs

Acknowledgments I want to thank Mary Shannon Johnstone for kindly giving me permission to use her photos. I am also immensely grateful to the editors of this volume for their thorough and thoughtful feedback at several stages of the writing process. Furthermore, I received invaluable suggestions from the members of the HumAnimal Group at the Centre for Gender Research, Uppsala University. This chapter was written as an extension of the research project *Intimate Sociality*, funded by the Swedish Research Council (no. 421-2014-1465). It is an expansion of ideas that I originally presented in a short text in Swedish in the journal *Fronesis* (no. 56–7, 2017).

References

Agamben, G. (1993) *The Coming Community*, Minneapolis: University of Minnesota.

Agamben, G. (1998) *Homo Sacer: Sovereign Power and Bare Life*, Stanford: Stanford University.

Agamben, G. (1999) 'Kommerell, or On Gesture', in D. Heller-Roazen (ed.) *Potentialities: Collected Essays in Philosophy*, Stanford: Stanford University.

Agamben, G. (2004) *The Open: Man and Animal*, Stanford: Stanford University.

Alt, S. (2011) 'Problematizing Life Under Biopower: A Foucauldian Versus an Agambenite Critique of Human Security', in D. Chandler and N. Hynek (eds.) *Critical Perspectives on Human Security: Rethinking Emancipation and Power in International Relations*, London: Routledge.

Antonello, P. and Farneti, R. (2009) 'Antigone's Claim: A Conversation with Judith Butler', *Theory & Event*, 12(1), http://muse.jhu.edu/journals/theory_and_event/v012/12.1.antonello.-html, accessed 12 July 2012.

Asdal, K., Druglitrø, T. and Hinchliffe, S. (eds.) (2016) *Humans, Animals and Biopolitics: The More-than-Human Condition*, London: Routledge.

Boggs, C. G. (2013) *Animalia Americana. Animal Representations and Biopolitical Subjectivity*, New York: Columbia University.

ten Bos, R. (2005) 'On the Possibility of Formless Life: Agamben's Politics of the Gesture', *Ephemera*, 5(1), 26–44.

Butler, J. (2004) *Precarious Life: The Powers of Mourning and Violence*, Verso: London.

Butler, J. (2009) *Frames of War: When Is Life Grievable?* Verso: London.

Charles, N. (2016) 'Post-Human Families? Dog-Human Relations in the Domestic Sphere', *Sociological Research Online*, 21(3), 1–12.

Chrulew, M. (2017) 'Animals as Biopolitical Subjects', in M. Chrulew and W. Dinesh (eds.) *Foucault and Animals*, Leiden: Brill.

Chrulew, M. and Wadiwel, D. (eds.) (2017) *Foucault and Animals*, Leiden: Brill.

Coile, D. C. (2003) *Chihuahuas*, Hauppauge: Barron's.

Collier, I. D. (2016) 'More than a Bag of Bones: A History of Animal Burials', in M. DeMello (ed.) *Mourning Animals: Rituals and Practices Surrounding Animal Death*, East Lansing: Michigan State University.

Dell'Aversano, C. (2010) 'The Love Whose Name Cannot Be Spoken: Queering the Human-Animal Bond', *Journal for Critical Animal Studies*, 8(1/2), 73–125.

Diken, B. (2004) 'From Refugee Camps to Gated Communities: Biopolitics and the End of the City', *Citizenship Studies*, 8(1), 83–106.

Foucault, M. (1977) *Discipline and Punish: The Birth of the Prison*, New York: Random House.

Foucault, M. (1978) *The History of Sexuality, Volume I: An Introduction*, New York: Pantheon Books.

Foucault, M. (2003) *Society Must Be Defended: Lectures at the Collège de France, 1975–6*, London: Penguin Books.

Fox, R. (2006) 'Animal Behaviours, Post-Human Lives: Everyday Negotiations of the Animal-Human Divide in Pet-Keeping', *Social & Cultural Geography*, 7(4), 525–537.

Francione, G. L. (2000) *Introduction to Animal Rights: Your Child or the Dog?* Philadelphia: Temple University Press.

Haraway, D. J. (2008) *When Species Meet*, Minneapolis: University of Minnesota.

Holmberg, T. (2017) *Urban Animals: Crowding in Zoocities*, London: Routledge.

Johnstone, M. S. (2016) 'Discarded Property', in M. DeMello (ed.) *Mourning Animals: Rituals and Practices Surrounding Animal Death*, East Lansing: Michigan State University.

Johnstone, M. S. (n.d.) 'Breeding Ignorance', http://www.shannonjohnstone.com/breed-ing_ignorance/breeding_ignorance.xml, accessed 5 June 2018.

Kirk, R. G. W. (2017) 'The Birth of the Laboratory Animal: Biopolitics, Animal Experimentation, and Animal Wellbeing', in M. Chrulew and W. Dinesh (eds.) *Foucault and Animals*, Leiden: Brill.

McHugh, S. (2011) *Animal Stories: Narrating Across Species Lines*, Minneapolis: University of Minnesota.

Morley, C. and Fook, J. (2005) 'The Importance of Pet Loss and Some Implications for Services', *Mortality*, 10(2), 127–143.

Nast, H. J. (2006) 'Critical Pet Studies?', *Antipode*, 38(5): 894–906.

O'Neil, J. (2008) *Chihuahuas for Dummies*, Indianapolis: Wiley.

Palmer, C. (2001) 'Taming the Wild Profusion of Existing Things? A Study of Foucault, Power, and Human/Animal Relationships', *Environmental Ethics*, 23(4), 339–358.

Palmer, C. (2003) 'Colonization, Urbanization, and Animals', *Philosophy & Geography*, 6(1), 47–58.

Power, E. (2008) 'Furry Families: Making a Human-Dog Family Through Home', *Social & Cultural Geography*, 9(5), 535–555.

Redmalm, D. (2013) *An Animal Without an Animal Within: The Powers of Pet Keeping*, dissertation, Örebro University.

Redmalm, D. (2014) 'Holy Bonsai Wolves: Chihuahuas and the Paris Hilton Syndrome', *International Journal of Cultural Studies*, 17(1), 93–109.

Redmalm, D. (2015) 'Pet Grief: When Is Non-Human Life Grievable?', *The Sociological Review*, 63(1), 19–35.

Redmalm, D. (2016) 'So Sorry for the Loss of Your Little Friend: Pets' Grievability in Condolence Cards for Humans Mourning Animals', in M. DeMello (ed.) *Mourning Animals: Rituals and Practices Surrounding Animal Death*, East Lansing: Michigan State University.

Redmalm, D. (2018) 'Sharing the Condition of Abandonment: The Beastly Topology of Condolence Cards for Bereaved Pet Owners', in J. Bull, T. Holmberg and C. Åsberg (eds.) *Animal Places: Lively Cartographies of Human-Animal Relations*, London: Routledge.

Redmalm, D. and Schuurman, N. (2017) 'Scandinavian Pet Cemeteries as Shared Spaces of Companion Animal Death', Presentation at the XXVII European Society for Rural Sociology Congress, Krakow, Poland, 24–27 July 2017.

Rose, N. (1999) *Powers of Freedom*, Cambridge: Cambridge University.

Scott, J. C. (2017) *Against the Grain. A Deep History of the Earliest States*, New Haven: Yale University.

Skoglund, A. and Redmalm, D. (2017) '"Doggy–Biopolitics": Governing via the First Dog', *Organization*, 24(2), 240–266.

Smith, J. A. (2003) 'Beyond Dominance and Affection: Living with Rabbits in Post-Humanist Households', *Society & Animals*, 11(2), 182–197.

Stanescu, J. (2012) 'Species Trouble: Judith Butler, Mourning, and the Precarious Lives of Animals', *Hypatia*, 27(3), 567–582.

Tuan, Y.-F. (1984) *Dominance and Affection: The Making of Pets*, New Haven: Yale University.

Wadiwel, D. J. (2017) 'Animal Friendship as a Way of Life: Sexuality, Petting and Interspecies Companionship', in M. Chrulew and W. Dinesh (eds.) *Foucault and Animals*, Leiden: Brill.

Witt, D. D. (2003) 'Pet Burial in the United States', in C. D. Bryant (ed.) *Handbook of Death and Dying, Volume One: The Presence of Death*, Thousand Oaks: Sage.

Wolfe, C. (2013) *Before the Law: Humans and Other Animals in a Biopolitical Frame*, Chicago: University of Chicago.

13

Mortality and Culture: Do Death Matters Matter?

Introduction

In the Peter Jackson directed film, *The Return of the King* (2003), the wizard Gandalf asserts:

> End? No, the journey doesn't end here. *Death is just another path, one that we all must take.* The grey rain-curtain of this world rolls back, and all turns to silver glass, and then you see it…. White shores, and beyond, a far green country under a swift sunrise. [emphasis added]

This widely quoted phrase creates a strong visualization of death in a highly successful and globally consumed film franchise as something that is to be embraced and not to be feared. It is, after all, "just another path." Hope and reassurance are offered about death turning it into a gateway leading to beauty and peace and the beginning of a greater journey. However, an actual physical demise must occur to begin this journey and

R. Penfold-Mounce (✉)
Department of Sociology, University of York, York, UK
e-mail: ruth.penfold-mounce@york.ac.uk

© The Author(s) 2019
T. Holmberg et al. (eds.), *Death Matters*,
https://doi.org/10.1007/978-3-030-11485-5_13

whether in Tolkien's fictional world of Middle Earth or in our real contemporary society, death and dying are something that in due course
everyone, and everything, encounters. We will all eventually die. As a
universal destination for living things, death demands our attention and
yet it is a topic that remains widely perceived as controversial territory to
discuss openly and commonly referred to as "taboo" by those living in the
West (Europe and North America). Although death is ultimately unavoidable, the view of actor, director and playwright Woody Allen seems to
have been widely adopted: "It's not that I'm afraid to die, I just don't want
to be there when it happens" (Allen, 1975). For many, Allen's sentiments
resonate strongly. Actively avoiding consideration of death or simply by
not making time to think about mortality seems to be a common
occurrence.

Intriguingly, although public wisdom in the West declares that death
is taboo, it is actually far from forbidden or denied. The visibility of the
hospice movement and the growing range of death awareness campaign-
ers such as Jon Underwood, founder of the Death Cafe, and Caitlin
Doughty, founder of The Order of the Good Death, seek to promote
death positivity and raise awareness of the need for end-of-life planning.
As stated by Tora Holmberg, Annika Jonsson and Fredrik Palm (Chap. 1,
this volume), death is in fact everywhere. It is not limited to just personal
experiences of loss or the process of dying and palliative care or the practicalities of body disposal within the death industry but extends into less
direct engagements with mortality. Death matters are not only an object
to be directly confronted but can also to be seen from the corner of one's
eye. In line with Žižek (1992), we might then suggest that we "look
awry" at death. By looking awry at an issue, in this instance, mortality, we
approach it from an alternative angle, just as Žižek does by explaining
Lacanian "high theory" by way of examples from "vulgar" popular culture (1992: viii). Looking at death indirectly, as is embraced in this
anthology, encourages a non-typical non-straightforward approach to
thanatology and allowing death matters to be revealed where we least
expect them such as in sex, our relationships to particular places and even
animals. As a death researcher, who chooses to investigate mortality by
not looking directly at death, I applaud this anthology's contributors who
have adopted a cultural sociological approach to death. In doing so they

join me at the edges of the typical domain of death scholarship and share the task of expanding the boundaries of thanatology and sociology by emphasizing the role and contribution of culture to understanding mortality. The importance of conducting this death edgework and looking at mortality from an unconventional angle lies at the heart of the contribution of this collected research to scholarship.

In this closing chapter to a collection of research focused on mortality, the question will be posed as to whether death matters *matter*. A cultural sociological approach is adopted to address this question, but it is important to acknowledge that the study of culture by sociologists is a contested space. Cultural sociologists struggle to achieve agreement over the content and boundaries of cultural sociological work particularly as it has not been embraced as a unified specialist sub-field on an international basis. The issue of mortality is one key cultural issue that has not attracted substantial attention. Therefore, this chapter argues a case that there is significant value in researching death culturally which is outside of its typical thanatological domain. First, using popular culture as an example of looking awry at death, it will be asserted that by adopting a cultural sociological approach to mortality allows for immersion in a rich, and underutilized, arena for both death scholarship and sociology. Second and finally, a reflection will be made upon the vital and compelling contribution of *Death Matters: Cultural Sociology of Mortal Life* to scholarship. It will be highlighted that not only does this volume contribute to thanatology via unique and original research but also emphasizes the significance of adopting a cultural sociological approach and using death as a springboard for new and creative thinking in sociology.

Looking Awry at Death: Being an Edgeworker

In the introduction to this anthology, Holmberg, Jonsson and Palm identify that much death research is conducted indirectly—almost out of the corner of your eye. This is a direct contrast to mainstream thanatological scholarship, which principally faces death head-on by focusing on issues of palliative care, grieving, death industry and increasingly digital legacies. Consequently, although cultural spheres are being studied in relation to death, dying and disposal, only a limited body of work has emerged that addresses diverse cultural components and approaches to mortality. In adopting a cultural sociological stance, this anthology expands the body of thanatological and sociological research by offering a collation of culturally focused approaches that are united through a research interest in death. Here, in this closing chapter, I want to add my own contribution to this anthology that looks awry (Žižek, 1992) at death and research outside of the typical boundaries of thanatology. As a cultural criminologist, with sociological roots, my research has gradually become consumed and defined by death although I still consider myself an edgeworker within thanatology. Lyng (2004a, b) proposed an "edgework" model focused on voluntary risk taking and I adapt this concept to refer to the risk and vitality of conducting work at the boundaries, or edges, of thanatology. As a death edgeworker, this does not mean my work is marginalized or fails to be part of the wider death research agenda but instead specifically seeks to push at the edges of death scholarship to expand the vision and agenda of studying mortality. Doing death edgework is about not looking directly at death matters. By doing non-typical death scholarship that is rooted in the intersection between death and culture, I have become a firm believer and advocate that there is still much to explore about mortality beyond the traditional thanatological domain and that sociology would benefit from recentralizing death to its research agenda. Therefore, cultural sociologists, looking at mortality from an alternative angle, have great potential to develop vibrant new insights for understanding death but also adding to, and expanding the discipline of sociology itself.

Like the researchers in this anthology, I adopt a cultural sociological stance to look awry at death and for me popular culture is what I gaze at from the corner of my eye and has subsequently become my research route into engaging with mortality. Through the huge range of popular culture forms in which death is present, there is rich potential for understanding notions of value and meaning in everyday practices, which lie at the heart of cultural sociological research. Popular culture, as defined by Hebdige, is a "set of generally available artefacts: films, records, clothes, TV programmes, modes of transport, etc." (1988: 47). As such, popular culture is comprised of a wide variety of objects and forms that can be used as data in order to examine society. Unfortunately, there remains a common perception that because popular culture is of huge public *interest*, it still struggles to be considered of public *value* (Beer & Penfold-Mounce, 2010; Penfold-Mounce, 2015). In researching death through popular culture, it can appear that the superficial, glossy and frivolous are being used to engage with a sensitive and weighty topic. However, as I argue in *Death, the Dead and Popular Culture* (2018), popular culture has something vital and important to say about contemporary society. It is a site for "cross-cultural and cross-generational understandings of global society" where it "embodies central tales for understanding society and the world around us" (Penfold-Mounce, 2018: 116). For just because popular culture is accessible and allows for regular, visual and entertaining ways of engaging with death and the dead it does not lessen its value as a tool to examine issues of mortality. In, and among, these entertaining popular sources, that are often globally consumed, I am able to examine death that has been normalized for consumption and is gazed upon through a "softening barrier" of unreality (Penfold-Mounce, 2015: 21). Using popular culture enables myself, as a researcher, and consumers to gaze upon and consider death without direct consequences.

Despite the value of popular culture as a data source for culturally shared narratives about death and the dead, both thanatologists and sociologists have not greatly expounded their research capabilities and resources to examine this phenomenon. Death scholars, of whom many are sociologists, have concentrated on looking at death directly by focusing on policy and the practicalities of death, dying and disposal of the dead. Nonetheless, some researchers do look awry at death and have become heavily influential on non-typical death scholarship including my own. One such scholar is Jacque Lynn Foltyn who looks at death from an alternative angle particularly through her examination of the relationship between fashion, beauty and mortality (1996, 2011). In fact, her work has been heavily influential in my conviction of the value of popular culture as a valuable data source. Through her concept of "corpse chic," (that reflects how modeling death to sell fashion is an increasingly common motif), she argues that alluring death imagery has moved into mainstream culture revealing contemporary Western culture to be immersed in a pornography of death (Gorer, 1955). Foltyn's ideas surrounding consumable and titillating representations of death have been central to the development of my own ideas about death matters particularly relating to crime porn (Penfold-Mounce, 2016b)—where crime drama casts dead female victims in a graphic and sexualized manner normalizing violence against women. The connection between death and crime is extensively explored in research focused on crime drama and forensic science television shows (Deutsch & Cavender, 2008; Foltyn, 2008; Penfold-Mounce, 2016a; Steenberg, 2013; Schweitzer & Saks, 2007). This reflects how criminologists as well as media and television researchers conduct thanatological edgework, where their work on the representation of crime and violence looks at death but from the corner of their eye rather than directly.

The relationship between celebrity and death, like crime and forensic science drama, has also garnered substantial research interest from scholars viewing death from a different angle. For instance, celebrities have provided an arena to consider public mediated dying as illustrated by publications focusing on the 2009 death of UK reality television star Jade Goody (Walter, 2009, 2010, 2011; Woodthorpe, 2010). Furthermore, celebrity individuals have also been used to explore grief and mourning particularly on a mass national or international scale (Garde-Hansen, 2010; Radford & Bloch, 2012; Sanderson & Hope Cheong, 2010). This body of work on celebrity death and mourning is added to by Magdalena Kania-Lundholm's work on processes of mourning celebrity death through social media (Chap. 9, this volume). In doing so, she makes an important contribution to extending debates around high-profile death and social media. Another arena of mortality scholarship that focuses on celebrity and is of particular interest to my research is work conducted about celebrity careers in terms of value, ownership and consumption after death (D'Rozario, 2016; D'Rozario & Bryant, 2013; Jensen, 2005; Kearl, 2010; Penfold-Mounce, 2018). For many celebrities, death is not an ending but a new stage of their career; their physical body may have gone but their image as intellectual property can continue on to have a vibrant posthumous career (Penfold-Mounce, 2018). These careers extending beyond the grave can have immense economic value. For example, singer-songwriter Michael Jackson has become the most financially successful recording artist alive or dead since his demise earning a spectacular $825 Million in 2016 according to the Forbes Magazine's Top Earning Dead Celebrity List (O'Malley Greenberg, 2016).

A recent voice among researchers conducting death edgework is Dina Khapaeva (2017) who has sought to examine the celebration of death through popular culture from a humanities viewpoint offering a comparison of Western culture with her knowledge as a native of Russia. She asserts that we are bearing witness to the rise of the cult of death where death, dying and disposal are bordering on veneration and that popular culture is key to this development. Popular culture forms are enabling and encouraging the celebration of death. Her claims tie neatly to my concept of "morbid space" (Penfold-Mounce, 2016a, 2018) where popular culture is forming a space in which consumers contemplate death matters in a safe and entertaining manner. Morbid spaces vary to include death, the process of dying and disposal of the dead in different formats such as fantasy television shows, such as *Game of Thrones* and *The Walking Dead*, but also comic book artwork and even children's television shows. These popular and globally consumed forms of death visualization ensure that death matters are a consistent component within entertainment consuming behaviors and enable both scholar and consumer to gaze upon death.

An older account than Khapaeva's work about the relationship between death and popular culture is Keith Durkin's chapter in a *Handbook of Death and Dying* (2003) where he approaches various manifestations of death, dying and the dead in popular culture. This has been influential on my own death edgework as it addresses examples of prominent portrayals of mortality. By examining television, cinema, music, print media and recreational activities such as games and jokes, Durkin highlights the social importance of thanatological themes in popular culture, and suggests a thematic outline for studying the relationship between popular culture and mortality (2003: 43). Like some contributions in this volume that focus on the relationship between death and phenomena such as eating and sexual excitement, what he raises is the role of humor in relation to death. Durkin focuses specifically and only on gallows humor and does not contemplate other humorous death representations that include black comedy shows and child-targeted death humor (2003).

Durkin's publication reveals not only a research gap on humor more broadly, but also regarding childhood and death, particularly popular culture produced for children. This latter research gap has come to fascinate me for it forms a unique "morbid space" in which death matters are portrayed and consumed. It is important to note that research has been conducted into childhood and death through research into children's literature (Clement & Jamali, 2018; Gibson & Zaidman, 1991), although Rudman does highlight that in the twentieth century, "books dealing realistically with the topic of death were almost in the same category as pornography" (1984: 326). So, mortality in children's literature has attracted researcher energies, but children's popular culture focusing on mortality has garnered less consideration. One exception is the work of Meredith Cox, Erin Garret and James Graham who investigate death in animated Disney films (2005). They highlight that the film narratives largely revolve around death and loss but "often present scenes that eclipse the permanence and irreversibility of death and often leave death (especially those of villains) emotionally unacknowledged" (Cox et al., 2005: 267). For example, in *The Lion King* (1994) the corpse of Mufasa is shown with his son Simba snuggling up to the body trying to get him to move. The finality of this death of a father is undermined later in the film when Mufasa returns to speak to an older Simba in a vision suggesting death is not the end and that loved ones remain with us after their demise. Significantly, animated Disney films succeed in introducing death to viewers at an early age. Death is far from forbidden or avoided by Disney instead it is regularly central to the narrative and consumed by children and adults alike.

Other visualizations of death and the dead in films targeting children and young people go further than the demise of key characters in animated Disney films. Some films principally focus on death matters such as Tim Burton's *The Corpse Bride* (2005) (see Kearl, 2010) and Disney-Pixar's *CoCo* (2018) of which the latter focuses on the beliefs and traditions surrounding the Mexican holiday, The Day of the Dead. In these instances, death directly defines the entire storyline and the dead are everywhere and impressively active considering they are not alive. Movies are not alone in portraying the dead as reflected in the immensely popular Terry Deary *Horrible Histories* book series adapted for television where the Grim Reaper features in a sequence of sketches entitled *Stupid Deaths* (2009–13). Here, death is humorous and the historical dead appear as they explain the circumstances of their death to the Grim Reaper who decides if they can enter the afterlife. Death and the dead have impressive appeal as an entertainment source and allow young consumers to engage with death matters.

To sum up popular culture representation of death and the dead for children and adults seem to be fascinating examples of what it could mean to look indirectly at death, not least due to the sheer plethora of varied portrayals that can range from playful, creative and funny to graphic, gruesome and frightening. What all these popular culture engagements with mortality have in common is that matters of death are commonplace and everywhere. Popular culture is a flexible and widely consumed "morbid space" (Penfold-Mounce, 2016a, 2018), where issues of death are able to demonstrate remarkable agency in influencing and provoking the living to engaging with mortality. For example, the portrayal of a Day of the Dead parade in Mexico City in the James Bond film *Spectre* (2015) led to city officials being inspired to host a similar parade the following year (Shephard, 2016). By embracing and celebrating mortality, popular culture has the potential in exerting direct influence over, and impact upon, the living. However, it is important to recognize that popular culture provides just one route to looking awry at death. This anthology represents a host of other scholars who look at death matters from the corner of their eye and through their death edgework they are expanding the contribution of cultural sociology to the fields of thanatology and sociology.

Reflecting on Cultural Sociology and Death Matters

Cultural sociology is comprised of sociologists who research culture. However, there are hotly debated differences of opinion regarding what the boundaries of cultural sociology should be. Scholars even struggle to agree over whether they are cultural sociologists or sociologists of culture! This lack of unity is only exacerbated when it comes to opinions over what research ideas and theories are central and most valuable to the intellectual field of cultural sociology. I do not intend to try to unpick these debates but instead choose to reflect upon the cultural sociological contribution of the scholars in this anthology. What they all have in common is an acceptance that when researching human groups culture is both central and integral. As a concept, it has the advantage of being "comfortably capacious" but also "notoriously difficult to define, [...as it] can seem misty, all encompassing, and ambiguous" (Spillman, 2002: 1). Accordingly, culture is broadly treated as processes of *meaning-making* and subsequently for cultural sociology a primary purpose is to:

> investigate how meaning-making happens, why meanings vary, how meanings influence human action, and the ways meaning making is important in social cohesion, domination, and resistance. (Spillman, 2002: 1)

As such, cultural sociology gives priority to cultural processes as a principal component in any social explanation (Back et al., 2012), meaning it is well placed to examine mortality and this anthology recognizes this. Due to cultural sociology overlapping with the different disciplinary boundaries of social science and humanities rather than challenging them, this has led to some empirical topics being underemphasized. Death has received limited consideration while other areas have attracted substantial attention such as class, political culture and social change. Therefore, cultural sociological research into mortality remains eclectic and scattered. It is the need to draw this scattered diversity together that this anthology seeks to address by creating a cohesive voice.

Similar to cultural sociology, thanatological research has achieved a large and comprehensive body of prominent literature, but it is dominated by the practicalities of death, dying and disposal practices. As such, many cultural death matters remain at the edges of death scholarship. This is not aided by the impressively diverse range of scholars who conduct death research including sociologists, film and television scholars, historians, policy researchers, anthropologists, theologians and even archaeologists. The interdisciplinary approach to looking at death as a cultural matter reveals it does indeed matter but the body of work lacks overall cohesion as it entails scholars whose work overlaps incidentally with thanatology rather than a planned strategic offering to the field.

Consequently, researchers, who do not identify themselves principally as death scholars or thanatologists, conduct much of existing death research. This means that death research is rife with different methods, approaches and ideas, which have many critical insights to contribute to societal and cultural understandings of death but struggle to produce a coherent and consistent contribution to thanatology.

Death Matters: Cultural Sociology of Mortal Life addresses the void in not only death scholarship but also cultural sociology by adopting the latter to address the former. It leads the way in international scholarship by providing a coherent collection of research that perceives death from a cultural sociology perspective. Distinctively for an edited collection of work it has been produced predominantly by Swedish scholars, most of whom are based in Uppsala University. Traditional standards for edited collections of work would suggest this to be a limitation to the text as typically the aim is to draw together key international experts from around the world who share a similar research agenda. However, this hub of Swedish scholars achieves something unique in an academic anthology because this text has grown organically from a group of sociological scholars debating the value of culture within sociological research. The Cultural Matters group at Uppsala has drawn together and unified researchers from different stages of their academic careers, who are from a predominantly sociological background. As a group, they have embraced the value of researching culture and identified a theme across their work in the form of mortality. This approach has subsequently not been restricted by asking for contributions from only those who identify as death and culture scholars (although I admittedly do!). Instead, its writers are drawn from a variety of different research interests—from gender and sexuality to science and technology studies, to space and place to celebrity—all of which have coalesced through the theme of death and embraced a cultural sociological stance. It highlights how researchers working in different sociological fields can unite and contribute valuable cultural sociological insights on a single theme, namely mortality. Death is far from an end in terms of research. Instead, it is a source of productivity, imagination and critical insights into human lives, identity and community. Consequently, the strength of this collection of research lies in the core value held by these scholars that *culture matters, do indeed, matter* and that death is a cultural matter through which wider social issues can be posited.

This anthology offers a true straddling of varied sociological inquiry seeking to cultivate a cultural sociological approach to mortality. The result is twofold: firstly, a dynamic and articulate collection of research drawing on diverse expertise in cultural sociology. Secondly, it manages to accomplish what many edited collections seek to do but struggle to truly achieve—it fulfills the ambition of providing a coherent and creative collation of exciting research that pushes the research field forward. As a book, it achieves this ambition and offers a much-needed broadening of what can be considered cultural sociology and thanatology. It does not seek to undermine what has been, and is being, achieved by others in these two research arenas. Instead, it seeks to look awry at death and offers an alternative angle to studying mortality as sociologists from a cultural perspective. It contributes to death edgework by seeking to challenge and expand established boundaries showing how death as a focus point for research can reveal so much about our contemporary world. In addition, it highlights how rich and captivating research can be when it seeks to be inclusive of work conducted under the banner of culture. Therefore, the value of this text lies in its ability to reveal that for the field of cultural sociology death can, should and *does* matter.

References

Allen, W. (1975) *Death: A Comedy in One Act*, London: Samuel French.

Back, L., Bennett, A., Desfor Edles, L., Gibson, M., Inglis, D., Jacobs, R. and Woodward, I. (2012) *Cultural Sociology: An Introduction*, Chichester: Wiley-Blackwell.

Beer, D. and Penfold-Mounce, R. (2010) 'Celebrity Gossip and the New Melodramatic Imagination', *Sociological Research Online*, 14(2), 1–12.

Clement, L. D. and Jamali, L. (eds.) (2018) *Global Perspectives on Death in Children's Literature*, Abingdon: Routledge.

Cox, M., Garrett, E. and Graham, J. A. (2005) 'Death in Disney Films: Implications for Children's Understanding of Death', *Omega-Journal of Death and Dying*, 50(4), 267–280.

D'Rozario, D. (2016) 'The Market for 'Delebs' (Dead Celebrities): A Revenue Analysis', *Journal of Customer Behaviour*, 15(4), 395–414.

D'Rozario, D. and Bryant, F. (2013) 'The Use of Dead Celebrity Images in Advertising and Marketing—Review, Ethical Recommendations and Cautions for Practitioners', *International Journal of Marketing Studies*, 5(2), 1–10.

Durkin, K. (2003) 'Death, Dying and the Dead in Popular Culture', in C. D. Bryant (ed.) *Handbook of Death and Dying*, Sage: London.

Deutsch, S. K. and Cavender, G. (2008) 'CSI and Forensic Realism', *Journal of Criminal Justice and Popular Culture*, 15(1), 34–53.

Foltyn, J. L. (1996) 'Dead Beauty: The Preservation, Memorialisation and Destruction of Beauty in Death' in P. C. Jupp (ed.) *Contemporary Issues in the Sociology of Death, Dying and Disposal*, London: Palgrave Macmillan.

Foltyn, J. L. (2008) 'Dead Famous and Dead Sexy: Popular Culture, Forensics, and the Rise of the Corpse', *Mortality*, 13(2), 153–173.

Foltyn, J. L. (2011) 'Corpse Chic: Dead Models and Living Corpses in Fashion Photography' in A. de Witt-Paul and M. Crouch (eds.) *Fashion Forward*, Oxford: Inter-Disciplinary Press.

Garde-Hansen, J. (2010) 'Measuring Mourning with Online Media: Michael Jackson and Real-Time Memories', *Celebrity Studies*, 1(2), 233–235.

Gibson, L. R. and Zaidman, L. M. (1991) 'Death in Children's Literature: Taboo or not Taboo?', *Children's Literature Association Quarterly*, 16(4), 232–234.

Gorer, G. (1955) 'The Pornography of Death', *Encounter*, 5(4), 49–52.

Hebdige, D. (1988) *Hiding in the Light: On Images and Things*, London: Routledge.

Jensen, J. (2005) 'Introduction – On Fandom, Celebrity, and Mediation: Posthumous Possibilities', in S. Jones and J. Jensen (eds.) *Afterlife as Afterimage: Understanding Posthumous Fame*, Oxford: Peter Lang.

Kearl, M. C. (2010) 'The Proliferation of Postselves in American Civic and Popular Cultures', *Mortality*, 15(1), 47–63.

Khapaeva, D. (2017) *The Celebration of Death in Contemporary Culture*, Ann Arbor: University of Michigan Press.

Lyng, S. (2004a) 'Crime, Edgework and Corporeal Transaction', *Theoretical Criminology*, 8(3), 359–375.

Lyng, S. (2004b). *Edgework: The Sociology of Risk-Taking*, New York: Routledge.

O'Malley Greenberg, Z. (12 October 2016) 'The Highest-Paid Dead Celebrities of 2016', *Forbes Magazine*. https://www.forbes.com/sites/

zackomalleygreenburg/2016/10/12/the-highest-paid-dead-celebrities-of-2016/#2eee8d9c11b1.

Penfold-Mounce, R. (2015) 'Conducting Frivolous Research in Neoliberal Universities: What Is the Value of Glossy Topics?', *Celebrity Studies*, 6(2), 254–257.

Penfold-Mounce, R. (2016a) 'Corpses, Popular Culture and Forensic Science: Public Obsession with Death', *Mortality*, 21(1), 19–35.

Penfold-Mounce, R. (24 October 2016b) 'How the Rise in TV 'Crime Porn' Normalises Violence Against Women', *The Conversation*. https://theconversation.com/how-the-rise-in-tv-crime-porn-normalises-violence-against-women-66877.

Penfold-Mounce, R. (2018) *Death, The Dead and Popular Culture*, Bingley, UK: Emerald Publishing.

Radford, S. K. and Bloch, P. H. (2012) 'Grief, Commiseration, and Consumption Following the Death of a Celebrity', *Journal of Consumer Culture*, 12(2), 137–155.

Rudman, M. K. (1984) *Children's Literature: An Issues Approach*, 2nd edn, New York: Longman.

Sanderson, J. and Hope Cheong, P. (2010) 'Tweeting Prayers and Communicating Grief over Michael Jackson Online', *Bulletin of Science, Technology & Society*, 30(5), 328–340.

Schweitzer, N. J. and Saks, M. J. (2007) 'The CSI Effect: Popular Fiction About Forensic Science Affects the Public's Expectations About Real Forensic Science', *Jurimetrics*, 47(3), 357–364.

Shephard, J. (27 October 2016) 'James Bond: Mexico City to Hold First Day of the Dead Parade Thanks to Spectre', *The Independent*. https://www.independent.co.uk/arts-entertainment/films/news/james-bond-spectre-mexico-city-day-of-the-dead-parade-a7382471.html.

Spillman, L. (2002) 'Introduction: Culture and Cultural Sociology', in L. Spillman (ed.) *Cultural Sociology*, Chichester: Wiley-Blackwell.

Steenberg, L. (2013) *Forensic Science in Contemporary American Popular Culture: Gender, Crime, and Science*. Abingdon: Routledge.

Walter, T. (2009) 'Jade's Dying Body: The Ultimate Reality Show', *Sociological Research Online*, 14(5), 1–11.

Walter, T. (2010) 'Jade and the Journalists: Media Coverage of a Young British Celebrity Dying of Cancer', *Social Science & Medicine*, 71(5), 853–860.

Walter, T. (2011) 'Angels Not Souls: Popular Religion in the Online Mourning for British Celebrity Jade Goody', *Religion*, 41(1), 29–51.

Woodthorpe, K. (2010) 'Public Dying: Death in the Media and Jade Goody', *Sociology Compass*, 4(5), 283–294.

Žižek, S. (1992) *Looking Awry: An Introduction to Jacques Lacan Through Popular Culture*. Cambridge, MA: MIT Press.

Index[1]

---

[1] Note: Page numbers followed by 'n' refer to notes.

Printed by Printforce, the Netherlands